The Primary Care Toolkit for Anxiety and Related Disorders

D1709356

The Primary Care Toolkit for Anxiety and Related Disorders

Quick, Practical Solutions for Assessment and Management

BIANCA LAURIA-HORNER, MD

Brush
Education Inc.

16 17 18 19 20   5 4 3 2 1

Brush Education Inc.
www.brusheducation.ca
contact@brusheducation.ca

Editorial: Alison Lilian, Nicholle Carrière

Cover Design: Dean Pickup; Cover image: Modified from Sergiy Gaydaenko | Dreamstime.com

Interior Design: Carol Dragich, Dragich Design

Printed and manufactured in Canada

Library and Archives Canada Cataloguing in Publication

Lauria-Horner, Bianca, author
    The primary care toolkit for anxiety and related disorders : quick, practical solutions for assessment and management / Bianca Lauria-Horner, MD.

Includes bibliographical references.

Issued in print and electronic formats.
ISBN 978-1-55059-660-1 (paperback).—ISBN 978-1-55059-661-8 (pdf).—
ISBN 978-1-55059-662-5 (mobi).—ISBN 978-1-55059-663-2 (epub)

1. Diagnostic and statistical manual of mental disorders. 5th ed.   2. Anxiety disorders.
3. Anxiety disorders—Diagnosis. 4. Anxiety disorders—Treatment. 5. Anxiety.
I. Title.

RC531.L39 2016   616.85'22   C2016-902458-X
                                 C2016-902459-8

We acknowledge the support of the Government of Canada.
Nous reconnaissons l'appui du gouvernement du Canada.   Canadä

Contents

Appendices

Toolkit Overview

Does This Sound Like You?

It is Friday afternoon at 4:30 p.m.; you are 1 hour behind schedule. A patient who was scheduled for a regular checkup breaks down crying because he or she is at the end of their rope.

Every medical professional knows this feeling well. You feel overwhelmed and helpless, and experience a sense of loss of control. You don't have the time or energy to help your patient adequately, but you want to carry out your duty to provide care.

Why Was This Toolkit Created?

This toolkit has been designed specifically for primary health care professionals. As a primary care provider, you may ask yourself: why invest time in learning about anxiety and related disorders, aren't all these conditions more or less managed the same? Anxiety and related disorders are extremely relevant to the primary health care professional as they are among the most common psychiatric conditions, with a lifetime prevalence rate of around 30%.[1] Most patients turn to their primary care provider first for assistance; however, almost one-third of patients will present with other symptoms, such as physical symptoms (e.g., headache, gastrointestinal distress, fatigue) or depression, and if the primary diagnosis is missed, it can lead to a chronic, difficult-to-treat disorder, depression, and/or suicidality. Management specific to anxiety and related disorder subtypes can be quite different depending on the disorder; therefore, early recognition and treatment can alter the course of illness and lead to much better outcomes, early recovery, and improved quality of life for patients.

These factors underscore the need to increase the knowledge and skills of primary care physicians in managing mental illness through education programs. Numerous training programs have been developed to improve the detection and management of mental illness.[2][3] Despite these efforts, most educational programs do not translate into changes in practice patterns. Although physicians invest a substantial amount of time in continuing medical education (CME) activities, studies have shown a lack of effect of formal CME if these CME initiatives are not associated with enabling or practice-reinforcing strategies.[4] A recent study conducted by Tamburrino et al. suggested that in order for education programs to be effective, family physicians may need to monitor mental illness symptoms closely with the help of protocols and prompts.[5] In addition, physicians best capitalize on professional development that offers distinct, finite opportunities to train for necessary skill sets that can be implemented immediately within the scope of their practice.

However, focusing solely on increasing knowledge and skills is not enough. Barriers that prevent physicians from applying this knowledge need to be taken into account. Studies suggest that one of the top barriers for family physicians in managing mental illness is lack of time.[6] To this end, an educational program that incorporates time-efficient assessment and management strategies would aid in increasing family physicians' interest and comfort in managing anxiety and related disorders.

How This Toolkit Will Benefit You

As a primary care provider, you probably encounter patients with anxiety and related disorders quite frequently. If you have a busy practice and need access to time efficient, user-friendly strategies and tools, this toolkit is for you. It will guide you through key features of common disorders with the help of case studies. You will work through time-efficient ways to screen, diagnose, and manage 7 common anxiety and related disorders over the course of multiple visits. Some examples of time-efficient assessment and management tools include the following:

- Short screening questionnaires (<6 questions) for each disorder
- Printable patient self-report validated scales
- Guidelines for pharmacotherapeutic and non-pharmacotherapeutic options
- Treatment algorithms
- Visit-by-visit guides

Particularly complicated or refractory cases will, however, require consultation with or referral to a psychiatric specialist.

As you begin to work through the elements of this toolkit, its benefits will soon become apparent. The toolkit consists of an approach to care that empowers patients and promotes partnership with professionals. Although you will encourage and facilitate the screening, assessment, treatment plan development, monitoring, and management process, the work is shared with your patient, therefore reducing your time involvement while improving patient engagement, compliance, and understanding of the importance of early and timely recovery. This toolkit also has an added bonus of example case studies reflecting real-life practice (e.g., patients presenting to you with somatic symptoms, chronic tension, and comorbid physical disorders, not just obvious psychiatric symptoms).

> Your patient schedules an office visit for a physical condition. He or she reveals an anxiety disorder. You don't have enough time to conduct a thorough assessment.
> » What are your choices?
> » What actions can you take?

Guidance on possible choices or actions available to you, combined with disorder-specific treatment strategies, will simplify treatment plan development for your patients, which increases the chances of treatment success. To learn about each disorder, you can follow the diagnosis, treatment, and management of our case study patient. You can progress through the case studies from start to finish, or you can select your own learning path in the Practice Case Study Index, p. xxv. The choice is yours. Well-developed directional strategies such as these empower you to take control.

What You Will Learn by Using This Toolkit

This book includes practical, concise tools that will enhance your ability to detect, assess, and diagnose patients with common anxiety disorders, obsessive-compulsive (OC) and related disorders, and trauma- and stressor-related disorders seen in primary care. You will also:

1. Understand the current treatment strategies that can optimize outcomes for patients with common anxiety, OC and related disorders, and trauma- and stressor-related disorders seen in primary care.
2. Obtain practical approaches for addressing long-term management challenges.
3. Appreciate the importance of functional recovery for patients.

Current Knowledge of Anxiety and Related Disorders

Self Pre-/Post-Test

To formally assess your current knowledge of anxiety disorders, try to answer the following questions. You might want to take the test again once you've finished the book to see how your knowledge has grown.

1. What percentage of primary care patients have symptoms of an anxiety or related disorder?
   a. 1–2%   c. 40–50%
   b. 8–20%   d. 34–40%

2. What is the most common comorbid condition with anxiety and related disorders?

3. Alprazolam is a first-line medication for which anxiety or related disorder?
   a. Generalized anxiety disorder
   b. Obsessive-compulsive disorder
   c. Posttraumatic stress disorder
   d. Alprazolam is not a first-line medication for any anxiety or related disorder

4. If an antidepressant causes sexual dysfunction, which of the following can help?
   1. Lowered dose of antidepressant
   2. Bupropion
   3. Lorazepam
   4. Sildenafil
   a. 1 and 4   c. 1 and 2
   b. 1, 3, and 4   d. 1, 2, and 4

5. When treating generalized anxiety disorder, the first medication should be given for how long before assessing response?
   a. 1 week   c. 6–8 weeks
   b. 2 weeks   d. 10–12 weeks

6. Obsessive-compulsive disorder and generalized anxiety disorder can both involve worries. However, the worries associated with obsessive-compulsive disorder are different because they
   1. are not simply worries about real-life problems that are out of proportion to the actual danger or threat in the situation
   2. are voluntary
   3. are about social or performance situations
   4. cause marked distress or significant impairment of functioning

   a. 1 and 4   c. 3 and 4
   b. 1 only   d. 2 and 3

7. Which of the following are typical stressors for posttraumatic stress disorder?
   1. Military combat
   2. Divorce
   3. Losing one's job
   4. Witnessing the sudden and unexpected death of a loved one
   a. 1 and 2   c. 1 and 4
   b. 2 and 3   d. 1 only

8. Anxiety or fear—being scared—interferes with one's normal functioning.
   a. True   b. False

9. Fear, anxiety, and avoidance are the main descriptors in phobias. The patient recognizes that their anxiety is excessive or unreasonable.
   a. True   b. False

10. A patient of yours is suffering from panic attacks. For a diagnosis of panic disorder to be made, which of the following criteria must be met?
    1. Unprovoked panic attack followed by 1 month or more of fear every day of having another panic attack or consequences of the attack
    2. Tachycardia related to untreated hyperthyroidism
    3. Anxiety for at least 6 months that another panic attack will occur
    4. Despite having panic attacks, there is no change in behavior
    a. All of the above   c. 2 and 4
    b. 1   d. 1, 2, and 3

11. Patients that start antidepressant treatment for panic disorder should be able to see improvement
    a. immediately   c. in 4 weeks
    b. in 1 week   d. in 6–8 weeks

12. For a patient with panic disorder, benzodiazepines would be most useful in which of the following situations?
    1. To reduce anxiety between panic attacks
    2. In the first few weeks of therapy, while waiting for the antidepressant to take effect
    3. As first-line treatment if comorbid depression exists
    a. 1 and 2   c. 2 only
    b. 1 and 3   d. All of the above

13. In assessing the severity of social anxiety disorder, which of the following scales can be self-administered by the patient?
    a. MINI Neural Psychiatric Interview for Social Anxiety Disorder
    b. Social Phobia Inventory (SPIN)

14. Which of the following is the most common?
    a. Generalized anxiety disorder
    b. Posttraumatic stress disorder
    c. Panic disorder
    d. Social anxiety disorder

15. Generalized anxiety disorder is characterized by anxiety that is out of proportion to the actual danger or threat in the situation, about a variety of events or activities, and occurring most days for a period of at least 3 months.
    a. True   b. False

16. Cognitive-behavioral therapy has been proven effective in treating generalized anxiety disorder.
    a. True   b. False

17. Patients with obsessive-compulsive disorder perform compulsions for which of the following reasons:
    1. To reduce anxiety
    2. As a response to auditory hallucinations
    3. To suppress obsessive thoughts
    4. As the result of a drug or medication
    a. All of the above   c. 1 only
    b. 1 and 2   d. 1 and 3

18. Obsessive-compulsive disorder typically starts
    a. during adolescence
    b. after age 25
    c. after age 35

19. To meet the DSM-5 criteria for obsessive-compulsive disorder, the patient's obsessions or compulsions must cause marked distress, significantly interfere with the patient's functioning, or consume how much time per day?
    a. 30 minutes per day
    b. 1 hour per day
    c. 2 hours per day
    d. 3 hours per day

20. Patients with obsessive-compulsive disorder may not respond promptly to their initial first-line medication. Consider which of the following before switching to a second-line medication or adding adjunctive medication?
    a. A trial of one SSRI
    b. Trials of two SSRIs
    c. Trials of two SSRIs and then clomipramine
    d. Trials of three SSRIs and then clomipramine

21. A patient of yours has difficulty falling asleep and difficulty concentrating. These are examples of which posttraumatic stress disorder symptom cluster?
    a. Re-experiences the event
    b. Avoids stimuli associated with the trauma
    c. Becomes numb
    d. Manifests increased arousal

22. For a patient with depression and mild posttraumatic stress disorder, what is the recommended treatment?
    a. Interpersonal therapy
    b. Cognitive-behavioral therapy alone
    c. Pharmacotherapy alone
    d. Cognitive-behavioral therapy and pharmacotherapy

23. For a diagnosis of panic attack, which of the following criteria must be met?
    1. Sudden onset of intense fear
    2. Four or more physical or cognitive symptoms such as palpitations, shortness of breath, fear of dying, trembling, and chest pain
    3. Symptoms peak within 30 minutes
    4. Symptoms peak within minutes
    5. Gradual development of fear over 1–2 days
    a. 1, 2, and 4   c. 2 only
    b. 1, 2, and 3   d. 2, 4, and 5

24. First-line non-pharmacological treatment for panic disorder is
    a. psychoeducation
    b. cognitive-behavioral therapy
    c. self-help manual
    d. exposure exercises

25. First-line pharmacological treatment for panic disorder is
    a. tricyclic antidepressants
    b. SSRIs and SNRIs
    c. benzodiazepines
    d. antipsychotics

26. For the treatment of social anxiety disorder, which of the following treatments is associated with a lower incidence of relapse following discontinuation?
    a. Cognitive-behavioral therapy with medication
    b. Medication alone

27. Which of the following are true?
    1. Shyness is a pre-requisite for social anxiety disorder.
    2. People with social anxiety disorder are always shy.
    3. Social anxiety disorder causes significant distress or functional impairment.
    a. 1 and 2   c. 3 only
    b. 1 and 3   d. All of the above

28. What tool(s) can you use to assess the severity of posttraumatic stress disorder?
    a. PTSD Checklist for DSM-5 (PCL-5)
    b. Severity of Posttraumatic Stress Symptoms—Adult
    c. GAD-7
    d. All of the above

29. Insight in OCD is the degree of the person's realization of their OCD beliefs. Which of the following are true?
    1. Good or fair insight (i.e., beliefs are definitely or probably not true)
    2. Poor insight (i.e., beliefs are probably not true)
    3. Absent insight/delusional beliefs (i.e., completely convinced beliefs are true)
    a. 1 and 2   c. 2 only
    b. 1 and 3   d. All of the above

30. In adjustment disorder, a person experiences an inability to cope with a particular event or situation (stressor). Emotional or behavioral symptoms develop
    a. within 3 months of the onset of stressors and end within 6 months of the onset of stressors
    b. within 3 months of the onset of stressors and end within 6 months of the end of the stressors
    c. with the onset of stressors and end within 9 months of the onset of stressor
    d. within 12 months of the onset of stressors and end within 24 months of the end of the stressors

Self Pre-/Post-Test Answer Key

1. b. 8–20%

2. Depression is by far the most common comorbid condition. Primary care providers should consider screening for depression in all cases of anxiety and related disorders.

3. d. Alprazolam is not a first-line medication for any anxiety or related disorder

4. d. 1, 2, and 4
The following can help in sexual dysfunction secondary to antidepressants: lowering the dose of antidepressant; adding bupropion (if no concern for drug interactions) or sildenafil; or switching to bupropion.

5. c. 6–8 weeks
A medication period of 6–8 weeks should be considered before assessing response when treating generalized anxiety disorder.

6. b. 1 only
By definition, obsessions are not simply worries about real-life problems that are out of proportion to the actual danger or threat in the situation. In contrast, the worries associated with generalized anxiety disorder are frequently of this nature.

7. c. 1 and 4
Military combat and witnessing the sudden and unexpected death of a loved one meet the criterion of PTSD involving actual or threatened death or serious injury, or sexual violence. Typically, divorce and losing one's job do not meet this criterion.

8. b. False
Anxiety or fear—being scared—is a natural, adaptive, and common biological response to danger. Mild anxiety actually improves our ability to perform in some situations, such as taking a test, and helps us live a safe and productive life. Anxiety also prepares our body to fight, freeze, or flee when faced with a dangerous situation. Expected anxiety is transient and does not interfere with a person's goals or normal daily functioning. Anxiety disorders interfere with functioning.

9. b. False
Fear, anxiety, and avoidance are the main descriptors in phobias, which must be out of proportion to the actual danger or threat in the situation (e.g., clinician judgment). The DSM-5 no longer requires patients to recognize that their anxiety is excessive or unreasonable. Individuals with these disorders often overestimate the danger in "phobic" situations.

10. b. 1 only

11. c. in 6–8 weeks
It can take up to 8 weeks with at least 2 weeks at maximum dose for initial response. Wait 8 weeks to decide if change of treatment is warranted, unless symptoms are severe (not feasible to wait). Decisions on management should be individualized for each patient.

12. a. 1 and 2
It is common to prescribe benzodiazepines as a short-term (2–3 weeks) adjunctive therapy. Give the benzodiazepines TID rather than PRN, and withdraw them promptly to avoid dependency.

13. b. Social Phobia Inventory (SPIN)
The Social Phobia Inventory is shorter and simpler than the physician-directed MINI Neural Psychiatric Interview for Social Anxiety Disorder Scale.

14. d. Social anxiety disorder
Social anxiety disorder has a lifetime prevalence of 13%.

15. b. False
The out-of-proportion worry and anxiety must occur most days for a period of at least 6 months.

16. a. True
In fact, cognitive-behavioral therapy is very effective with most anxiety and related disorders.

17. d. 1 and 3
Patients with obsessive-compulsive disorder can perform compulsions to reduce their own anxiety or to suppress their obsessive thoughts (among other reasons). The compulsions are performed in response to persistent ideas, thoughts, urges, or images, not auditory hallucinations.

18. a. during adolescence

19. b. 1 hour per day

20. c. Trials of two SSRIs
For obsessive-compulsive disorder, first-line medications (SSRIs) and clomipramine are more effective than most second-line medications. Clomipramine is as effective as SSRIs; however, it is considered second-line due to tolerability and safety issues. Therefore, first-line medications should be explored thoroughly before resorting to second-line medications. An adequate trial for the initial SSRI is 10–12 weeks.

21. d. Manifests increased arousal
The other symptoms from this cluster include:
- Irritability or outbursts of anger
- Hypervigilance
- Exaggerated startle response

22. d. Cognitive-behavioral therapy and pharmacotherapy
If posttraumatic stress disorder is accompanied by any comorbid psychiatric disorder, consider starting with both cognitive-behavioral therapy and pharmacotherapy, if the patient is willing.

23. a. 1, 2, and 4

24. b. cognitive-behavioral therapy, specifically exposure therapy (e.g., systematic desensitization)

25. b. SSRIs and SNRIs

26. a. Cognitive-behavioral therapy with medication
Studies suggest that CBT with pharmacotherapy, in particular when exposure therapy is included, is more effective than pharmacotherapy alone in maintaining gains achieved, and this for up to 5 years.

27. c. Social anxiety disorder causes significant distress or functional impairment.

28. d. All of the above

29. b. 1 and 3

30. b. within 3 months of the onset of stressors and end within 6 months of the end of the stressors

NOTES

OVERVIEW

1 Kessler RC, Chiu WT, Demler O, Walters E.
Prevalence, severity, and comorbidity of twelve-month
DSM-IV disorders in the National Comorbidity
Survey Replication (NCS-R). Arch Gen Psychiatry.
2005 [cited 2015 March]; 62(6):617–627. Available
from: http://doi.org/10.1001/archpsyc.62.6.617

2 Van Os TW, Ormel J, van den Brink RH, Jenner
JA, Van der Meer K, Tiemens BG, et al. Training
primary care physicians improves the management
of depression. Gen Hosp Psychiatry. 1999; 21(3):168–
176.

3 Kroenke K, Taylor-Vaisey A, Dietrich A, Oxman TE.
(2000). Interventions to improve provider diagnosis
and treatment of mental disorders in primary care. A
critical review of the literature. Psychosomatics. 2000;
41(1):39–52.

4 Davis D, Thomson M, Oxman A, Haynes R. Changing
physician performance. A systematic review of the
effect of continuing medical education strategies.
JAMA. 1995; 274(9):700–705.

5 Tamburrino M, Nagel R, Lynch D. Managing
antidepressants in primary care: physicians' treatment
modifications. Psychol Rep. 2011; 108(3):799–804.

6 Wittchen HU, Mühlig S, Beesdo K. Mental disorders
in primary care. Dialogues Clin Neurosci. 2003;
5(2):115–128.

Tools for Primary Care Practice

The following is a list of tools included in this book; however, there is additional important information on the tools within each respective section. For example, some tools have been validated for the stated purpose and some are meant solely as memory aids. In addition, you will find information and links to other assessment tools readily available online from sites such as the American Psychiatric Association.

🖨 The printer icon indicates print-ready tools available on the CD included with this book or by downloading from www.brusheducation.ca/toolkit.

Practice Case Study Index

SECTION I
Anxiety and Related Disorders

Introduction

During a board meeting, Sandra had already left the room 4 times to go to the bathroom. She was tapping her foot on the floor and fidgeting with her hands. Her eyes were darting across the room, and suddenly the boardroom felt small and stuffy. Sandra knew she was next in line to speak, and she felt her heart beating very fast. She began to feel light-headed and nauseous; it seemed as though her heart would beat out of her chest. She felt she was going to have a heart attack, and suddenly the urge came to rush out of the room again.

What Is Anxiety?

The terms *anxiety* and *anxiety disorders* are sometimes used interchangeably but have very different meanings and implications. Many people feel anxious at times. We can all think of situations when we felt on edge and not quite comfortable in certain situations. Anxiety or fear—being scared—is a natural, adaptive, and common biological response to danger. Most of us feel at least a little scared when we are about to experience a new or potentially dangerous situation. When we are scared, we are more alert, and we react more quickly. Mild anxiety actually improves our ability to perform in some situations, such as taking a test, and helps us live a safe and productive life. Anxiety also prepares our body to fight, freeze, or flee when faced with a dangerous situation. Expected anxiety is transient and does not interfere with a person's goals or normal daily functioning.

When Is Anxiety a Disorder?

An anxiety disorder is different from normal fear. When anxiety significantly interferes with a person's daily life (work, family, school, or social life), it becomes a problem—an anxiety disorder. The individual experiences significant distress and cannot control the anxiety, even though there is no evidence of danger or external threat to justify the exaggerated fear response.

There is *mental* unease (e.g., fear, worry) and a *physical* reaction (e.g., nervous tension, palpitations). When in an anxiety-provoking situation, an individual may overreact or try to avoid the situation at all cost to avoid the distressful feelings. To meet the criteria for a diagnosis of an anxiety or related disorder, 3 ingredients are required:[1]

1. Hallmark signs and symptoms specific to each disorder
2. Signs and symptoms lasting for a minimum specified duration depending on the disorder
3. Interference with at least 1 area in day-to-day life—home, school, work, or social life

Impact in the Primary Care Setting

As a primary health care provider, you already know that anxiety disorders are some of the most common mental illnesses seen in practice. Rates of these disorders are fairly consistent across cultures,[2, 3] and although data varies from study to study, systematic reviews have found that lifetime prevalence is reported to be as high as 31% of the population worldwide.[4, 5] Untreated, anxiety and related disorders cause unnecessary suffering, chronic disability, decreased work productivity, high utilization of psychiatric and non-psychiatric medical services, and high economic and social burdens. According to Katzman et al., the annual risk of suicide is tenfold in patients with an anxiety disorder compared to the general population.[6]

Primary care providers are ideally placed to intervene early, improving both remission rates and quality of life. Figure 1.1 highlights the prevalence of common disorders in the general population. Average (mean) lifetime prevalence rates are used for ease of reporting.

Eight to twenty percent of primary care patients have symptoms of an anxiety disorder.[7] Women are more affected than men, with a lifetime prevalence of 19.5% compared to 10% in men. In youth, fewer studies have been done, and anxiety and related disorders are under-reported in this population group. Therefore, although the reported lifetime prevalence rate for youth can range between 9% and 27%, the true rate of illness is relatively unknown.[8]

Patients presenting with frequent undiagnosed somatic complaints should be screened for anxiety or a related disorder.

Comorbidity

Depression is by far the most common comorbid condition. Primary care providers should consider screening for depression in all cases of anxiety and related disorders. Illicit drug or alcohol abuse or dependency (substance use disorder [SUD]) is also frequent. The substance-related disorders encompass 10 separate classes of drugs, which are are not fully distinct: alcohol; caffeine; cannabis; hallucinogens; inhalants;

FIGURE 1.1 LIFETIME PREVALENCE OF SPECIFIC ANXIETY AND RELATED MOOD DISORDERS

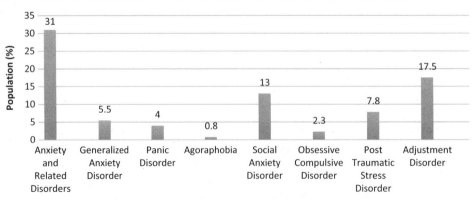

opioids; sedatives, hypnotics, and anxiolytics; stimulants (amphetamine-type substances, cocaine, and other stimulants); tobacco; and other (or unknown) substances.

Patients will often self-medicate and turn to alcohol or sedative drugs to help them cope with their symptoms. Finally, anxiety and related disorders are also highly comorbid with each other. The presence of a comorbid condition will affect treatment. For example, if your patient has a missed primary or comorbid substance use disorder, the illness may become treatment resistant. Using a tool that screens for common comorbid conditions may be quite useful. This will be discussed in future chapters.

DSM-5 Changes in Categorizing Anxiety Disorders

The *Diagnostic and Statistical Manual of Mental Disorders* (DSM)[9] is the gold-standard resource guide for health care professionals and provides a standardized approach to diagnosing mental illnesses. The development of the DSM-5,[10] the most recent edition, involved an evidence-based process to incorporate changes that reflect advances in the field. The goal was to enhance reliability, validity, and clinical utility for clinicians and researchers, and to improve patient care. The American Psychiatric Association (APA) board of trustees and others involved in the updating process felt changes were warranted to improve the accuracy of diagnosis and thus increase the effectiveness of treatments.

The biggest change pertaining to the anxiety disorders chapter is that it no longer includes, for example, obsessive-compulsive disorder (OCD) or posttraumatic stress disorder (PTSD). The DSM-5 now recognizes 3 distinct disorder groups, each with its own

chapter, that we refer to collectively as *anxiety and related disorders*:

1. Anxiety disorders
2. Obsessive-compulsive (OC) and related disorders
3. Trauma- and stressor-related disorders

This change was made to group closely related disorders—related in terms of shared clinical features, biology, shared assessment measures, comorbidity, and treatment approaches—within the same chapter, with closely related chapters adjacent. For example, in the OC and related disorders group, there appears to be a dysfunction in the prefrontal cortical striatal-thalamo-cortical loops compared to the anxiety disorders group, where there is thought to be a dysfunction in the amygdala. New disorders found to be problematic to patients requiring treatment have been added. In addition, the multiaxial system has been eliminated in the DSM-5. Figure 1.2 lists those disorders found in the DSM-5 chapters that pertain to anxiety and related disorders.

In this book, we discuss some of the most commonly seen or commonly managed disorders in primary care. To this end, the following 7 disorders are included:

Anxiety Disorders
- Generalized anxiety disorder (GAD)
- Panic disorder
- Agoraphobia
- Social anxiety disorder (also called social phobia)

Obsessive-Compulsive and Related Disorders
- Obsessive-compulsive disorder (OCD)

FIGURE 1.2 DSM-IV TO DSM-5 ANXIETY DISORDERS CHAPTER CHANGES

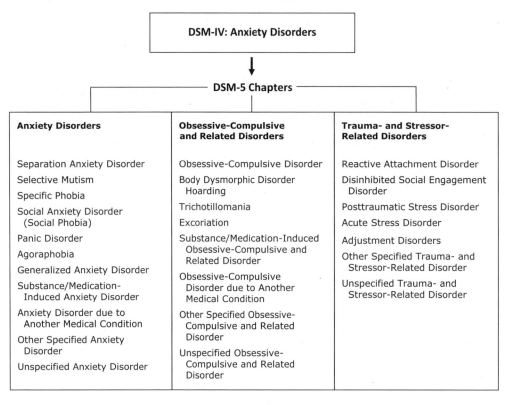

Trauma- and Stressor-Related Disorders

- Posttraumatic stress disorder (PTSD)
- Adjustment disorder

In the next section, we describe the specific changes from the DSM-IV to the DSM-5 for the 7 disorders discussed in this book. Full DSM-5 criteria will be described in each specific disorder section.

Changes to Anxiety Disorders Criteria

General Changes

- Fear, anxiety, and avoidance are the main descriptors in phobias; this fear, anxiety, and avoidance must be out of proportion to the actual danger or threat in the situation (i.e., according to clinician judgment); there is no longer a requirement that the patient recognize that their anxiety is excessive or unreasonable.
- Except for panic disorders, the duration criteria—"typically lasting for 6 months or more"—has been added for adults to minimize over-diagnosis of transient fears.

Specific Changes

GENERALIZED ANXIETY DISORDERS

- The criteria are unchanged except that GAD can be diagnosed even if it occurs only during major depressive disorder (MDD) episodes or in mood, psychotic, or pervasive developmental disorders. In the DSM-IV, the diagnosis of GAD was not assigned if it occurred only during episodes of MDD. This resulted in an under-diagnosis of GAD.

PANIC ATTACK, PANIC DISORDER, AND AGORAPHOBIA

- Panic disorder and agoraphobia are now 2 distinct diagnoses, each with separate criteria (in the DSM-IV, agoraphobia is associated with panic disorder; i.e., panic disorder with or without agoraphobia).

PANIC ATTACK

- Different types of panic attacks have been deleted (i.e., situationally bound/cued, situationally predisposed, and unexpected/uncued).
- The terms *unexpected* and *expected panic attacks* have been introduced.

Of note, panic attacks can also be a specifier in all DSM-5 disorders in which the attacks are triggered by that disorder. For example, if someone suffers from PTSD and a situation triggers a re-experience of the traumatic event, which in turn triggers a panic attack, the panic attack would be a specifier of the PTSD diagnosis because it is cued by a specific determinant (event or situation) of the disorder. Panic attack as a specifier in a disorder is a prognostic factor for severity of illness, illness course, suicidality, comorbidity, and poorer response to treatment, including, but not limited to, anxiety disorders.

PANIC DISORDER

- Panic attacks can arise from a calm or anxious state.

AGORAPHOBIA

- Agoraphobia is no longer required to be associated with panic disorder

(i.e., individuals with agoraphobia do not necessarily experience panic symptoms or panic disorder).
- Anxiety must be out of proportion to the actual danger or threat in the situation (according to clinician judgment).
- The individual must have experienced fear in 2 or more agoraphobic situations (to distinguish agoraphobia from specific phobias).
- The symptoms must last for at least 6 months.

SOCIAL ANXIETY DISORDER

- Individuals are no longer required to be over 18 years of age.
- An individual is no longer required to recognize that their anxiety is excessive or unreasonable. This decision is now made according to the clinician's judgment that the anxiety is out of proportion to the actual danger or threat in the situation, after taking cultural contextual factors into account. (Individuals with these disorders often overestimate the danger in "phobic" situations, and older individuals often misattribute "phobic" fears to aging.) For example, a patient might say, "No, I don't think my fear is unreasonable. I really will do something stupid or embarrassing."
- The requirement for symptoms to last at least 6 months or more, which was limited to individuals under 18 years of age in the DSM-IV, is now extended to all ages (to minimize over-diagnosis of transient fears).
- The specifier "generalized" has been removed as the definition was unclear. The DSM-5 now recognizes individuals who fear only performance situations (e.g., public speaking), as this is a distinct group respective to age of onset, etiology, and physiologic and treatment response.

Changes to Obsessive-Compulsive and Related Disorders Criteria

OBSESSIVE-COMPULSIVE DISORDER

- The word "impulse" has been replaced with the word "urge" to describe obsessions more accurately.
- The word "inappropriate" when referring to obsessions has been replaced with the word "unwanted" (the meaning of "inappropriate" can vary with culture, gender, age, and other factors).
- There is a new "tic" specifier: past or current. There is a close relationship and high comorbidity between OCD and tics; OCD and comorbid tics have earlier onset, are more common in males, and tend to respond better when a selective serotonin uptake inhibitor (SSRI) is augmented with an antipsychotic.
- Patients are no longer required to recognize that their obsessions and compulsions are excessive or unreasonable. (These descriptors can have different meanings for different people: many patients have poor insight, and 2–4% have no insight.[11])
- Insight specifiers in the DSM-5 have been changed to "good" or "fair," "poor," and and "absent insight/delusional beliefs." The DSM-IV only had "poor insight" as a specifier (inconsistent with patients being required to recognize that their obsessions and compulsions were excessive or unreasonable).
  - Good insight: The individual knows he or she won't catch a deadly germ but feels anxious that maybe they will.
  - Poor insight: The individual is pretty sure he or she will get a dangerous germ if they don't wash their hands 25 times.
  - Absent insight/delusional beliefs: The individual is absolutely convinced that consequences will occur; he or she will catch a deadly germ if they don't wash their hands 25 times.
  - The delusional variant (a person is convinced that the belief or the consequence will occur; the house will burn down if he or she doesn't check the stove 50 times) has been moved from the psychosis section into the parent OCD section.

  The most important clinical significance of this change in the DSM-5 is to decrease the misdiagnosis of OCD comorbid with delusional beliefs and schizophrenia or another psychotic disorder, and subsequently the mistreatment with monotherapy antipsychotics. Research shows that the former responds better with an SSRI followed by an augmented antipsychotic if there is no response.

Changes to Trauma- and Stressor-Related Disorders Criteria

Exposure to a traumatic or stressful event is required as a diagnostic criterion. The order of the disorders listed in this chapter is reflective of developmental perspective. Those with earlier onset are listed earlier in the chapter. Here we describe the changes for PTSD.

Posttraumatic Stress Disorder

The DSM-IV was unclear with regard to what was considered a traumatic event, which resulted in an over-diagnosis of PTSD.

- The diagnostic A1 criterion is more specific for the definition of "traumatic event"; it is limited to actual or threatened death, serious injury, or sexual violence. It clarifies that you do not get PTSD from watching television.
- The trauma must precede the symptoms as they have to be linked to the trauma.

- In the A2 criterion, the "fear of helplessness and horror" is eliminated (it was unclear, and not all patients experience these symptoms; e.g., police officers who are trained to suppress these feelings).
- There are now 4 symptom clusters rather than 3 and "avoidance" and "numbing of responsiveness" have been separated. A person must experience the following symptoms for at least 1 month or more:
  - Re-experiencing
  - Avoidance
  - Persistent negative alterations in cognition and mood with at least 2 of the following:
    → Inability to recall important aspects of the trauma
    → Decreased interest in pleasurable activities
    → Negative beliefs
    → Detachment from others
    → Fear
    → Helplessness
    → Guilt
    → Anger
    → Shame
    → Horror
  - Increased arousal with at least 2 of the following:
    → Irritable or aggressive behavior
    → Reckless or self-destructive behavior
    → Hypervigilance
    → Exaggerated startle response
    → Problems with concentration
    → Sleep disturbance
- Acute and chronic PTSD specifiers have been deleted.
- The PTSD diagnostic criteria apply to adults, adolescents, and children >6 years of age.
- The following subtypes have been added:
  - Children ≤6 years of age
  - Dissociative symptoms—detachment from physical and emotional experience—is now a specifier for patients of all ages

As with all specifiers, patients must meet all the criteria of PTSD, and if they have a high degree of derealization or depersonalization, this would warrant the dissociative subtype.

Adjustment Disorders

In the DSM-5, adjustment disorders are covered in the Trauma- and Stressor-Related Disorders chapter as they are considered to be caused by a stress response that occurs after exposure to a distressing event. The DSM-IV subtypes (depressed mood, anxious symptoms, and disturbances in conduct) are unchanged. The distinction between chronic (duration of more than 6 months) and acute (less than 6 months) has been removed and replaced with "persistent" if the disorder lasts longer than 12 months.

Theories on the Causes of Anxiety and Related Disorders

To date, the exact cause of anxiety disorders is still not known; however, researchers propose a great number of theories: a combination of genetic vulnerability, biological factors, temperament, family context, life experiences, or situational factors.

Genetic Theory

Research suggests that there is a genetic tendency to develop anxiety disorders. In other words, the illness runs in families. For example, the risk of developing a panic disorder among first-degree relatives with panic disorder is 41% compared to 4% among controls.[12] Other anxiety disorders have similar but lower associated risks. This genetic tendency could either predispose someone to developing a specific anxiety disorder or perhaps a general anxiety characteristic is passed on to offspring. Specific genes have not been identified to date.

Biological Theory

CHANGES IN THE BRAIN

Anxiety disorders
The hypothalamic-pituitary-adrenocortical (HPA) axis, illustrated in Figure 1.3, is a complex biofeedback loop or regulatory system that controls the release of stress hormones. Simply put, when the HPA axis is stimulated, 3 main hormones are released—corticotropin-releasing factor (CRF), arginine vasopressin (AVP), and adrenocorticotropic hormone (ACTH). Subsequently, this stimulates the adrenal gland to release the stress hormones responsible for the stress reaction. The sudden increase in the bloodstream of the stress hormone cortisol has a negative

FIGURE 1.3 THE HYPOTHALAMIC-PITUITARY-ADRENOCORTICAL (HPA) AXIS

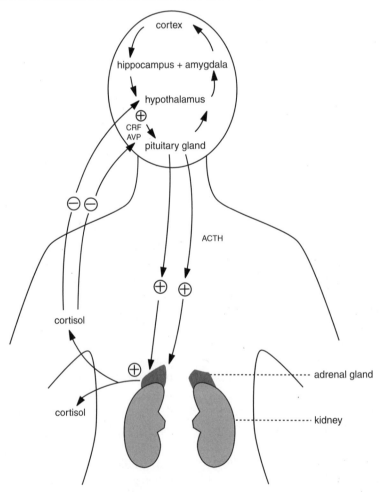

stimulatory effect on the hypothalamus and the pituitary gland (negative feedback) of the HPA axis, suppressing or inhibiting the release of more stress hormones.

When an individual is not experiencing stress, normal quantities of stress hormones fluctuate throughout the day by stimulation and inhibition of this feedback mechanism. Under stressful conditions, there is an increase in the release of stress hormones, particularly adrenaline, which speeds up the heart rate, constricts blood vessels, raises blood pressure and breathing rate, increases sweating, and tenses the muscles to prepare a person to fight, flee, or freeze. This physiologic reaction subsides once the stressful stimulus ends.[13, 14]

The biological theory for anxiety disorders proposes that there is an imbalance in the stress hormones regulated by this mechanism. The hippocampus and the amygdala are centers of the brain thought to be responsible for emotions (Figure 1.4). These centers are connected via nerve circuits

FIGURE 1.4 BRAIN EMOTION CENTERS

Hippocampus and Amygdala

Brain viewed from the underside and front

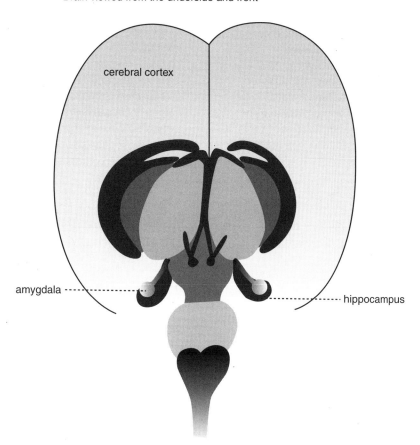

cerebral cortex

amygdala

hippocampus

to the hypothalamus. Changes in activity in these centers can therefore influence the HPA axis. In anxiety disorders, researchers propose that there exists an abnormal process that lowers the *excitement* response level (arousal thresholds) in the hippocampus and the amygdala, resulting in overstimulation of the hypothalamus and pituitary glands and a greater release of stress hormones.

Obsessive-compulsive and related disorders

A different mechanism is proposed in OCD. People with OCD show hyperactive changes in functional brain imaging studies in 3 areas of the brain: the caudate nucleus, the prefrontal orbital cortex, and the cingulate gyrus.

- The caudate nucleus filters thoughts coming in from other areas and controls repetitive behaviors. In OCD, it is believed that the nucleus is unable to control or filter the worries or thoughts between the thalamus and the cortex. This changes the impact of the information received, which in turn alters actions and decisions.
- The prefrontal orbital cortex is responsible for appropriate social behavior. Decreased activity in this area reduces inhibitions. With increased activity, which is the case for OCD, people overly worry about social behaviors, acting inappropriately and becoming, for example, meticulous, neat, and preoccupied with cleanliness.
- The cingulate gyrus may be responsible for the emotional response to obsessive thoughts, which leads to the compulsion to reduce the anxiety related to the obsessive thoughts.

SSRIs, which increase serotonin levels in the brain and enable better transmission of messages, may change the level of activity in these areas of the brain.

Trauma- and stressor-related disorders

For trauma- and stressor-related disorders, in particular PTSD, another theory has been proposed. First, people experience at least 1 traumatizing or distressing event in their lifetime. Three areas of the brain have been identified in which function may be affected by traumatic events: the prefrontal cortex, amygdala, and hippocampus.

- The volume of the hippocampus, which is responsible for memory, discriminating between past and present experiences, and interpreting environmental situations correctly, decreases. The hippocampus cannot filter past memories, hence exposure to any situation or event resembling the past trauma triggers an increased stress response.
- The volume and functioning of the ventromedial prefrontal cortex, which regulates negative emotions such as fear when exposed to stimuli, decreases.
- The amygdala is normally involved in processing emotions and is activated with exposure to fear. Exposure to stimuli (fear) from the past launches the stress response, resulting in anxiety, panic, and extreme stress. Hyperactivity of the amygdala is positively related to the severity of PTSD symptoms.[15, 16, 17]

NEUROCHEMICAL IMBALANCE

Another common biological theory is that anxiety and related disorders are caused by an imbalance in brain neurochemicals. At least 5 neurochemicals could be implicated and thought to be unbalanced in anxiety and related disorders: serotonin, norepinephrine, gamma-aminobutyric acid (GABA), corticotropin-releasing hormone (CRH), and cholecystokinin. Serotonin and GABA are chemicals that prevent and quiet the stress response. The contribution of the neurotransmitters to each type of anxiety or related disorder differs depending on the disorder. For example, when patients with PTSD are exposed to stress, the hypothalamic paraventricular nucleus secretes CRH, which through a chain reaction stimulates the release of glucocorticoids (cortisol) from the adrenal cortex.[18] In addition, there is also an abnormal regulation of catecholamine (norepinephrine), serotonin in brain circuits that regulates fear responses.

Psychological Theory

Several psychological theories attempt to explain the causes of anxiety and related disorders. The most common ones are based on psychodynamic, behavioral, and cognitive principles.

PSYCHODYNAMIC THEORIES

Psychodynamic theories suggest that the development of anxiety disorders is a result of an underlying emotional conflict. The theory proposes that an individual's defense mechanisms cause them to suppress and store underlying emotionally traumatic memories, thoughts, or wishes in the subconscious because these thoughts are threatening, cause psychic pain, or are socially or ethically unacceptable to the individual. These thoughts or memories will have a natural tendency to surface from time to time, so the person can either attempt to resolve them or seek pleasure from them. Because the resurfacing of these memories or thoughts is no less threatening to the person than actual events, anxiety is triggered. The underlying emotional conflict, which is the basis of this theory, is the contradiction

between the attempt to deny the painful emotions and the natural urge for emotional traumatic memories to surface. People will develop defense mechanisms, such as a disconnect between intellectually recognizing the emotions and being able to physically experience them (isolation of affect) and unconsciously pushing painful emotions into the body (repression of affect). Even though the individual is not aware of this subconscious battle, he or she may be affected throughout their lifetime.

Psychoanalysis and other dynamic therapies assist with recovery by helping the individual become aware of repressed emotions and mental conflicts. A therapist will help the individual feel the visceral emotions of rage, guilt, and sadness that have been suppressed over several years of conflict, along with giving the individual an understanding of the influence of these emotions on his or her past history and present difficulties. When these feelings are experienced in a professional's office setting, the individual usually experiences relief from symptoms and improved mental functioning.[19]

BEHAVIORAL THEORIES

Behavioral theories suggest that classical conditioning and observational learning are the root of anxiety disorders. In classical conditioning, a non-frightening situation is repeatedly paired with a frightening situation, so that eventually the non-frightening situation triggers fear. In observational learning, an individual learns a behavior by observing the reactions of others to a fearful stimulus. An example of this is when children observe their parents' behavior when faced with fearful objects or situations. The children learn to be afraid of these objects or situations and start avoiding them just like their parents. This avoidance behavior only serves to reinforce and maintain the anxiety, which becomes a vicious circle.

COGNITIVE THEORIES

Cognitive theories explain that how an individual thinks about or perceives various events is determined by specific attitudes, assumptions, or rules learned from past experiences during the developmental years. These theories propose that if we learn faulty assumptions, rules, or attitudes, we will attribute these rules to current events and perceive them in a faulty manner, leading to psychological problems. For example, a child may have learned that if you are smart, you will be successful. Later in life, if the person is not successful in finding a good job after graduating from college, he or she would make the assumption "I am not smart." These thoughts are automatic without us being aware of them. When we find ourselves thinking about things automatically, we can sometimes assume those thoughts are

true without ever really examining them. Cognitive behavior therapy (CBT) focuses on changing the way a person perceives and thinks about a feared event so that the individual adopts a more rational thought process.[20]

Environmental Theory

Environmental theory proposes that environmental factors are at the root of the development of anxiety disorders; for example, early stressful life events (e.g., the loss of a parent) and psychosocial stressors (e.g., dysfunctional family).[21, 22, 23]

Temperamental Theory

Temperamental theory proposes that the temperament of the child is at play in anxiety disorders. Character traits such as irritability, shyness, fearfulness, cautiousness, quietness, or introversion give an individual the tendency to withdraw in unfamiliar situations and are thought to increase the likelihood of the individual developing anxiety disorders.[24, 25]

Summary

Although several theories have been put forth, the consensus among experts is that anxiety disorders are the result of a combination of factors, rather than any given one. For example, an individual could have so-called *anxiety genes*, which would make the individual susceptible to developing an anxiety disorder. These genes would stay dormant until the individual was exposed to an environmental factor or life stressor. The combination would trigger an actual disorder (the study of gene-environment interaction is called epigenetics). To date there are no laboratory or genetic tests, biomarkers, or brain imaging studies to help guide the choice of treatment in specific anxiety and related disorders.

NOTES

1 American Psychiatric Association. Diagnostic and statistical manual of mental disorders (DSM-5). 5th ed. Arlington, VA: American Psychiatric Association; 2013.

2 Sadock B, Kaplan HI, Sadock VA. Kaplan & Sadock's synopsis of psychiatry: behavioral sciences/clinical psychiatry. 10th ed. Philadelphia: Lippincott Williams & Wilkins; 2007.

3 Somers J, Goldner E, Waraich P, Hsu L. Prevalence and incidence studies of anxiety disorders: a systematic review of the literature. Can J Psychiatry. 2006; 51(2):100–113.

4 Martín-Merino E, Ruigómez A, Wallander M, Johansson S, García-Rodríguez L. Prevalence,

incidence, morbidity and treatment patterns in a cohort of patients diagnosed with anxiety in UK primary care. Family Practice. 2009; 27(1):9–16.

5 Kessler RC, Angermeyer M, Anthony JC, De Graaf R, Demyttenaere K, Gasquet I, et al. Lifetime prevalence and age-of-onset distributions of mental disorders in the World Health Organization's World Mental Health Survey Initiative. World Psychiatry. 2007; 6(3):168–176.

6 Katzman MA, Bleau P, Blier P, Chokka P, Kjernisted K, Van Ameringen M, et al. Canadian clinical practice guidelines for the management of anxiety, posttraumatic stress and obsessive-compulsive disorders. BMC Psychiatry. 2014; 14 Suppl 1:S1.

7 Canadian Psychiatric Association. Clinical practice guidelines for the management of anxiety disorders. Can J Psychiatry. 2006; 51 Suppl 2:9S–91S.

8 Sadock B, Kaplan HI, Sadock VA. Kaplan & Sadock's synopsis of psychiatry: behavioral sciences/clinical psychiatry. 10th ed. Philadelphia: Lippincott Williams & Wilkins; 2007.

9 American Psychiatric Association. Diagnostic and statistical manual of mental disorders (DSM-5). 5th ed. Arlington, VA: American Psychiatric Association; 2013.

10 American Psychiatric Association. Diagnostic and statistical manual of mental disorders (DSM-5). 5th ed. Arlington, VA: American Psychiatric Association; 2013.

11 American Psychiatric Association. Diagnostic and statistical manual of mental disorders (DSM-5). 5th ed. Arlington, VA: American Psychiatric Association; 2013.

12 Crowe R, Noyes R, Pauls D, Slymen D. A family study of panic disorder. Arch Gen Psychiatry. 1983; 40(10):1065–1069.

13 Varghese FP, Brown ES. The Hypothalamic-pituitary-adrenal axis in major depressive disorder: a brief primer for primary care physicians. Prim Care Companion Journal of Clin Psychiatry. 2001; 3(4):151–155.

14 Hardman JG, Limbird LE, Gilman AG, editors. Goodman and Gilman's the pharmacological basis of therapeutics. 10th ed. New York: McGraw-Hill; 2001. Chapter 59, Adrenocorticotropic Hormone; Adrenocortical Steroids and Their Synthetic Analogs; Inhibitors of the Synthesis and Actions of Adrenocortical Hormones, p. 1649–1678.

15 Bremner J, Elzinga B, Schmahl C, Vermetten E. Structural and functional plasticity of the human brain in posttraumatic stress disorder. Progress in Brain Research. 2008; 167:171–86.

16 Koenigs, M., Grafman, J. Posttraumatic stress disorder: the role of medial prefrontal cortex and amygdala. Neuroscientist. 2009; 15(5), 540–548.

17 Rocha-Rego V, Pereira M, Oliveira L, Mendlowicz M, Fiszman A, Marques-Portella C et al. Decreased premotor cortex volume in victims of urban violence with posttraumatic stress disorder. PLoS ONE. 2012; 7(8):e42560.

18 Sherin JE, Nemeroff CB. Post-traumatic stress disorder: the neurobiological impact of psychological trauma. Dialogues Clin Neurosci. 2011; 13(3): 263–278.

19 Keefe JR, McCarthy KS, Dinger U, et al. A meta-analytic review of psychodynamic therapies for anxiety disorders. Clin Psychol Rev. 2014; 34(4): 309–323.

20 Beck AT, Rush JA, Shaw BF, Emery G. Cognitive theory of depression. John Rush, Brian F Shaw, Gary Emery. New York: Guilford Press; 1979.

21 Brook CA, Schmidt LA. Social anxiety disorder: a review of environmental risk factors. Neuropsychiatric Disease and Treatment. 2008; 1:123–143.

22 Ballash NG, Pemble MK, Usui WM, et al. Family functioning, perceived control, and anxiety: a mediational model. J Anxiety Disord. 2006; 20(4): 486–497.

23 Grover RL, Ginsburg GS, Ialongo N. Childhood predictors of anxiety symptoms: a longitudinal study. Child Psychiatry Hum Dev. 2005; 36(2):133–153.

24 Ballenger JC, Davidson JR, Lecrubier Y, Nutt DJ, Bobes J, Beidel DC, et al. Consensus statement on social anxiety disorder from the International Consensus Group on Depression and Anxiety. J Clin Psychiatry. 1998; 59 Suppl 17:54–60.

25 Svihra M, Katzman MA. Behavioural inhibition: a predictor of anxiety. Paediatrics & Child Health. 2004; 9(8):547–550.

2

Assessment

Common Presentation of Anxiety and Related Disorders

Common anxiety symptoms will manifest in varying degrees in all anxiety and related disorders. Typically, patients will present with complaints that fall into 3 categories: mental unease, physical symptoms, and behavior changes. Patients will almost always try to avoid the situations they fear (Table 2.1).

In some cases, symptoms can be more severe and crystallize into a panic attack. The DSM-5 recognizes that panic attacks can be isolated or a specifier of another disorder. People describe a panic attack as a strong feeling of fear or discomfort, a fear of dying, a feeling of going crazy, or a feeling that they are about to lose control, which peaks and gradually subsides. A panic attack on its own is not a considered a disorder. In some cases, the panic attack reoccurs and can be debilitating, causing behavioral changes, such as avoidance of situations or fear of certain objects, interfering with the individual's day-to-day functioning. A panic attack is central to the development of a panic disorder; however, it can be a common occurrence in anxiety and related disorders such as social phobia and specific phobia (see Chapter 5: Panic Disorder, p. 57). Patients with anxiety or related disorders typically experience their symptoms for many years.

TABLE 2.1 ANXIETY AND RELATED DISORDERS PRESENTATION[1]

PSYCHOLOGICAL SYMPTOMS	PHYSICAL SYMPTOMS	BEHAVIOR CHANGES
Fear; chronic nervous tension; worry; concentration, memory, and decision-making problems	Pounding heart; sweating; chest pains; butterflies in stomach; nausea; shakes; chills; dizziness; light-headedness or feeling faint; difficulty breathing; tension headaches; sleep problems; fatigue	Avoidance of anxiety-provoking situations; poor relationships; self-medicating with drugs or alcohol to reduce anxiety; becoming housebound

Factors to Consider When Assessing Anxiety and Related Disorders

Non-psychiatric conditions can present with anxiety symptoms, but rarely to the point of being a complete disorder. Common triggers to consider include, for example, excessive caffeine intake and certain medications, such as methylphenidate. Other medical conditions, such as hyperthyroidism, can present as tenseness and irritability. It is also important to consider the impact that medications or other substances may have on emotional, cognitive, and behavioral symptoms (e.g., drug and alcohol abuse/ misuse). Finally, the presence of another psychiatric condition, such as a depressive disorder, can precede, occur concurrently with, or be the result of a primary condition. If such a condition remains unknown or undiscovered, it can interfere with conventional treatment.

> To further your assessment, use the tool Factors to Consider When Assessing Anxiety Symptoms, Appendix I, p. 155.

Provisional Diagnosis

Anxiety and Related Disorders: Types and Subtypes

Once you rule out non-psychiatric causes, you are ready to begin assessing for anxiety and related disorders. The Patient Self-Report Screening Tool for Mental Illnesses (Appendix VI, p. 161) contains screening questions to guide your provisional diagnosis. The tool is not validated; however, it serves as a *memory aid* for questions ordinarily asked in the screening phase and helps orient the subsequent choice of validated assessment scales. These scales will be discussed in each of the specific disorder chapters. Identifying the specific anxiety or related disorder will improve the patient's rate of recovery, as management can be tailored appropriately. The main difference between disorders is the nature of the fear (worry) or the stressor/trauma involved. Table 2.2 helps clarify the issue and provides a quick reference. Another useful tool is the DSM-5 Self-Rated Level 1 Cross-Cutting Symptom Measure—Adult developed by the American

TABLE 2.2 REFERENCE GUIDE FOR ANXIETY AND RELATED DISORDERS

TYPE OF ANXIETY DISORDER	WHAT DOES THE PATIENT WORRY ABOUT? WHAT IS THE STRESSOR?
Generalized anxiety disorder (GAD)	Fear of several activities, including everyday, routine life events or multiple non-specific situations; fear is out of proportion to the actual danger or threat—broad scope. This is the typical "worry wart" or "what if this happens" type of individual.
Panic disorder	Fear of the fear itself—fear of recurrent, unexpected panic attacks.
Agoraphobia	Fear of places, situations, or events from which escape might be difficult or in which help may not be available.
Social anxiety disorder	Fear of negative evaluation by others in social interactions or of performing in front of others (fear that the scrutiny or judgment of others will cause embarrassment or humiliation).

(Table 2.2 continued on next page)

TABLE 2.2 (CONTINUED)

TYPE OF ANXIETY DISORDER	WHAT DOES THE PATIENT WORRY ABOUT? WHAT IS THE STRESSOR?
Obsessive-compulsive disorder (OCD)	Fear related to intrusive, recurrent, and persistent ideas, thoughts, urges, or images (e.g., becoming contaminated), which can result in compulsive behavior meant to neutralize the fear related to the obsessions (e.g., washing hands repeatedly for fear of germs, checking repeatedly that doors are locked or appliances are unplugged for fear that a catastrophe will occur, such as the house burning down).
Posttraumatic stress disorder (PTSD)	Fear or distress caused by remembering/reliving a specific traumatic event.
Adjustment disorder	An abnormal reaction to or distress caused by a major life event that occurs within 3 months of an identifiable stressor (e.g., loss of a relationship, conflict in the workplace) and resolves within 6 months, once the stressor has resolved.

Psychiatric Association (APA). This measure can be reproduced without permission by researchers and clinicians for use with their patients. The tool and rating information can be accessed and downloaded at http://www .psychiatry.org/psychiatrists/practice/dsm /dsm-5/online-assessment-measures.

> The tool Differentiating Anxiety, Obsessive-Compulsive, and Trauma- and Stressor-Related Disorders (Appendix II), p. 156, helps differentiate the types of anxiety and related disorders.

Confirming the Diagnosis

The DSM-5 formal diagnostic criteria for anxiety and related disorders have been developed by the APA and will be included in each disorder chapter.[2] Although not validated as diagnostic tools, self-report assessment scales combined with reviewer confirmation of the duration of hallmark symptoms as listed in the DSM-5, plus functional impairment, are useful in primary care to help guide the diagnosis, in particular if time is of the essence. Examples of how

these tools can be used will be included in each disorder section.

Baseline Assessment

Once you have confirmed the diagnosis of the specific anxiety or related disorder, the next step is to conduct a baseline assessment. Structured, validated screening and assessment scales can be used to identify the frequency and severity of symptoms. Scales are visually inspected by providers for significant responses, reviewed for areas of agreement, and scored.

> » What should be included in a baseline assessment?
> » What tools are useful at baseline and follow-up visits?

Primary care providers can use both clinician-based measures and self-report measures. Self-report rating scales are used by health care professionals in many medical conditions, including mental health assessments. These tools are time efficient and helpful in guiding thought processes. However, there is no substitute for a careful clinical assessment. Ultimately, decisions about diagnosis and management should be based on a clinical assessment that comes from listening to a patient's story and questioning the individual about what they reported on a rating scale. A careful assessment and rating of each of the following parameters will establish a baseline state from which to measure treatment response:

- Safety (suicide) assessment
- Anxiety and related disorder symptom severity
- Comorbid conditions
- Somatic complaints
- Functional impairment

Assessing Patient Safety

Assessment of suicide risk should be considered at baseline and when clinically warranted at follow-up visits.[3] Ask about thoughts of death or suicide and feelings of hopelessness or that life is not worth living. Ask about the intensity and frequency of these thoughts and whether there is intent or plans for suicide. The Suicide Assessment Questionnaire (Appendix III, p. 157) and the Suicide Risk Factors Summary (Appendix IV, p. 158) can help assess the level of risk. Case studies in this book purposely do not reflect patients at imminent risk of suicide as this would change the course of action, and the goal of the book is to support primary health care professionals to work through the entire assessment and management of mild, moderate, and severe anxiety and related disorders.

Assessing Anxiety Symptom Severity

The severity of a patient's condition can influence treatment options. The generalized anxiety disorder 7-item scale, or GAD-7 (Appendix V, p. 160), is a validated practical tool to assess anxiety symptom severity. This 7-item questionnaire assesses both psychological and physiologic symptoms[4] and can be used to monitor treatment efficacy as well. It yields a single score between 0 (no anxiety) and 21 (severe anxiety), plus the scoring is easy to remember because levels 5, 10, and 15 are cutpoints for increasing severity:

$$0–4 = \text{no anxiety}$$
$$5–9 = \text{mild anxiety}$$
$$10–14 = \text{moderate anxiety}$$
$$>15 = \text{severe anxiety}$$

Using the threshold score of 10, the GAD-7 has a sensitivity of 89% and a specificity of 82% for GAD. It is moderately good at screening 3 other common anxiety disorders: panic disorder (sensitivity 74%, specificity 81%), social anxiety disorder (sensitivity 72%, specificity 80%), and PTSD (sensitivity 66%, specificity 81%).[5, 6] The treatment goal is to achieve complete remission (a score of <5). However, the scoring system should be interpreted along with clinical presentation because a patient can score low (e.g., 10), yet exhibit substantial functional impairment and be suicidal. In this example, the severity may not reflect the true clinical picture.

Other useful tools that can be used to assess illness severity, such as the Disorder-Specific Severity Measures developed by the APA,[7] can be downloaded directly from their site at http://www.psychiatry.org/psychiatrists/practice/dsm/dsm-5/online-assessment-measures. These measures can be reproduced without permission by researchers and by clinicians for use with their patients. Rating information is provided as well.

Screening for Comorbid Conditions

Depression is by far the most common comorbid condition with anxiety disorders. Anxiety and related disorders are also highly comorbid with each other and with substance use disorder because patients with anxiety and related disorders often turn to alcohol or sedative drugs to help them cope with their symptoms. The presence of another psychiatric condition such as a depressive disorder or substance use disorder can precede (i.e., be a primary condition for), occur concurrently with, or be the result of a primary condition. If a comorbid condition is unknown or undiscovered, it can interfere with conventional treatment and impact recovery.

» How do you screen for common anxiety disorders?

» How do you screen for common comorbid psychiatric conditions?

PATIENT SELF-REPORT SCREENING TOOL FOR MENTAL ILLNESSES

If not done at the screening/provisional diagnosis phase, primary care providers can screen for comorbid conditions with the Patient Self-Report Screening Tool for Mental Illnesses (Appendix VI, p. 161). It can be used to do the following:

- Screen and help differentiate between anxiety disorders
- Briefly screen for key symptoms of other psychiatric conditions
- Screen for substance use disorder
- Assess functional impairment
- Guide providers towards the next step specific disorder scale to be used

Note: The Patient Self-Report Screening Tool for Mental Illnesses is not a validated tool; however, it serves as a memory aid for questions ordinarily asked when assessing patients, helping providers to decide which validated assessment or diagnostic tools to use. In this book, specific assessment scales/tools can be found in each disorder chapter. Providers can use the tools as is or to help generate additional questions as per usual assessment practices. The DSM-5 Level 1 Cross-Cutting Symptom Measure—Adult, developed by the APA, can also be used.[8] It can be downloaded directly from the APA site at http://www.psychiatry.org/psychiatrists/prac tice/dsm/dsm-5/online-assessment-measures. These measures can be reproduced without permission by researchers and by clinicians for use with their patients. Rating information is provided as well.

PHQ-9

If screening for depression returns a positive result (section 1 of the tool), the Patient Health Questionnaire-9, or PHQ-9 (Appendix VII, p. 165) can be used. The PHQ-9, developed by Dr. Robert L. Spitzer and Dr. Janet B.W. Williams specifically for primary care settings, is a self-report tool that takes only a few minutes to complete. The tool is highly sensitive and specific for the diagnosis of depression and scores each of the nine DSM-5 criteria for depression, as well the effect of the major depressive episode (MDE) on functioning. When combined with clinical judgment, the tool can be used for screening, diagnosis, severity assessment, and monitoring progress. The scoring interpretation is as follows.

Major depressive disorder is suggested if:

1. Question 1 or 2: Need 1 or both of the first 2 questions endorsed as 2 = "More than half the days" or 3 = "Nearly every day"
2. Need a total of 5 or more of the 9 items endorsed within the shaded area of the form (questions 1–8 must be endorsed as a 2 or a 3; question 9 must be endorsed as a 1, or a 2 or a 3)

3. Question 10 must be endorsed as "Somewhat difficult," "Very difficult," or "Extremely difficult"

To use the PHQ-9 to assess severity and monitor treatment, add the total score and use the scoring interpretation as follows:

0–4 = not depressed
5–9 = mild depression
10–14 = moderate depression
15–19 = moderate-severe depression
20–27 = severe depression

Assessing Somatic Complaints

Assessing somatic complaints at baseline provides practitioners with valuable information on 2 fronts: differentiating between anxiety-related somatic complaints and somatic complaints related to other factors (e.g., secondary to medication side effects). This distinction could prove useful in guiding decisions about the best way to manage a patient. Somatic symptoms can be assessed with the Symptom Assessment Checklist (Appendix VIII, p. 167).

Assessing Functional Impairment

Anxiety and related disorders can cause considerable functional impairment.

Addressing functional impairment is critical when evaluating treatment efficacy. To assess the big picture of the patient's psychological, social, and occupational functioning, you can use the Functional Impairment Assessment Scale (Appendix IX, p. 168), a patient self-report tool that assesses functioning across the following domains: work, social/leisure activities, family life/home responsibilities, relationship with spouse/partner. It is not a validated tool; however, it serves as a user-friendly *visual aid* for patients to self-assess functioning, which can then be verified by a health care professional. The validated Sheehan Disability Scale, which can be found in the DSM-5 or accessed in the public domain by Google search, can also be used for this purpose.[9] Aim for full remission of symptoms and complete psychosocial functioning, as complete remission is associated with decreased likelihood of recurrence and long-term morbidity. Consider assessing functional impairment at baseline and monthly thereafter. Table 2.3 summarizes how the various tools can be used.

TABLE 2.3 PROGRAM TOOLS

DIFFERENTIAL DIAGNOSIS TOOLS		
Step 1	Administer the Patient Self-Report Screening Tool for Mental Illnesses (Appendix VI, p. 161).	Can be self-administered by the patient at home, in the office, or by a health care professional.
		Helps screen for common psychiatric illnesses seen in primary care.
		Screens for comorbid disorders.
		Review responses with patient to verify accuracy.
Step 2	Apply the algorithm Differentiating Anxiety, Obsessive-Compulsive, and Trauma- and Stressor-Related Disorders (Appendix II, p. 156)	Quick reference to help differentiate the anxiety and related disorders.

(Table 2.3 continued on next page)

TABLE 2.3 (CONTINUED)

DIFFERENTIAL DIAGNOSIS TOOLS						
Step 3	Administer provisional diagnostic scale consistent with positive screen in steps 1 and 2, to be reviewed against the DSM-5 criteria to confirm diagnosis.					
Step 4	Administer disorder-specific severity assessment tool, consistent with positive diagnosis in step 3, as well as baseline measures.					

DISORDER-SPECIFIC SCREENING/SEVERITY ASSESSMENT TOOLS						
GAD	GAD-7	✓	VDS	VDSA		PUB
	Severity Measure for Generalized Anxiety Disorder–Adult	✓		VDSA	APA	PUB
Panic Disorder	GAD-7*	✓	VDS	VDSA		PUB
	Panic Disorder Severity Scale Self-Report Form (PDSS)	✓		VDSA		PUB
	Severity Measure for Panic Disorder–Adult	✓		VDSA	APA	PUB
Agoraphobia	Severity Measure for Agoraphobia–Adult	✓		VDSA	APA	PUB
Social Anxiety Disorder	Social Phobia Inventory (SPIN)	✓	VDS	VDSA		
	Severity Measure for Social Anxiety Disorder–Adult	✓		VDSA	APA	PUB
	GAD-7*	✓	VDS	VDSA		PUB
OCD	Level 2–Repetitive Thoughts and Behaviors–Adult	✓		VDSA	APA	PUB
	Brief Obsessive-Compulsive Scale (BOCS)	✓	VDS	VDSA	TC	PUB
PTSD	PTSD Checklist for the DSM-5 (PCL-5)	✓	VDS	VDSA		PUB
	Severity of Posttraumatic Stress Symptoms–Adult	✓		VDSA	APA	PUB
	GAD-7*	✓	VDS	VDSA		PUB
Depression	PHQ-9	✓	VDS	VDSA		PUB
Overall Functioning	Global Assessment of Functioning (GAF) Scale	✓		VDSA		PUB
	Sheehan Disability Scale			VDSA		PUB
	Functional Impairment Assessment Scale	✓				

VDS: Validated disorder screening tool

VDSA: Validated disorder severity assessment tool

APA: Available on the APA website; no copyright restrictions for downloading, printing or clinicians' use with patients

TC: More time-consuming to administer

PUB: Available in the public domain, by Google search, or accessible on the APA website

√: Permission to reproduce tool has been obtained from the author of the scale; tool is included in appendices and/or is available in the public domain

*Moderately sensitive to screen these disorders. Confirm the presence of hallmark symptoms.

Note: Combined with clinical judgment based on the DSM-5 criteria, these tools can be used to confirm diagnosis.

Common Presentation

When patients consult primary care providers, they generally do not come with a "psychiatric illness diagnosis." Often, the first signs of an anxiety or related disorder may not be obvious. Rather, patients complain of common anxiety symptoms, or symptoms come disguised as "somatic symptoms" such as tenseness, irritability, sleep problems, fatigue, and a loss of interest. Primary care providers will then begin the process to narrow the diagnosis: rule-out non-psychiatric causes, explore comorbid conditions, assess safety risk, and so on. In chapters 4 to 10, practice case studies will guide you through various options reflecting this real-life process. The case study below illustrates this point.

It is late in the afternoon; you are 1 hour behind schedule. A patient who was scheduled for a regular checkup breaks down crying because he is at the end of his rope. The patient complains of the following symptoms:

- Excessive anxiety
- Chronic restlessness and nervous tension
- Difficulty concentrating
- Physical symptoms including tension headaches, tightness in the abdomen, palpitations, and difficulty breathing, sleeping only 3 hours per night, and fatigue

Common anxiety symptoms will manifest in varying degrees in all anxiety and related disorders. The main difference between disorders is the nature of the fear (worry) or the stressor/trauma involved. (See Table 2.2). Table 2.4 provides a quick reference linking the patient's type of worry or stressor/trauma to the associated practice case study in this book.

TABLE 2.4 TYPE OF WORRY OR STRESSOR/TRAUMA ASSOCIATED TO CASE STUDY

TYPE OF WORRY OR STRESSOR/TRAUMA	CASE STUDY
Fear of several activities, including everyday, routine life events or multiple non-specific situations; fear is out of proportion to the actual danger or threat—broad scope. This is the typical "worry wart" or "what if this happens" type of individual.	Go to Generalized Anxiety Disorder Case Study: Meet Mr. AG, p. 46.
Fear of the fear itself—fear of recurrent unexpected panic attacks.	Go to Panic Disorder Case Study: Meet Mrs. RM, p. 59.
Fear of going to places, situations, or events from which escape might be difficult or in which help may not be available.	Go to Agoraphobia Case Study: Meet Dr. GC, p. 72.
Fear of negative evaluation by others in social interactions or of performing in front of others (fear that the scrutiny or judgment of others will cause embarrassment or humiliation).	Go to Social Anxiety Disorder Case Study: Meet Ms. SA, p. 87.
Fear related to intrusive, recurrent, and persistent ideas, thoughts, urges, or images (e.g., becoming contaminated), which can result in compulsive behavior meant to neutralize the fear related to the obsessions (e.g., washing hands repeatedly for fear of germs, checking repeatedly that doors are locked or appliances are unplugged for fear that a catastrophe will occur, such as the house burning down).	Go to Obsessive-Compulsive Disorder Case Study: Meet Mr. DH, p. 104.

(Table 2.4 continued on next page)

TABLE 2.4 (CONTINUED)

TYPE OF WORRY OR STRESSOR/TRAUMA	CASE STUDY
Fear or distress caused by remembering/reliving a specific traumatic event.	Go to Postraumatic Stress Disorder Case Study: Meet Mrs. BD, p. 125.
An abnormal reaction to or distress caused by a major life event that occurred within 3 months of an identifiable stressor (e.g., loss of a relationship, conflict in the workplace), and resolves within 6 months once the stressor has resolved.	Go to Adjustment Disorder Case Study: Meet Mr. CF, p. 141.

NOTES

1 Adapted from Evans M, Bradwejn J, Dunn L, editors. Ontario guidelines for the treatment of anxiety disorders in primary care. 1st ed. Toronto: Queen's Printer of Ontario; 2000.

2 American Psychiatric Association. Diagnostic and statistical manual of mental disorders (DSM-5). 5th ed. Arlington, VA: American Psychiatric Association; 2013.

3 Sareen J, Cox B, Afifi T, De Graaf R, Asmundson G, Ten Have M, Stein M. Anxiety disorders and risk for suicidal ideation and suicide attempts: a population-based longitudinal study of adults. Arch Gen Psychiatry. 2005; 62(11):1249–1257.

4 Spitzer R, Kroenke K, Williams J, Löwe B. A brief measure for assessing generalized anxiety disorder: the GAD-7. Arch Intern Med. 2006; 166(10):1092–1097.

5 Swinson R. The GAD-7 scale was accurate for diagnosing generalised anxiety disorder. J Evid Based Med. 2006; 11(6):184.

6 Kroenke K, Spitzer R, Williams J, Monahan P, Löwe B. Anxiety disorders in primary care: prevalence, impairment, comorbidity, and detection. Ann Intern Med. 2007; 146(5):317–325.

7 American Psychiatric Association. Diagnostic and statistical manual of mental disorders (DSM-5). 5th ed. Arlington, VA: American Psychiatric Association; 2013.

8 American Psychiatric Association [Internet]. Arlington (VA): American Psychiatric Association; 2013. Online assessment measures; c2013 [cited 2015 August 29]. Available from: http://www.psychiatry.org/psychiatrists/practice/dsm/dsm-5/online-assessment-measures

9 Sheehan D, Harnett-Sheehan K, Raj B. The measurement of disability. Int Clin Psychopharmacol. 1996; 11 Suppl 3:89–95.

3

Management

The ultimate goal of management in anxiety and related disorders is threefold: to reduce the frequency and intensity of or to eliminate symptoms; to eliminate phobic avoidance; and finally, to restore the patient's ability to carry out normal day-to-day functioning at home, at work or school, and in social situations. Comorbid psychiatric conditions should be treated. Primary care providers should aim for remission whenever possible as partial improvement increases risks of reoccurrence. The choice of treatment will depend on several factors, for example:[1, 2]

- Patient opinions about treatment
- Patient receptivity to counseling
- Patient receptivity to medication
- Severity of symptoms
- Comorbidity
- Previous response (or lack of response) to treatment
- Availability of resources in the community

In addition, decision making regarding management should be individualized, therefore the Table 3.1 is provided solely to serve as a guide.

TABLE 3.1 GUIDE FOR EVIDENCE-BASED OPTIONS BASED ON BASELINE PRESENTATION

GAD-7	SEVERITY OF ANXIETY	DIAGNOSIS	ACTION
0–4	Absent or minimal	GAD unlikely or minimal.	Watchful monitoring.*
5–9	Mild	Mild anxiety symptoms with mild impairment in 1 or more domains of functioning.	Watchful monitoring; psychotherapy can be considered if psychosocial stressors, intrapsychic conflict, etc. are present.
10–14	Moderate	Moderate anxiety with moderate to significant impairment in multiple domains of functioning.	Psychotherapy; pharmacotherapy can be considered as first line if patient is not receptive to psychotherapy.

(Table 3.1 continued on next page)

TABLE 3.1 (CONTINUED)

GAD-7	SEVERITY OF ANXIETY	DIAGNOSIS	ACTION
>15	Severe anxiety (warning level)	Severe anxiety with significant impairment in multiple domains of functioning.	Pharmacotherapy treatment; psychotherapy should be part of management; may need to subside symptoms first with pharmacotherapy for patient to be receptive.
>15	Extreme	Severe anxiety symptoms with severe impairment in multiple domains of functioning and/or high suicide risk.	Consider referral to specialized mental health services.

*Watchful monitoring is recommended for a mild or unclear diagnosis and includes ongoing psycho-education, regularly scheduled telephone and face-to-face contacts, continuous evaluation of symptoms, function, and suicidality, and supportive counseling.

Non-Drug Therapy

Self-Management Strategies

All patients, regardless of the type or severity of the anxiety disorder, should be encouraged to incorporate self-management strategies as part of the treatment plan.[3] Some common-sense lifestyle changes can help reduce anxiety symptoms. Self-management strategies also include the development of coping and stress-management skills. Health care professionals can provide patients with information on self-management resources,[4, 5] and based on the availability of resources in your community, refer patients to self-management community programs. Patients should become familiar with the following strategies:

- Psychoeducation
- Healthier eating
- Reduced caffeine intake
- Active lifestyle
- Adequate sleep
- Setting goals and problem solving
- Improving self-confidence
- Managing distressful symptoms such as fear, anger, and frustration
- Making daily tasks easier
- Improving communication with health care providers, family, and friends

Psychotherapeutic Treatment

COGNITIVE BEHAVIOR THERAPY

While there are many types of psychotherapy available, cognitive behavior therapy (CBT) still remains, in most instances, the first-line recommendation for the management of anxiety disorders, particularly OCD, PTSD, and social anxiety disorder.[6, 7]

Cognitive behavior therapy is the combination of cognitive therapy and behavior therapy. The cognitive element tries to modify patients' mistaken automatic thoughts and perceptions, while the behavioral element tries to modify patients' automatic physical responses to triggers. Patients learn to face their fears with repeated exposure to a stressful situation, thereby increasing their tolerance for the distressful feelings associated with the situation until such time as the feelings gradually decrease. This allows the patients to assign an appropriate level of threat to the feelings, which decreases avoidance. The therapy is brief, focused, active, and directional, and is probably best suited to the busy primary care provider interested in delivering this service. Typically, CBT involves 12–14 weekly sessions, which is considered an adequate treatment trial to assess effectiveness, and can last for as many as 20 sessions. Response can occur in as few as 6 sessions. Cognitive behavior strategies are individualized and focus on factors that trigger the anxiety. Strategies can include the following:

- Psychoeducation (especially important)
- Cognitive restructuring
- Exposure therapy
- Response prevention
- Developing greater tolerance for uncertainty
- Applied relaxation training (relearning how to relax)
- Anxiety management

Furthermore, there is mounting evidence that CBT can be effective in most types of anxiety disorders if delivered face to face, in groups, by telephone when guided by a mental health coach, or in self-directed, credible online programs.[8, 9, 10, 11] For appropriate patients, a mobile app downloadable on smartphones or other devices can provide a convenient way to learn skills and complete homework anywhere or anytime, based on personal schedules. Information is available at http://www.trureachhealth.com/.[12]

When facing real-life anxiety-provoking situations is difficult, virtual-reality exposure therapy is the best choice.[13] Brain-imaging studies demonstrate that CBT can result in similar changes as pharmacotherapy with regard to a patient's return to normal patterns of behavior. It has both short-term and long-term efficacy, and it is more effective than either cognitive or behavioral therapy alone. To learn more about CBT targeted approaches for specific disorders, refer to the Canadian clinical practice guidelines for the management of anxiety, posttraumatic stress, and obsessive-compulsive (OC) disorders.[14]

ADVANCES AND NOVEL APPROACHES IN COGNITIVE BEHAVIOR THERAPY PSYCHOTHERAPY

More studies are required to apply the following approaches clinically, but these types of novel treatments do show promising results. Recently, d-cycloserine has received much attention as an augmenting agent with CBT therapy in the treatment of anxiety and related disorders. Study results are varied regarding its efficacy in the treatment of these disorders. The drug, used as an antibiotic to treat tuberculosis, is thought to activate specific receptors in the amygdala, increasing a person's ability to unlearn certain patterns of fear.

According to Dr. Pine, another interesting advance is attentional bias. Attentional bias is a type of cognitive bias in which a person focuses on a few possibilities and overlooks some options and possible outcomes. Patients with anxiety disorders tend to assign their attention selectively towards threat-related information. The bias is deployed so rapidly that patients are not even aware of it. It is thought to at least partially reflect perturbations in the amygdala. Studies are underway using computer-generated training to help shift patients' biases.[15]

OTHER PSYCHOTHERAPIES

Interpersonal therapy (IPT) is also effective; however, it is more complicated and time-consuming to deliver. Acceptance-based behavior therapy, meta-cognitive therapy,[16, 17] adjunctive mindfulness-based cognitive therapy,[18, 19] and pre-treatment motivational interviewing[20] can also be beneficial. Many resources are available to interested patients who want to learn more about mindfulness strategies.[21, 22, 23]

Other Strategies

See each specific disorder chapter for a brief overview of research in support of other evidence-based strategies.

Drug Therapy

Second-Generation Antidepressants

Second-generation antidepressants are the first-line pharmacological therapy for anxiety and related disorders. Generally speaking, second-generation antidepressants such as SSRIs and serotonin and norepinephrine reuptake inhibitors (SNRIs) have better side effect and safety profiles than reversible monoamine oxidase inhibitors (RIMAs). Table 3.2 gives a brief overview of commonly used second-generation antidepressant recommendations for anxiety and related disorders.

Typically, a new medication is initiated at the initial recommended dose (or half the recommended dose in the elderly or patients who are highly anxious and likely to have difficulties with compliance due to side effects) and increased gradually to the recommended typical average dose (target dose). Refer

to the specific disorder sections for more information on optimum dose and titration. Once the target dose has been achieved, it is maintained for up to 6–8 weeks to assess the response (this can be 10 weeks for OCD). The dosage is increased gradually every 2 weeks until the optimum effective dose is reached, and it is maintained on average for 1–3 years or longer, depending primarily on the severity and duration of the illness.

Tricyclic Antidepressants, Monoamine Oxidase Inhibitors, Reversible Monoamine Oxidase Inhibitors, and Benzodiazepines

Older antidepressants such as tricyclic antidepressants (TCAs) and monoamine oxidase inhibitors (MAOIs), as well as anticonvulsants are also effective; however, they are second- and third-line treatment recommendations due to their side effects profile and tolerability. In particular, the combination of MAOIs with selected foods with high tyramine content (aged cheeses, cured meats, potentially spoiled meats or fish, sauerkraut, soy, Marmite, tap beer, excess wine) can result in a hypertensive crisis.

Buspirone is a Health Canada–approved second line monotherapy indication in GAD. It is not recommended if depression is comorbid with GAD and has been shown to be less effective if patients have previously been treated with benzodiazepines. The consensus is to consider buspirone in benzodiazepine-naïve patients who cannot tolerate, or fail to respond to, an SSRI or SNRI, in particular in the elderly when sedation, psychomotor impairment, and cognitive effects are of concern. Mokhber et al. found that in the elderly, buspirone is well-tolerated, safe, and decreased clinical symptoms of GAD at an average dose of

TABLE 3.2 BRIEF OVERVIEW OF COMMONLY USED SECOND-GENERATION ANTIDEPRESSANT RECOMMENDATIONS FOR ANXIETY AND RELATED DISORDERS (CURRENT FDA– AND/OR HEALTH CANADA–APPROVED INDICATIONS)[24]

INDICATIONS	CITALOPRAM	ESCITALOPRAM	VENLAFAXINE	SERTRALINE	PEROXETINE	FLUVOXAMINE	FLUOXETINE	DULOXETINE
Generalized anxiety disorder		✓	✓	✓	✓	✓		✓
Panic disorder	✓	✓	✓	✓	✓	✓	✓	
Agoraphobia	✓	✓	✓	✓	✓	✓	✓	
Social anxiety disorder		✓	✓	✓	✓	✓	✓	
Posttraumatic stress disorder			✓	✓	✓		✓	
Obsessive-compulsive disorder	✓	✓		✓	✓	✓	✓	

Note: Drug time-release options (e.g., extended-release [XL, XR], sustained-release [SR], etc.) can be found in each specific disorder chapter.

Note: Studies on the management of agoraphobia as a distinct disorder are lacking. Recommendations are based on a meta-analysis of randomized controlled trials including patients with agoraphobia associated with panic disorders. Specific criteria for treating with CBT, pharmacotherapy, or both are difficult to establish. As new information becomes available, evidence-based management guidelines for agoraphobia will be updated in future editions of this book.

Note: More studies are required to evaluate the effectiveness of pharmacological agents in treating adjustment disorder. If another comorbid psychiatric disorder is present, treat the disorder that predominates.

10–15 mg twice daily. [25, 26, 27] Buspirone can be prescribed 2 or 3 times daily; however, 3 times daily dosing can affect compliance rates.

Note: The approved initial dose of buspirone for GAD is 7.5 mg twice daily (5 mg twice daily in the elderly). The dose may be increased every 2 to 3 days in increments of 2.5 mg twice daily as tolerated to a target dose of 20–30 mg/day. Consider maintaining at the target dose for 4–6 weeks before further increases (maximum 30 mg twice daily). Onset of action may be delayed and only evident at 2 weeks or longer.

ADD-ON THERAPY

When considering long-term add-on therapy, several options are available and will be discussed in each disorder section. The usefulness of benzodiazepines is offset by several downsides (i.e., increased risk of falls, motor vehicle accidents, memory problems, and dependency). If benzodiazepines are prescribed as an add-on therapy, they should be used in the short-term (2–3 weeks) only.[28] Benzodiazepines have a rapid onset of action and relieve symptoms of anticipatory anxiety quickly, but to avoid dependency, they should be prescribed 3 times daily rather than as needed until the antidepressant medications take effect, and withdrawn gradually as soon as possible. Some studies have shown that switching from benzodiazepines to buspirone may be useful; however, more recent studies are non-conclusive. Also, buspirone may not be effective in patients previously treated with long-term benzodiazepines. If buspirone is considered, patients may not tolerate withdrawal from benzodiazepines; therefore, it is recommended to prescribe buspirone 20–40 mg 2–4 weeks before benzodiazepine withdrawal by tapering 25% of the daily dose per week.[29] Cochrane reviews on atypical antipsychotics as add-ons in the treatment of anxiety and related disorders are too limited to draw any conclusions.[30, 31]

Some off-label-use drugs (i.e., drugs not approved for a particular disorder by the U.S. Food and Drug Administration, Health Canada, or other drug regulatory agencies) are included in the general practice guidelines; for example, pregabalin as an add-on in GAD. The off-label use of drugs is a common and supported practice when guided by credible sources such as the APA practice guidelines, scientific literature, and clinical experience.

Starting dosages, usual dosages, maximum dosages, considerations for special populations, common side effects, and toxic interactions are summarized in the table of Pharmacological Therapies (Appendix X, p. 170).

SUICIDALITY

An extensive review of the literature by mental health experts using meta-analyses, forensic databases, pharmacoepidemiological studies, and naturalistic and observational studies has shown that there is no increase in the incidence of completed suicide in adult patients who take antidepressants.[32, 33, 34, 35, 36] Studies also show there is a trend towards protection in older groups.[37] The number needed to harm (NNH) (i.e., attempted suicide) is around 700–1000.[38] The NNH is the number of subjects on average needed to treat before causing an iatrogenic complication.

Addressing Challenges in Long-Term Management

There are common challenges associated with the long-term management of anxiety and related disorders. Effectively addressing these challenges will result in a better physician-patient experience and increased patient compliance to treatment. This section will provide an overview of common, troubling, and clinically significant challenges. Online resources or mobile apps are particularly important as a real-time resource, particularly when combining drugs. For example, RxTx, free for Canadian Medical Association members,[39, 40] provides a wealth of information, including medication description, side effects, "Compendium of Pharmaceuticals and Specialties," and important drug-drug interactions.[41] Primary care providers can verify with their respective associations what similar tools are available to them.

Medication Side Effects

Physicians can play a very important role in patient medication compliance and preventing patients from discontinuing drugs due to side effects. Patients who get the following educational messages are more likely to comply during the first month of therapy:

- Take the medication daily.
- It takes 2–4 weeks for a noticeable effect.
- Continue to take the medication even if you are feeling better.
- Do not stop taking antidepressant medication without checking with your physician.
- Most side effects begin to subside after 2–3 weeks.

Treatment of Emergent Sexual Dysfunction

One of the most troublesome side effects of many second-generation antidepressants is sexual dysfunction (i.e., loss of desire, arousal, erectile ability, orgasm, and ejaculation). Many primary care physicians underestimate the impact that the sexual-adverse effects of antidepressants can have on compliance. Almost all antidepressants are associated with decreased libido, erectile dysfunction, and anorgasmia. Serotonergic drugs are probably more closely associated with sexual-adverse effects than noradrenergic compounds.

There is very little or no spontaneous remission of antidepressant-induced sexual dysfunction. Very few strategies have been shown to be effective despite several reports of the possible effectiveness of other pharmaceutical and natural products. A dose reduction can be considered if appropriate. Combination treatment with mirtazapine (Remeron) is sometimes beneficial.[42] Bupropion and sildenafil add-ons have the best evidence of effectiveness for erectile dysfunction secondary to second-generation antidepressants.[43]

Clinically Significant Side Effects

- SSRIs and SNRIs have an increased risk of upper GI bleeding.[44] Consider mianserin, mirtazapine, moclobemide, or trazodone (less risk). In patients at risk of GI bleeding, consider gastroprotection medicines (proton pump inhibitors), especially if the combination of SSRIs and SNRIs with nonsteroidal anti-inflammatory drugs (NSAIDs) cannot be avoided.
- Bleeding risk increases with SSRIs and SNRIs, in particular with concomitant use of drugs that interfere with hemostasis (NSAIDs, aspirin, warfarin, heparin, etc.); consider mirtazapine (when taken with warfarin, the International Normalized Ratio [INR] may increase slightly); use SSRIs and SNRIs with caution when combined with aspirin.
- TCAs have a higher risk for seizures (0.4–1.2%). Bupropion does not exceed the risk when prescribed within the recommended dose range. Avoid bupropion if there is a history of seizures

or eating disorders, significant central nervous system lesions, or recent head trauma.

- TCAs may be contraindicated in patients with recent myocardial infarction, cardiac conduction defects, urinary retention, narrow-angle glaucoma, orthostatic hypotension, or cognitive impairment, and they have not been shown to be effective in youth.
- Venlafaxine has a significantly greater cardiotoxicity than SSRI agents.[45] Offer citalopram 20 mg or sertraline 50–100 mg daily in cases of postmyocardial infarction or acute coronary syndrome.
- When prescribing atypical antipsychotics, monitor for metabolic syndrome (i.e., obesity, glucose intolerance, insulin resistance, weight gain, dyslipidemia) and risk of extrapyramidal side effects. Aripiprazole has the lowest risk (8% incidence), and clozapine and olanzapine are associated with the highest risk (20%).[46] There is a 69% relative risk reduction for aripiprazole compared with olanzapine.

Clinically Significant Drug-Drug Interactions

It is difficult to remember the multitude of important drug-drug interactions in an ever-changing medical field. The use of credible resources, such as the *Compendium of Pharmaceuticals and Specialties*, or mobile apps, such as RxTx, could prove invaluable.

Serotonin syndrome is the result of one of the most important drug-drug interactions to be aware of. This syndrome can be mild or life-threatening. Common symptoms include agitation, autonomic instability (labile HR/BP), hyperthermia, sweating, shivering, tremors, nausea, diarrhea, rigidity, myoclonus, confusion, hypomania, delirium, lack of coordination, hyper-reflexes, seizures, and coma. The risk of serotonin syndrome is increased in particular when SSRIs and MAOIs are combined, but it can occur with several drug combinations, including the interaction of SSRIs or SNRIs with any medication that increases the blood level of serotonin. If a patient develops serotonin syndrome, discontinue the serotonin agent and treat with supportive care. If severe, the patient should be sent to a hospital emergency department. Table 3.3 provides some of the most clinically significant drug-drug interactions.

Escitalopram, venlafaxine, desvenlafaxine, and duloxetine have a relatively low risk

TABLE 3.3 CLINICALLY SIGNIFICANT DRUG-DRUG INTERACTIONS

DRUG 1	DRUG 2	EFFECT/MECHANISM
SSRI or SNRI	MAOIs	Serotonin syndrome; excessive brain 5-HT
	L-tryptophan	
	Fenfluramine	
	St. John's wort	
	Lithium	
	TCAs	
	Trazadone in high doses	
	Buspirone	

DRUG 1	DRUG 2	EFFECT/MECHANISM
Escitalopram	Amoxicillin/clarithromycin Lansoprazole	Dose-dependent prolongation of the QT interval and increased risk of ventricular arrhythmias, including torsade de pointes and sudden death
SSRI or SNRI	Drugs that interfere with hemostasis (NSAIDs, aspirin, warfarin, heparin)	Bleeding risk
MAOI	TCA Heterocyclics	Serotonin syndrome; excessive brain 5-HT
MAOI	TCA SSRIs	Hypertensive episodes, excitement, hyperactivity
MAOI	Bupropion	Seizures
MAOI	Meperidine dextromethorphan	Serotonin syndrome; excess brain 5-HT; decreased hepatic metabolism of the narcotic
MAOI	Levodopa	Severe hypertension; decreased degradation of dopamine and norepinephrine
Lithium	Diuertics (especially thiazides), ACE, ARB, NSAID	Increased lithium concentration causing toxicity/reduced renal clearance of lithium
Clozapine	Benzodiazepines	Respiratory collapse
Clozapine	Carbamazepine	Increased risk of agranulocytosis/increased serum level in both drugs; risk of toxicity
SSRIs	3A4 substrates	Fatal arrhythmias have been reported (i.e., with cisapride, terfenidine, astemizole)
Fluvoxamine		Fluvoxamine carries the most risk of drug-drug interactions
Olanzapine	Fluoxetine Fluvoxamine	Olanzapine toxicity increase by 50% with fluoxetine and 3–4-fold with fluvoxamine

for drug interactions due to having a more selective mechanism of action and receptor profile. Citalopram and sertraline also have a lower propensity for drug interactions and should be considered in patients with chronic physical health problems.[47] Fluoxetine, fluvoxamine, and paroxetine have a higher propensity for drug interactions.[48]

Special Populations

Pregnancy and Breastfeeding
With pregnant patients, use caution when

prescribing medication. Physicians should offer psychotherapy when possible as the evidence regarding the risks of drug use during pregnancy is limited due to a very small number of studies and case control and cohort designs. In addition, there are many confounding variables and conflicting results. Seven meta-analyses examining the safety of antidepressants during pregnancy published since 2000 concluded that SSRIs and newer antidepressants are not associated with an increased risk of major or minor malformations.[49, 50] SSRIs (particularly fluoxetine) and tricyclic antidepressants are generally the agents of choice. In breastfeeding, if high doses of SSRIs and TCAs are required for extended periods, consider discontinuing breastfeeding. Table 3.4 provides an overview of the risks of taking antidepressants in pregnancy and breastfeeding.

Youth, Elderly, Medically Ill, or Those with Symptoms of Intolerance

In the treatment of youth, individual, group, and Internet-based CBT approaches should be considered first. They are effective in social anxiety disorder, panic disorder, OCD, PTSD, and separation anxiety disorder. Cognitive behavior therapy benefits were

TABLE 3.4 RECOMMENDATIONS FOR DRUG TREATMENT OF ANXIETY AND RELATED DISORDERS IN PREGNANCY AND BREASTFEEDING

PREGNANCY	
DRUG	COMMENTS
SSRIs	In some studies but not others, associated with persistent newborn pulmonary hypertension with maternal use after 20 weeks of gestation, slight decrease in gestational age, lower birth weight.
	Associated with neonatal withdrawal or adaptation syndrome.[51]
Paroxetine	First-trimester cardiovascular malformations (ventricular and atrial septal defects), avoid first trimester.
TCAs	Neonatal withdrawal symptoms and anticholinergic adverse effects.
Bupropion	Spontaneous abortion;[52, 53, 54] however, questionable when only high-quality studies are reviewed.[55]
Other newer antidepressants	Insufficient data.
Benzodiazepines	Data controversial and limited.
	No increased risk of major malformation or cardiac defect.
	Questionable increased low risk of oral cleft.[56]
	Neonatal withdrawal syndrome.
Atypical antipsychotics	Data limited; consider risk/benefit ratio. A meta-analysis published in 2015 on adverse obstetric and neonatal outcomes (statistically significant correlation) showed[57] the following: • Increased risk of major malformations (odds ratio [OR] 2.12) • Increased risk of cardiac defects (OR 2.09) • Increased risk of preterm delivery (OR 1.86) • Lower birth weight (weighted mean difference −57.89 g) • Small for gestational age (OR 2.44) • Questionable increase of metabolic syndrome in the mother for second-generation antipsychotics. • In the infant, in some studies but not in others, abnormal muscle movement and neonatal withdrawal symptoms associated with maternal use after 20 weeks of gestation.

BREASTFEEDING	
GENERAL	
Choose the antidepressant with the lowest excretion in breast milk, lowest infant serum concentrations, and fewest adverse reactions.	
ANTIDEPRESSANT/BENZODIAZEPINE	**COMMENTS**
Sertraline Paroxetine Nortriptyline	Sertraline and paroxetine are preferred as plasma levels in breast-fed infants are normally undetectable; however, avoid paroxetine if likely to be used long term when future pregnancy is possible (avoid first trimester of pregnancy, see above).
	Citalopram and fluoxetine have the highest concentrations in breast milk and more reports of infant adverse effects.
	40% decrease in breast milk by switching to escitalopram at 25% citalopram dose.
Venlafaxine	Detectable in the serum and associated with less weight gain in breast-fed infants.
Doxepin	Low excretion in breast milk.
	Shallow respiration and sedation have been reported.
	Effect on breast-fed infants unknown and may be of concern.[58]
Burpropion Mirtazapine Trazodone	Little information available, but concentrations in breast milk infant serum are low.
Benzodiazepines	Concentrations in breast milk infant serum are low; side effects such as sedation are minimal.
Atypical antipsychotics	Data limited.

maintained for up to 7 years posttreatment.[59] Pharmacotherapy recommendations and challenges in youth are beyond the scope of this publication.

The elderly, patients with liver or renal impairment, and highly anxious patients are more sensitive to antidepressant side effects and may require lower starting doses of medication and slower medication titration. In this population group, initiate treatment at half the manufacturer's suggested daily dose or every other day until tolerated. Medication should be slowly increased to reach the suggested target dosage—usually 1–2 weeks for SSRIs or SNRIs. For TCAs, the titration rate will depend on the side effects; attempts should be made to increase the dosage every 1–2 weeks.

In medically ill patients, consultation of resources (RxTx, credible online drug interaction sources, local pharmacists, specialists) can play an invaluable role in assisting in the decision-making process.

Switching from One Antidepressant to Another

The first-line recommendation when initial treatment is not effective is to switch to another drug rather than adding a second drug due to better tolerability and less potential for

TABLE 3.5 SWITCHING FROM DRUG TO DRUG

SWITCH FROM	SSRI	SNRI	SARI	NDRI	TETRACYCLIC	TCA	RIMA	MAOI
SSRI	NWN	NWN	NWN	NWN	NWN	**5 times the half-life	**5 times the half-life	1 week
SNRI	NWN	NWN	NWN	NWN	NWN	**5 times the half-life	**5 times the half-life	1 week
SARI	NWN	NWN	NWN	NWN	NWN	NWN	NWN	1 week
NDRI	NWN	NWN	NWN	NWN	NWN	2 days	3–5 days	1 week
Tetracyclic	1 week	1 week	1 week	1 week	1 week	1 week	1 week	1 week
TCA	**5 times the half-life	**5 times the half-life	NWN	**5 times the half-life	NWN	NWN	**5 times the half-life	**5 times the half-life
RIMA	2 days	2 days	2 days	2 days	2 days	2 days	NWN	*Crossover technique
MAOI	2 weeks	2 weeks	2 weeks	2 weeks	2 weeks	2 weeks	NWN	2 weeks

NWN = No washout necessary

* Use a crossover technique—the first medication should be tapered to a lower dose for at least 5–7 days, and then the second medication can be started, but at a low dose. Gradually, the first medication is discontinued, and the second medication is increased to therapeutic dosage.

** Five times the half-life for most medications is up to 1 week; for fluoxetine, it is about 5 weeks. Therefore wait to start a new medication (e.g., if an MAOI is being started) or watch for side effects for 1 month.

side effects. Physicians can follow the same titration schedule as the first treatment trial; however, the dose can be increased sooner—after 2 weeks—if tolerated. Table 3.5 provides the recommended "washout" period for switching from drug to drug.[60]

Treatment Efficacy

- No consistent differences have been shown in the effectiveness of CBT, medication, and their combination over the short term.[61]
- Several studies involving long-term patient follow-up show that CBT has produced lasting remission from anxiety symptoms.

- Recent studies in depression management have shown that patient choice over evidence-based treatment options of medication or behavioral interventions improves outcomes.[62] It needs to be determined if this is the case for anxiety and related disorders.
- In panic disorder, there is clear evidence of better outcomes with a combination of psychotherapy and pharmacotherapy.[63, 64]
- To increase the rate of long-term remission and prevent relapse, studies support the combination of psychotherapy and pharmacotherapy treatment when psychotherapy or pharmacotherapy alone do not result in optimal improvement.[65, 66]

Treatment Sequence

More research is needed on the best way to sequence different treatments. For many anxiety and related disorders, the advantage of combination therapy (antidepressants and CBT) is still under debate compared to pediatric treatment studies for anxiety disorders, which support increased effectiveness with combination treatment over either therapy alone in certain anxiety disorders.[67] For the treatment of panic disorder in adults, there is evidence to suggest that pharmacotherapy alone may not be as effective as a combination of psychotherapy and pharmacotherapy, hence the latter should be considered first-line.[68] The decision to start treatment with psychotherapy versus pharmacotherapy depends on several factors, including the patient's views of treatment and receptivity to either therapy. In severe cases, it may be necessary to subside the symptoms with pharmacotherapy first for the patient to be receptive to CBT. In addition, including spouses in CBT improves response.

> Progress can be monitored with commonly used assessment scales. Assessment scales can be found in the appendices. A list can also be found in the Tools for Primary Care Practice section on p. xxi.

Visit-by-Visit Guides for Anxiety and Related Disorders

A visit-by-visit guide is included in each disorder chapter. The following describes common terms found throughout the scenarios:

- *Minimal clinical response to treatment* refers to a >25% to <50% symptom reduction as evidenced by a severity assessment scale score.
- *Significant clinical response to treatment* refers to a >50% symptom reduction as evidenced by a severity assessment scale score.

Symptom relief can begin as early as 2 weeks, and it can take 12 weeks for a significant response to treatment.

> Severity assessment scales can be found in each disorder chapter.

Remission and Functional Recovery

The focus of treatment is on maximum functional recovery. Targeting symptom improvement alone is associated with an increased relapse rate and is predictive of negative long-term outcomes.[69] Achieving and maintaining functional remission is critical. If pharmacotherapy is part of the treatment plan, offer an optimum dose for an adequate length of time, which is usually at least 12–24 months. Psychotherapy visits usually occur weekly for 12–20 sessions. Monitor symptoms as well as functioning with clinician-directed and/or patient self-report validated assessment scales in the maintenance phase. Advise patients that remission and return to full functioning is the goal. A clear explanation of this goal by the physician at the outset of treatment will influence patients' compliance, engagement, and potential for recovery. A visit-by-visit guide is included in each specific anxiety and related disorder chapter.

Remission

Remission is most frequently defined by 3 items: the presence of features of positive mental health such as optimism and self-confidence; a return to one's usual, normal self; and a return to a usual level of functioning. Remission is defined also by the person no longer meeting diagnostic criteria and there being no functional impairment.

Relapse
Relapse is defined as the return or worsening of symptoms before achieving full remission. Relapse usually occurs within 4–6 months of the initial response to treatment and is a continuation of the initial episode.

Recurrence
Recurrence is the appearance of a new episode after 6 months of full remission.

Referral Guidelines
Consider referral for patients in the following situations:

- Need for a second opinion; unclear diagnosis
- Elderly, confused patient with an unclear history
- Severe disorder symptoms (e.g., severe weight loss or gain)
- Physical damage from drinking or failure to quit drinking
- Failed response to adequate therapy
- Resistance to multiple therapies
- Concurrent complex medical or mental illness
- Acute deterioration in a previously stable course
- Suicidal ideation or tendencies, or recent suicide attempt

Summary
The lifetime prevalence of anxiety and related disorders is reported to be as high as 31% of the population worldwide.

- Early detection is important.
- Treat aggressively and longer term if symptoms have been present for some time and interfere with normal daily functioning.
- Cognitive behavior therapy is the first-choice psychological treatment.
- SSRIs and SNRIs are the first drugs of choice.
- Anxiolytics have their place in the treatment of anxiety disorders; however, be aware of the addiction potential, and withdraw the drug as soon as feasible.

NOTES

1 Swinson R, Antony M, Bleau P, Chokka P, Craven M, Fallu A, et al. Clinical practice guidelines. Management of anxiety disorders. Can J Psychiatry. 2006; 51(8 Suppl 2):9S–91S.

2 Kennedy SH, Lam RW, Parikh SV, Patten SB, Ravindran AV. Canadian Network for Mood and Anxiety Treatments (CANMAT) clinical guidelines for the management of major depressive disorder in adults. J Affect Disord. 2009; 117 Suppl 1:S1–S2.

3 Schrank B, Bird V, Rudnick A, Slade M. Determinants, self-management strategies and interventions for hope in people with mental disorders: systematic search and narrative review. Soc Sci Med. 2011; 74(4): 554–564.

4 Lewis C, Pearce J, Bisson J. Efficacy, cost-effectiveness and acceptability of self-help interventions for anxiety disorders: systematic review. Br J Psychiatry. 2012 Jan; 200(1):15–21.

5 HeretoHelp [Internet]. Vancouver, BC: HeretoHelp (a project of BC Partners for Mental Health and Addictions Information); c2015 cited 2015 March 8. Available from: http://www.heretohelp.bc.ca/

6 Hunot V, Churchill R, Silva de Lima M, Teixeira V. Psychological therapies for generalised anxiety

disorder. Cochrane Database Syst Rev. 2007; (1):CD001848.

7   Hofmann, SG, Smits, JA. Cognitive-behavioral therapy for adult anxiety disorders: a meta-analysis of randomized placebo-controlled trials. J Clin Psychiatry. 2008; 69(4):621–632.

8   Mohr D, Ho J, Duffecy J, Reifler, D, Sokol L, Burns M., et al. Effect of telephone-administered vs face-to-face cognitive behavioral therapy on adherence to therapy and depression outcomes among primary care patients: a randomized trial. JAMA. 2012; 307(21):2278–2285.

9   Robinson E, Titov N, Andrews G, McIntyre K, Schwencke G, Solley K. Internet treatment for generalized anxiety disorder: a randomized controlled trial comparing clinician vs. technician assistance. PLoS ONE. 2010; 5(6):e10942.

10 Paxling B, Almlöv J, Dahlin M, Carlbring P, Breitholtz E, Eriksson T, Andersson G. Guided Internet-delivered cognitive behavior therapy for generalized anxiety disorder: a randomized controlled trial. Cogn Behav Ther. 2011; 40(3):159–173.

11 Landreville P, Gosselin P, Grenier S, Hudon C, Lorrain D. Guided self-help for generalized anxiety disorder in older adults. Aging Ment Health. 2015:1–14.

12 TruReach Health [Internet]. [Place unknown]: TruReach Health; 2015 [cited 2015 October 30]. Available from: http://www.trureachhealth.com/

13 Opriş D, Pintea S, García-Palacios A, Botella C, Szamosközi S, David D. Virtual reality exposure therapy in anxiety disorders: a quantitative meta-analysis. Depress Anxiety. 2012; 29(2):85–93.

14 Katzman MA, Bleau P, Blier P, Chokka P, Kjernisted K, Van Ameringen M, et al. Canadian clinical practice guidelines for the management of anxiety, posttraumatic stress and obsessive-compulsive disorders. BMC Psychiatry. 2014; 14 Suppl 1:S1.

15 Psych Central [Internet]. [Place unknown]: Psych Central; 1995–2016. Pine D. Anxiety disorders in DSM-5 & beyond; 2009 Sep [cited 2015 Sep 10]. Available from: http://pro.psychcentral.com/anxiety-disorders-in-dsm-5-beyond/006381.html

16 Wells A, Welford M, King P, Papageorgiou C, Wisely J, Mendel E. A pilot randomized trial of metacognitive therapy vs applied relaxation in the treatment of adults with generalized anxiety disorder. Behav Res Ther. 2010; 48(5):429–434.

17 Van Der Heiden C, Muris P, Van Der Molen H. Randomized controlled trial on the effectiveness of metacognitive therapy and intolerance-of-uncertainty therapy for generalized anxiety disorder. Behav Res Ther. 2012; 50(2):100–109.

18 Kim YW, Lee SH, Choi TK, Suh SY, Kim B, Kim CM, et al. Effectiveness of mindfulness-based cognitive

therapy as an adjuvant to pharmacotherapy in patients with panic disorder or generalized anxiety disorder. Depress Anxiety. 2009; 26(7):601–606.

19 Hofmann S, Sawyer A, Witt A, Oh D, La Greca AM. The effect of mindfulness-based therapy on anxiety and depression: a meta-analytic review. J Consult Clin Psychol. 2010; 78(2):169–183.

20 Westra HA, Arkowitz H, Dozois DJ. Adding a motivational interviewing pretreatment to cognitive behavioral therapy for generalized anxiety disorder: a preliminary randomized controlled trial. J Anxiety Disord. 2009; 23(8):1106–1117.

21 Stahl B, Goldstein E. A mindfulness-based stress reduction workbook. Oakland, CA: New Harbinger; 2010.

22 Siegel R. The Mindfulness solution: everyday practices for everyday problems. New York: Guilford Press; 2010.

23 Williams M, Penman D. Mindfulness: an eight-week plan for finding peace in a frantic world. New York: Rodale; 2011.

24 Bandelow B, Sher L, Bunevicius R, Hollander E, Kasper S, Zohar J, et al. Guidelines for the pharmacological treatment of anxiety disorders, obsessive-compulsive disorder and posttraumatic stress disorder in primary care. Int J Psychiatry Clin Pract. 2012; 16(2):77–84.

25 Treating GAD: Is Buspirone a Good Option? Last accessed September 10, 2015 at http://www.medscape.com/viewarticle/828221

26 Flint AJ. Generalised anxiety disorder in elderly patients: epidemiology, diagnosis and treatment options. Drugs Aging. 2005;22(2):101–114.

27 Mokhber, N., Azarpazhooh, M., Khajehdaluee, M., Velayati, A., & Hopwood, M. (2010). Randomized, single-blind, trial of sertraline and buspirone for treatment of elderly patients with generalized anxiety disorder. Psychiatry and Clinical Neurosciences. 64(2), 128–133.

28 Evans M, Bradwejn J, Dunn L, editors. Ontario guidelines for the management of anxiety disorders in primary care. 1st ed. Toronto: Queen's Printer of Ontario; 2000.

29 Canadian Network for Mood and Anxiety Treatment (CANMAT) [Internet]. [Place unknown]: Canadian Network for Mood and Anxiety Treatment; c2010. Disorder information: generalized anxiety disorder; c2010. [cited 2011 Dec 13]. Available from: http://www.canmat.org/di-anxiety-generalized-anxiety-disorder.php

30 Komossa K, Depping A, Meyer M, Kissling W, Leucht S. Second-generation antipsychotics for obsessive compulsive disorder. Cochrane Database Syst Rev. 2010; (12):CD008141.

31 Depping A, Komossa K, Kissling W, Leucht S. Second-generation antipsychotics for anxiety disorders. Cochrane Database Syst Rev. (12):CD008120.

32 Hammad T, Laughren T, Racoosin J. Suicide rates in short-term randomized controlled trials of newer antidepressants. J Clin Psychopharmacol. 2006; 26(2):203–207.

33 Lam RW, Kennedy SH. CPA Position statement: prescribing antidepressants for depression in 2005: recent concerns and recommendations. Can J Psychiatry. 2004: 49(12):1–6 (insert).

34 Gunnell D, Saperia J, Ashby D. Selective serotonin reuptake inhibitors (SSRIs) and suicide in adults: meta-analysis of drug company data from placebo controlled, randomised controlled trials submitted to the MHRA's safety review. BMJ. 2005; 330(7488):385.

35 Möller H, Baldwin D, Goodwin S, Kasper G, Okasha S, Stein A, et al. Do SSRIs or antidepressants in general increase suicidality? Eur Arch Psychiatry Clin Neurosci. 2008; 258(3):3–23.

36 Barbui C, Esposito E, Cipriani A. Selective serotonin reuptake inhibitors and risk of suicide: a systematic review of observational studies. CMAJ. 2009; 180(3):291–297.

37 Friedman RA, Leon AC. Expanding the black box—depression, antidepressants, and the risk of suicide. N Eng J Med. 2007; 356(23):2343–2346.

38 Kauffman JM. Selective serotonin reuptake inhibitor (SSRI) drugs: more risks than benefits? Journal of American Physicians and Surgeons. 2009; 14(1):7–12.

39 Canadian Medical Association, Clinical Resources [Internet]. Ottawa (ON): Canadian Medical Association; 1995–2016. The CPS on the RxTx mobile app; c2015 [cited 2015 Nov 6]. Available from: https://www.cma.ca/En/Pages/cps-mobile-app.aspx

40 Canadian Medical Association, Clinical Resources [Internet]. Ottawa (ON): Canadian Medical Association; 1995–2016. The CPS on the RxTx mobile app; c2015 [cited 2015 Nov 6]. Available from: https://www.cma.ca/En/Pages/cps-mobile-app.aspx

41 Canadian Pharmacists Association, Drug & Therapeutic Products [Internet]. Ottawa (ON): Canadian Pharmacists Association; n.d. RxTx mobile app; c2015 [cited 2015 Nov 6]. Available from: http://www.pharmacists.ca/index.cfm/products-services/rxtxmobile/

42 Kennedy SH, Lam RW, Parikh SV, Patten SB, Ravindran AV. Canadian Network for Mood and Anxiety Treatments (CANMAT) clinical guidelines for the management of major depressive disorder in adults. J Affect Disord. 2009; 117 Suppl 1:S1–S2.

43 Taylor MJ, Rudkin L, Hawton K. Strategies for managing antidepressant-induced sexual dysfunction: systematic review of randomised controlled trials. J Affect Disord. 2005; 88(3):241–254.

44 Loke Y, Trivedi A, Singh S. Meta-analysis: Gastrointestinal bleeding due to interaction between selective serotonin uptake inhibitors and non-steroidal anti-inflammatory drugs. Aliment Pharmacol Ther. 2008; 27(1):31–40.

45 Deshauer D. Venlafaxine (Effexor): Concerns about increased risk of fatal outcomes in overdose. CMAJ. 2007; 176(1):39–40.

46 Riordan HJ, Antonini P, Murphy MF. Atypical antipsychotics and metabolic syndrome in patients with schizophrenia: risk factors, monitoring, and healthcare implications. Am Health Drug Benefits. 2011; 4(5):292–302.

47 National Collaborating Centre for Mental Health (UK) [Internet]. Depression in adults with a chronic physical health problem: treatment and management. Leicester (UK): British Psychological Society; 2010. Available from: http://www.ncbi.nlm.nih.gov/books/NBK82916/

48 Marken PA, Munro JS. Selecting a selective serotonin reuptake inhibitor: clinically important distinguishing features. Prim Care Companion J Clin Psychiatry. 2000; 2(6):205–210.

49 Einarson TR, Einarson A. Newer antidepressants in pregnancy and rates of major malformations: a meta-analysis of prospective comparative studies. Pharmacoepidemiol Drug Saf. 2005; 14(12):823–827.

50 Kennedy SH, Lam RW, Parikh SV, Patten SB, Ravindran AV. Canadian Network for Mood and Anxiety Treatments (CANMAT) clinical guidelines for the management of major depressive disorder in adults. J Affect Disord. 2009; 117 Suppl 1:S1–S2.

51 Katzman MA, Bleau P, Blier P, Chokka P, Kjernisted K, Van Ameringen M, et al. Canadian clinical practice guidelines for the management of anxiety, posttraumatic stress and obsessive-compulsive disorders. BMC Psychiatry. 2014; 14 Suppl 1:S1.

52 Hemels ME, Einarson A, Koren G, Lanctôt KL, Einarson TR. Antidepressant use during pregnancy and the rates of spontaneous abortions: a meta-analysis. Ann Pharmacother. 2005; 39(5):803–809.

53 Rahimi R, Nikfar S, Abdollahi M. Pregnancy outcomes following exposure to serotonin reuptake inhibitors: a meta-analysis of clinical trials. Reprod Toxicol. 2006; 22(4):571–575.

54 Kjaersgaard M, Parner E, Vestergaard M, Sørensen M, Olsen J, Christensen J, et al. Prenatal antidepressant exposure and risk of spontaneous abortion—a population-based study. PloS One. 2013; 8(8):e72095.

55 Ross L, Grigoriadis S, Mamisashvili L, Vonderporten E, Roerecke M, Rehm J, et al. Selected pregnancy and delivery outcomes after exposure to antidepressant

medication: a systematic review and meta-analysis. JAMA Psychiatry. 2013; 70(4):436–443.

56 Dolovich L, Addis A, Vaillancourt J, Power J, Koren G, Einarson T. Benzodiazepine use in pregnancy and major malformations or oral cleft: meta-analysis of cohort and case-control studies. BMJ. 1998; 317(7162):839–843.

57 Coughlin C, Blackwell K, Bartley C, Hay M, Yonkers K, Bloch M. Obstetric and neonatal outcomes after antipsychotic medication exposure in pregnancy. Obstet Gynecol. 2015; 125(5):1224–1235.

58 American Academy of Pediatrics Committee on Drugs. The transfer of drugs and other chemicals into human milk. Pediatrics [Internet]. 2001 [cited 2015 Nov 23]; 108(3):776–789. Available from: http://pediatrics.aappublications.org/content/pediatrics/108/3/776.full.pdf

59 Katzman MA, Bleau P, Blier P, Chokka P, Kjernisted K, Van Ameringen M, et al. Canadian clinical practice guidelines for the management of anxiety, posttraumatic stress and obsessive-compulsive disorders. BMC Psychiatry. 2014; 14 Suppl 1:S1.

60 Clinical guidelines for the treatment of depressive disorders. Can J Psychiatry. 2001; 46 Suppl 1:44S–46S.

61 Bandelow B, Seidler-Brandler U, Becker A, Wedekind D, Rüther E. Meta-analysis of randomized controlled comparisons of psychopharmacological and psychological treatments for anxiety disorders. World J Biol Psychiatry. 2007; 8(3):175–187.

62 Sherbourne CD, Wells KB, Duan N, Miranda J, Unützer J, Jaycox L, et al. Long-term effectiveness of disseminating quality improvement for depression in primary care. Arch Gen Psychiatry. 2001; 58(7): 696–703.

63 Bandelow B, Seidler-Brandler U, Becker A, Wedekind D, Rüther E. Meta-analysis of randomized controlled comparisons of psychopharmacological and psychological treatments for anxiety disorders. World J Biol Psychiatry. 2007; 8(3):175–187.

64 Hofmann SG, Sawyer AT, Korte KJ, Smits JA. Is it beneficial to add pharmacotherapy to cognitive-behavioral therapy when treating anxiety disorders? A meta-analytic review. Int J Cogn Ther. 2009; 2(2): 160–175.

65 Canadian Psychiatric Assocation. Clinical practice guidelines. Management of anxiety disorders. Can J Psychiatry. 2006; 51(8 Suppl 2):9S–91S.

66 Craske MG, Stein MB, Sullivan G, Sherbourne C, Bystritsky A, Rose RD, et al. Disorder-specific impact of coordinated anxiety learning and management treatment for anxiety disorders in primary care. Arch Gen Psychiatry. 2011; 68(4):378–388.

67 Walkup J, Albano A, Piacentini J, Birmaher B, Compton S, Sherrill J, et al. Cognitive behavioral therapy, sertraline, or a combination in childhood anxiety. N Eng J Med. 2008; 359(26):2753–2766.

68 Furukawa T, Watanabe N, Churchill R. Combined psychotherapy plus antidepressants for panic disorder with or without agoraphobia. Cochrane Database Syst Rev. 2007; (1):CD004364.

69 Stein D, Bandelow B, Dolberg O, Andersen H, Baldwin D. Anxiety symptom severity and functional recovery or relapse. Ann Clin Psychiatry. 2009; 21(2):81–88.

SECTION II
Anxiety Disorders

In the DSM-5, the "Anxiety Disorders" chapter includes the following:

- Separation anxiety disorder
- Selective mutism
- Specific phobia
- Social anxiety disorder (social phobia)
- Panic disorder
- Agoraphobia
- Generalized anxiety disorder (GAD)
- Substance/medication-induced anxiety disorder
- Anxiety disorder due to another medical condition
- Other specified anxiety disorder
- Unspecified anxiety disorder

Here we will describe the screening, assessment, and management of 4 common anxiety disorders seen in primary care: GAD, panic disorder, agoraphobia, and social anxiety disorder.

4

Generalized Anxiety Disorder

Introduction

Patients with GAD have frequent office visits for unexplained physical symptoms; consequently, as a primary care physician, you will most likely encounter GAD in the course of investigating a patient who has come in for one of GAD's associated symptoms, such as restlessness, fatigue, concentration problems, headaches, and myalgia.[1] To learn about GAD, you can follow the diagnosis, treatment, and management of our patient, Mr. AG. You can progress through the practice case study from start to finish, or you can select your own learning path in the Practice Case Study Index, p. xxv. The choice is yours.

Clinical Presentation

Patients with GAD experience anxiety for most days during a 6-month period that is out of proportion to the actual danger or threat in a situation, a variety of events, or activities. This is the typical "worry wart." Patients worry about "what if" scenarios—these types of worries are a key distinguishing feature of GAD. They worry about a number of future events or activities— about what might happen, not what is already happening. This is the hallmark feature of GAD patients. Worries typically involve the following:[2]

- Health
- Job and finances
- Competence
- Acceptance
- Family, friends, relationships
- Minor matters

The worry is difficult to control and is accompanied by a variety of associated symptoms, such as restlessness, fatigue, and muscle tension.[3] The symptoms cause significant distress or impairment in social, occupational, or other important areas of functioning.[4]

GAD is often chronic. When patients with GAD discontinue their medication,

- 25% relapse in the first month
- 60–80% relapse over the course of the next year.[5]

> The diagnostic criteria for GAD can be found in Appendix XI, p. 182.

Prevalence

The lifetime prevalence of GAD is approximately 4–7% of the general population.[6]

GAD is highly comorbid. It has been estimated that 90% of patients with GAD have lifetime comorbidity with either substance use disorder (SUD) or a psychiatric disorder.[7, 8] Lifetime comorbidity includes:

- Major depressive disorder (MDD) (62%)
- Dysthymia (40%)

- Alcohol use disorder (38%)
- Simple phobia (35%)
- Social anxiety disorder (34%)

GAD is diagnosed twice as often in women as in men. The disease typically starts around 31 years of age.[9]

Generalized Anxiety Disorder Case Study: Meet Mr. AG

Mr. AG, a 39-year-old male lawyer, presents to your office with the following symptoms:

- Excessive anxiety for 20 years
- Chronic restlessness and nervous tension
- Difficulty concentrating
- Physical symptoms including tension headaches, tightness in the abdomen, palpitations, and difficulty breathing
- Sleeps only 3 hours per night
- Fatigue

> » What should or can you do?
> » What are your options?

Upon chart review, you notice that Mr. AG had a full cardiopulmonary workup 2 months ago that failed to reveal any abnormalities. You realize that you will not be able to offer him the time required for an in-depth investigation at this visit as your office assistant booked him for only a single appointment.

ASSESSMENT: SCREENING AND PROVISIONAL DIAGNOSIS

If you are pressed for time and there is no safety risk or clinical judgment of urgency, you can tell Mr. AG you understand his suffering and will help, but that you need him to schedule an appointment that will give you the time to assess him properly. Advise him to return should his condition get worse in the meantime. This is a very important step, particularly if time is an issue. This takes 1–2 minutes and reassures him that even if you don't have time to spend with him this visit, you are still concerned about him and want to take the time to address his complaints properly. He will feel heard and relieved that someone will help. This lessens his distress while gaining his trust.

Note: You can arrange for any additional investigative workup as appropriate to rule out underlying non-psychiatric conditions and schedule a follow-up appointment. Some non-psychiatric conditions and factors can present with anxiety symptoms, but rarely to the point of a complete disorder. Refer to Chapter 2: Assessment, p. 16, for further information on factors to consider when assessing anxiety symptoms or go directly to Factors to Consider When Assessing Anxiety Symptoms, (Appendix I, p. 155).

Screening for Anxiety and Related Disorders

Mr. AG's blood tests return normal and further investigation reveals no abnormalities. You are considering an anxiety or related disorder, keeping in mind that depressive disorders are comorbid 60% of the time.

> » How do you screen for common anxiety and related disorders?
> » How do you screen for common comorbid mental disorders?
> » What is the provisional diagnosis?

Provisional Diagnosis

Mr. AG provides the following answers to the questions in section 2 of the Patient Self-Report Screening Tool for Mental Illness (Appendix VI, p. 161), which supports your suspicion that Mr. AG may be suffering from an anxiety or related disorder.

Have you worried excessively or been anxious about several things with regard to day-to-day life while at work, at home, or in your close circle, which is out of proportion considering your life circumstances for at least the last 6 months?	"Yes, 6 months at least! I worry all the time and about several things."
What do you worry about?	"I worry about how I will pay my bills, if my wife will get cancer, if I will lose my job, if my children are going to be okay, and if they will have a good job when they grow up."
Are you a worrier by nature or is this new for you?	"I have been a worrier for years, but usually I can change my thoughts by doing other things like jogging or watching a movie, but in the last 8 months, I seem to not be able to do so as easily. I know the worries are more frequent, and I worry about more things."
Do you think you worry more than most other people?	"I definitely worry more than most people. People tell me that I have to stop worrying so much about things that haven't happened yet."
Have you been unable to stop or control your worries or let go of them, holding your worries inside?	"Yeah, I'd say I keep my worries inside. I can't stop my worries, Doctor, no matter how hard I try to change my thoughts. I have trouble controlling them. When I'm trying to fall asleep, I try to not think about my worries, but I can't." *(With this response, Mr. AG satisfies an important criterion for GAD. By definition, patients with GAD find it difficult to control their worry.)*
In the last 6 months, have you been feeling physically unwell because of your worrying (feeling exhausted, having problems sleeping, getting headaches, having trouble focusing, having sore muscles)?	"My worries make me physically tense, and I can never seem to relax. I can't sleep, which makes me tired at work, and it is really hard to focus on my job duties." (You notice that Mr. AG is clenching his fists.) ***Note:*** *Diagnosis requires at least 3 physical symptoms (see next page).*

Do the worries get in the way of your day-to-day life at home, work, or when you are with friends?	"I am tired because I don't sleep as well as I used to. It is starting to affect my work performance, plus I snap at the kids now."
On a scale of 0–10, how problematic is this for you?	"I would say that it is problematic—about a 4 out of 10."

PHYSICAL SYMPTOMS OF GAD

A diagnosis of GAD requires at least 3 of the following symptoms:
- Restlessness or feeling keyed up or on edge
- Becoming easily fatigued
- Difficulty concentrating or mind going blank
- Irritability
- Muscle tension
- Sleep disturbance (difficulty falling or staying asleep, or restless, unsatisfying sleep)

You ask, "Are you having financial troubles?" He replies, "No, but what if I lose my job? What if my wife or children get sick?"

When you discuss these worries further, it becomes apparent that there is no basis for his worries (his job is stable; his wife and children are healthy). He has admitted that he finds it difficult to control his worries. He denies symptomatology related to panic disorder, social anxiety disorder, PTSD, OCD, or substance use disorder.

Mr. AG's GAD-7 score is consistent with GAD. Based on his responses, you make a provisional diagnosis of GAD.

CONFIRMING THE DIAGNOSIS

The next step is to confirm Mr. AG's diagnosis.

The diagnosis of GAD is confirmed by using the DSM-5 Criteria for GAD[10] (see Appendix XI, p. 182). Physicians can employ user-friendly tools adapted from the DSM-5 to recall diagnostic features:

- Patient-directed tools: GAD-7 (sensitivity 89%, specificity 82%)[11] (Appendix V, p. 160).
- A physician-directed, validated tool, the Mini International Neuropsychiatric Interview (MINI) for GAD, a proprietary tool, is also a widely used instrument, but it is time-consuming so it may not be feasible for a busy primary care office.[12]

> » What factors must you consider to confirm Mr. AG has GAD?
> » What instruments can be used to confirm the diagnosis?

In Mr. AG's case, the DSM-5 supports your diagnosis of GAD. For at least 6 months, he has worried most days about finances, his wife getting sick, and his children's future. However, there is no objective basis for these worries. In addition:

- He has difficulty controlling his worries.
- For at least 6 months, more days than not, he has experienced the following symptoms:

- Restlessness
- Being easily fatigued
- Difficulty concentrating
- Irritability
- Sleep problems

These worries cannot be accounted for by the direct physiological effects of a substance (e.g., a drug of abuse, a medication) or a general medical condition. More importantly, his symptoms are causing dysfunction in Mr. AG's day-to-day life—he is unable to focus at work, which has resulted in a decline in his work performance.

Generalized Anxiety Disorder versus Nonpathological Anxiety

To differentiate GAD from nonpathological (normal) anxiety, remember that GAD worries are

- out of proportion to the patient's life circumstances
- difficult to control, which results in significant distress or functional impairment.

BASELINE ASSESSMENT

The next step is to conduct a baseline assessment. This will provide you and your patient with important information to tailor a treatment plan specific to your patient.

> » What should be included in a baseline assessment?
> » What tools are useful at baseline and follow-up visits?

Patient self-report tools are used in primary care for many medical conditions. These are practical, time-efficient tools that can be used in mental health assessments as well; however, responses should be interpreted by clinicians together with the DSM-5 criteria and clinical judgment. A careful assessment and rating of each of the following parameters will also establish a baseline from which to measure treatment response:

- Suicide Assessment Questionnaire (Appendix III, p. 157)
- GAD symptom severity
  - GAD-7 (Appendix V, p. 160)
  - Severity Measure for Generalized Anxiety Disorder—Adult[13] (see note below)
- Comorbid conditions
- Somatic complaints; Symptom Assessment Checklist (Appendix VIII, p. 167)
- Functional impairment; Functional Impairment Assessment Scale (Appendix IX, p. 168)

Note: The Severity Measure for Generalized Anxiety Disorder—Adult can be downloaded directly from the APA site at http://www.psychiatry.org/psychiatrists/practice/dsm/dsm-5/online-assessment-measures. These measures can be reproduced without permission by researchers and clinicians for use with their patients. Rating information is provided as well.

Note: You can arrange for any additional investigative workup as appropriate to rule out underlying non-psychiatric conditions and schedule a follow-up appointment. Some non-psychiatric conditions and factors can present with anxiety symptoms, but rarely to the point of a complete disorder. Refer to Chapter 2: Assessment, p. 16, for further information on factors to consider when assessing anxiety symptoms or go directly to Factors to Consider When Assessing Anxiety Symptoms, (Appendix I, p. 155).

The GAD-7 (Appendix V, p. 160) can be used to assess illness severity. You can also refer to the "Baseline Assessment" section of Chapter 2, p. 18.

Mr. AG's Baseline Assessment

Mr. AG denies any suicidal thoughts. The GAD-7 yields a score of 8 (mild). On the Symptom Assessment Checklist, he reports headaches (1), tiredness (1), difficulty concentrating (2), nervousness (2), tightness in the abdomen (1) and sleep problems—he describes waking up intermittently through the night (2). The Functional Impairment Assessment Scale (Appendix IX, p. 168) reveals that his performance at work is 80% as he has felt less productive during 2 out 5 days. He remembers his mother worrying a lot but is unsure if she saw a doctor for this. He smokes half a pack of cigarettes per day and drinks 5–6 cups of coffee at work. The rest of his history is unremarkable.

MANAGEMENT GUIDELINES

Now that you have confirmed the diagnosis of GAD and have a general idea of Mr. AG's illness severity and how it affects him, you can begin to develop a care plan. Information collected to date will guide your management plan; however, the choice of treatment will depend on several factors, for example:[14, 15]

- Patient opinions about treatment
- Receptivity to counseling
- Receptivity to medication
- Severity of symptoms
- Comorbidity
- Previous response (or lack of response) to treatment
- Availability of resources in the community

Table 4.1 summarizes the psychotherapy and pharmacological agents used to treat GAD.

You can also refer to Chapter 3: Management, p. 25. First-, second-, and third-line treatments for GAD are listed in Table 4.1.

Biological Therapies

Although more studies are needed, repetitive transcranial magnetic stimulation (rTMS), a noninvasive form of brain stimulation, shows promise. This therapy uses magnetic pulses instead of electricity to activate parts of the brain. A magnetic field generator placed near the patient's head sends small electrical currents to different regions of the left and right prefrontal cortex, penetrating up to 5 cm.[16] The effect of this stimulation depends on the location, intensity, and frequency of the magnetic pulses. Repetitive transcranial magnetic stimulation is an FDA-approved therapy in treatment-resistant depression, and researchers are exploring its efficacy in the treatment

TABLE 4.1 PSYCHOTHERAPY AND PHARMACOTHERAPY RECOMMENDATIONS FOR GENERALIZED ANXIETY DISORDER***

	PSYCHOTHERAPY	PHARMACOLOGICAL AGENT
First-line	CBT (usually 12–20 weekly sessions) Cognitive therapy (usually 12–20 weekly sessions) Applied relaxation therapy (helps people relax during anxiety-provoking situations)	Agomelatine, duloxetine, escitalopram, paroxetine, paroxetine CR, pregabalin**, sertraline, venlafaxine XR
Second-line	Acceptance and commitment therapy (ACT) Mindfulness	Alprazolam*, bromazepam*, bupropion XL*, buspirone, diazepam*, hydroxyzine, imipramine, lorazepam*, quetiapine XR*, vortioxetine
Third-line		Citalopram, divalproex chrono, fluoxetine, mirtazapine, trazodone
Adjunctive therapy		**Second-line:** pregabalin** **Third-line:** aripiprazole, olanzapine, quetiapine, quetiapine XR, risperidone

CR = controlled release; XL or XR = extended release

*These drugs have distinct mechanisms, efficacy, and safety profiles. Within these second-line agents, consider benzodiazepines first; however, consider risk of substance abuse. Bupropion XL should be reserved for later. Quetiapine XR is effective; however, due to metabolic concerns associated with atypical antipsychotics, it should be reserved for patients who cannot be provided antidepressants or benzodiazepines. Please refer to Katzman et al.[17] for further rationale for the recommendations.

** Study results with pregabalin as monotherapy are positive; more studies are needed.

***Adapted from Katzman et al. (2014).[18]

of anxiety disorders. More information on these therapies can be found in an open-access publication by Katzman et al. at http://www.biomedcentral.com/1471-244X/14/S1/S1.

Complementary and Alternative Medicine

Evidence is limited on the effectiveness of complementary and alternative medicines (CAMs), although they are often used. Variation in the standardization of products makes recommendations difficult. Furthermore, the use of some common botanicals and supplements with second-generation antidepressants can induce serotonin syndrome.

VISIT-BY-VISIT GUIDE: MILD GENERALIZED ANXIETY DISORDER

Mr. AG expresses a strong preference for pharmacotherapy over psychotherapy. "I don't have time for therapy," he says. "I won't go, and I really want these worries to stop. I am afraid because I think I am slowly getting worse. Please help me, Doctor!"

Because Mr. AG strongly prefers pharmacotherapy alone, you choose to respect his wishes. After considering the possible pharmacological therapies, you initiate escitalopram 10 mg daily. You also advise him to reduce the number of cups of coffee he drinks per day. You schedule a follow-up appointment in 2 weeks.

> What treatment should you initiate with Mr. AG?
> » Should you insist on psychotherapy due to the diagnosis of mild GAD?
> » Should you prescribe pharmacotherapy alone?
> » Should you use a combination of psychotherapy and pharmacotherapy?
> » What about exercise and self-management strategies?

After 2 weeks of taking escitalopram 10 mg daily, Mr. AG returns, feeling much better. He tells you that he is now drinking only 2 cups of coffee in the morning. The following assessments should be made:

- Suicide Assessment Questionnaire (Appendix III, p. 157)
- GAD symptom severity (GAD-7) (Appendix V, p. 160)
- Symptom Assessment Checklist (Appendix VIII, p. 167)
- Functional Impairment Assessment (Appendix IX, p. 168)

Mr. AG's GAD-7 score is 5 (mild), and he has minimal side effects. Functional impairment assessment reveals that he has missed no days of work (mild). "My body is physically relaxed in a way it hasn't been for years," he says. The escitalopram is maintained at 10 mg daily, and in 6 weeks, his GAD-7 score is 3 (complete remission). You decide to maintain the escitalopram for at least 6 months with the intention of discussing CBT again at that time to see if he might be willing to consider this option. You see him monthly initially, and at 6 months, he is not receptive to CBT because of time constraints. You decide to maintain the drug for 12 months due to the long-standing presence of symptoms. The frequency of visits is reduced as warranted.

VISIT-BY-VISIT GUIDE: MODERATE GENERALIZED ANXIETY DISORDER

First Visit	Nine months after initiating escitalopram, Mr. AG comes in for his scheduled appointment. He says that his symptoms have gradually returned over the past month, and he now feels much worse. His worries are more pervasive, and he finds it difficult at times to get through the day. He reports headaches, which he rates at 2. You reassess the diagnosis and comorbidity, asking Mr. AG to complete the Patient Self-Report Screening Tool for Mental Illnesses (Appendix VI, p. 161). Your assessment once again is consistent with GAD and excludes comorbid conditions, although there is evidence of subthreshold depression.
	Mr. AG's GAD-7 score has risen to 12 (moderate). His functional impairment is moderate. He reports having missed 2 days of work in the last week, but when he is at work, he feels his performance is at 60% of what it used to be. In addition, he rates his ability to socialize at 50% and denies any trouble at home.

What is your next step?

- Switch to another medication.
- Add a second first-line drug.
- Maintain the escitalopram at 10 mg daily and reassure.
- Increase dose, titrating every 2 weeks.

Mr. AG is not on a maximum dose of escitalopram. The next step would be to titrate the drug until remission or the maximum dose is achieved, unless he experiences intolerable side effects. You ask him to increase the dose of escitalopram he is taking to 20 mg daily (the maximum dose for escitalopram). After 4 weeks, Mr. AG responds slightly. His GAD-7 score is now at 10 (i.e., mild to moderate anxiety). However, he now kicks his partner in his sleep and wakes up with nightmares.

You explain that restless leg syndrome is one of the side effects of escitalopram, but usually side effects subside after 3–4 weeks of treatment. You also advise him that combined psychotherapy and pharmacotherapy can be more effective over the long term in maintaining treatment gains. At this point, his symptoms are problematic; therefore, he decides to try psychotherapy and is referred for CBT. You schedule a follow-up appointment in 2 weeks.

Subsequent Visits	After 2 weeks, Mr. AG returns and reports that he is not feeling better. His scores are unchanged. An adequate treatment trial with CBT is about 6–8 sessions, so you explain to him that psychotherapy can take up to 8 sessions for an initial response. You both agree to continue on the same treatment regime and allow enough time for the CBT to take effect. Finally, at the maximum dose of escitalopram and after an additional 4 sessions of CBT, he reports that the combination is "really starting to work." His symptoms subside, and he is once again in remission.
Maintenance Visits	You advise Mr. AG to finish the recommended CBT sessions (usually 12–20 weekly sessions) and continue his pharmacotherapy for an additional year. Aim for optimum functional recovery as focusing solely on symptom reduction increases the likelihood of relapse with decreased quality of life.

VISIT-BY-VISIT GUIDE: SEVERE GENERALIZED ANXIETY DISORDER

First Visit	After a year in remission, Mr. AG returns. He is visibly sweating and has developed uncontrollable fidgeting. His worries are quite severe, and he now must use considerable effort to get through the day.

Mr. AG has been compliant taking escitalopram 20 mg daily, and he tells you that the psychotherapist taught him strategies, which he has been performing faithfully, to maintain the treatment gains before releasing him from his care. You reevaluate the diagnosis and reassess comorbidity using the Patient Self-Report Screening Tool for Mental Illnesses (Appendix VI, p. 161). His answers are consistent with a comorbid depressive disorder. He reports fleeting thoughts of suicide but is adamant he would never consider this option as he would not hurt his family in this way. His GAD-7 score has risen to 21 (severe). During the functional impairment assessment, he reports that he has not been at work for the last 2 weeks. Prior to his leave, he admits to not being at all productive. His boss spoke to him about a few serious mistakes, which not only concerned Mr. AG, but also aggravated his condition to the point of triggering him to not being able to work. He tells you he is constantly tired because he is unable to sleep. His worries keep him up all night, which affects his concentration. He has not been socializing much with his friends and is really not interested in doing so. He tells you that it slipped his mind, but 5 years ago, his previous doctor gave him paroxetine for the same problem, which he discontinued after 6 weeks. "I was feeling really good, doctor, so I stopped it, but I remember it worked well."

You decide to switch to paroxetine, 20 mg daily, quickly titrating upwards to a maximum dose of 60 mg daily (see Table 3.5, p. 36, for details on switching medications).

Subsequent Visits	At maximum dosage, Mr. AG has partially improved—his GAD-7 score falls from 21 to 10 (borderline mild-moderate). He is still on medical leave from work.
	He reports some fatigue but agrees to stay on the medication. You feel this is important to maintain the therapeutic gains and negotiate adding another drug. Mr. AG agrees. You decide to add pregabalin as studies have shown its effectiveness as an add-on, particularly in comorbid GAD and depression.[19, 20] Pregabalin add-on is considered an off-label use for GAD;[21] you explain this to Mr. AG, as well as the expected side effects from the combination. Mr. AG agrees to give this option a try. The dose is gradually increased to 200 mg daily. He reports substantial improvement.
Maintenance Visits	At follow-up, Mr. AG states that he is feeling much better and is at his previous functioning state. He tells you that he is no longer depressed, is functioning well at work, and has regained his will to socialize. Due to his previous relapse and his long-standing GAD, you decide to continue his therapy for at least 2 years, and to reassess at that time.

Refer to the GAD Treatment Guide Summary in Appendix XII, p. 183.

Patients should be on maintenance therapy for a minimum of 6–12 months after the onset of improvement and up to 24 months depending on the duration and severity of the GAD. In severe cases, consider maintaining pharmacotherapy for longer and watch for relapse.[22, 23] Remember, when patients with GAD discontinue their medication

- 25% relapse in the first month
- 60–80% relapse over the course of the next year.

RELAPSE PREVENTION FOR GENERALIZED ANXIETY DISORDER

- Have a summary of strategies that helped.
- Identify expected stressors (exams, taxes, Christmas, etc.) and plan for them.
- Identify early signs of relapse.
- Match strategies with signs of relapse.
- Know when to seek help.

SUMMARY

You have completed reading a case study that illustrates the screening, diagnosis, treatment, and management of GAD. This case study is only a guide. Decision making should be individualized and based on clinical judgment. For an overview of management guidelines, refer to the GAD Treatment Guide Summary (Appendix XII, p. 183).

GENERALIZED ANXIETY DISORDER KEY POINTS

- Generalized anxiety disorder is a common, chronic, and often disabling condition.
- Patients have "what if" worries that are out of proportion to life circumstances.
- Patients have difficulty controlling their worries.
- Patients have 3 or more associated symptoms, such as restlessness, fatigue, muscle tension, irritability, and sleep problems.
- More than 60% of patients with GAD have lifetime comorbid MDD.
- Among non-pharmacological treatments, first-line treatment is CBT or therapy with CBT-based principles.
- SSRIs and SNRIs are the first-line pharmacological treatments.
- To prevent relapse, medication should be maintained for 12 months after the onset of symptom improvement before tapering. Maintain medication longer based on duration and severity of condition.

NOTES

1 Locke AB, Kirst N, Shultz CG. Diagnosis and management of generalized anxiety disorder and panic disorder in adults. Am Fam Physician. 2015; 91(9):617–624.

2 American Psychiatric Association. Diagnostic and statistical manual of mental disorders (DSM-5). 5th ed. Arlington, VA: American Psychiatric Association; 2013.

3 Sadock B, Kaplan HI, Sadock VA. Kaplan & Sadock's synopsis of psychiatry: behavioral sciences/clinical psychiatry. 9th ed. Philadelphia: Lippincott Williams & Wilkins; 2003.

4 Adapted from American Psychiatric Association. Diagnostic and statistical manual of mental disorders (DSM-5). 5th ed. Arlington, VA: American Psychiatric Association; 2013.

5 Gliatto, MF. Generalized anxiety disorder. Am Fam Physician. 2000; 62(7):1591–1600.

6 Kessler R, Berglund P, Demler O, Jin R, Merikangas K, Walters E. Lifetime prevalence and age-of-onset distributions of DSM-IV disorders in the National Comorbidity Survey Replication. Arch Gen Psychiatry. 2005; 62(6):593–602.

7 Kushner M, Abrams K, Thuras P, Hanson K, Brekke M, Sletten S. Follow-up study of anxiety disorder and alcohol dependence in comorbid alcoholism treatment patients. Alcohol Clin Exp Res. 2005; 29(8):1432–1443.

8 Judd L, Kessler R, Paulus M, Zeller P, Wittchen H, Kunovac J. Comorbidity as a fundamental feature of generalized anxiety disorders: results from the National Comorbidity Study (NCS). Acta Psychiatr Scand Suppl. 1998; 393:6–11.

9 Kessler R, Berglund P, Demler O, Jin R, Merikangas K, Walters E. Lifetime prevalence and age-of-onset distributions of DSM-IV disorders in the National Comorbidity Survey Replication. Arch Gen Psychiatry. 2005; 62(6):593–602.

10 American Psychiatric Association. Diagnostic and statistical manual of mental disorders (DSM-5). 5th ed. Arlington, VA: American Psychiatric Association; 2013.

11 Benjamin S, Herr NR, McDuffie J, et al. Performance characteristics of self-report instruments for diagnosing generalized anxiety and panic disorders in primary care: a systematic review [Internet]. Washington (DC): Department of Veterans Affairs (US); 2011 Aug. Available from: http://www.ncbi.nlm.nih.gov/books/NBK82545/

12 Sheehan DV, Lecrubier Y, Sheehan KH, Amorim P, Janavs J, Weiller E, et al. The Mini-International Neuropsychiatric Interview (MINI): the development and validation of a structured diagnostic psychiatric interview for DSM-IV and ICD-10. J Clin Psychiatry. 1998; 59 Suppl 20:22–33.

13 American Psychiatric Association [Internet]. Arlington (VA): American Psychiatric Association; 2013. Online assessment measures; c2013 [cited 2015 August 29]. Available from: http://www.psychiatry. org/psychiatrists/practice/dsm/dsm-5/online-assessment-measures

14 Evans M, Bradwejn J, Dunn L, editors. Ontario guidelines for the treatment of anxiety disorders in primary care. 1st ed. Toronto: Queen's Printer of Ontario; 2000.

15 Kennedy SH, Lam RW, Parikh SV, Patten SB, Ravindran AV. Canadian Network for Mood and Anxiety Treatments (CANMAT) clinical guidelines for the management of major depressive disorder in adults. J Affect Disord. 2009; 117 Suppl 1:S1–S2.

16 White D, Tavakoli S. Repetitive transcranial magnetic stimulation for treatment of major depressive disorder with comorbid generalized anxiety disorder. Ann Clin Psychiatry. 2015; 27(3):192–196.

17 Katzman MA, Bleau P, Blier P, Chokka P, Kjernisted K, Van Ameringen M, et al. Canadian clinical practice guidelines for the management of anxiety, posttraumatic stress and obsessive-compulsive disorders. BMC Psychiatry. 2014; 14 Suppl 1:S1.

18 Adapted from Katzman MA, Bleau P, Blier P, Chokka P, Kjernisted K, Van Ameringen M, et al. Canadian clinical practice guidelines for the management of anxiety, posttraumatic stress and obsessive-compulsive disorders. BMC Psychiatry. 2014; 14 Suppl 1:S1. This is a PMC Free Article; copyright and licence information can be found at: http://www.ncbi.nlm.nih.gov/pmc/articles/PMC4120194/.

19 Karaiskos D, Pappa D, Tzavellas E, Siarkos K, Katirtzoglou E, Papadimitriou G, Politis A. Pregabalin augmentation of antidepressants in older patients with comorbid depression and generalized anxiety disorder—an open-label study. Int J Geriatr Psychiatry. 2013; 28(1):100–105.

20 Strawn J, Geracioti T. The treatment of generalized anxiety disorder with pregabalin, an atypical anxiolytic. Neuropsychiatr Dis Treat. 2007; 3(2):237–243.

21 Some off-label use drugs (not an approved indication for the particular disorder by the U.S. Food and Drug Administration, Health Canada, or other drug regulatory agents) are included in the practice guidelines. Off-label use of drugs is a common and supported practice when guided by credible sources such as APA practice guidelines, scientific literature, and clinical experience (e.g., pregabalin add-on in GAD).

22 Sadock B, Kaplan HI, Sadock VA. Kaplan & Sadock's synopsis of psychiatry: behavioral sciences/clinical psychiatry. 9th ed. Philadelphia: Lippincott Williams & Wilkins; 2003.

23 Bandelow B, Boerner JR, Kasper S, Linden M, Wittchen H, Möller H. The diagnosis and treatment of generalized anxiety disorder. Dtsch Ärztebl Int. 2013; 110(17):300–309.

5

Panic Disorder

Introduction

Panic attacks as part of panic disorder are an "out of the blue" discrete period of intense fear that is out of proportion to the situation. Panic attacks can also occur as part of other psychiatric or medical conditions. In this case, the DSM-5 refers to panic attacks as a specifier in all DSM-5 disorders in which the attacks are triggered by that disorder. For example, if someone suffers from PTSD and a situation triggering a re-experience of the traumatic event triggers a panic attack, the panic attack would be a specifier of a PTSD diagnosis because it does not come out of the blue, but is cued by a specific determinant (event or situation) of the disorder.

A panic attack is not a mental disorder (not codable in the DSM-5). However, panic attacks can lead to *panic disorder*: an unprovoked panic attack followed by 1 month or more of daily fear of having another panic attack or of the consequences of the attack, which begins to affect functioning (avoidance). Patients become aware of and worry about physical changes that might happen with the panic attacks (DSM-5).[1] Patients may consult physicians about the fear of "having a heart attack," "dying," or "going crazy."

Many patients with panic disorder develop *agoraphobia* (anxiety about or the avoidance of places or situations from which escape might be difficult, or in which help might not be available in the event of a panic attack). Some will present with an Internet addiction, as this may be their only means of socializing.[2]

> In the DSM-5, panic disorder and agoraphobia are now considered distinct disorders. This stems from the understanding that agoraphobia is not a complication of panic disorder.[3] Diagnostic criteria for panic disorder can be found in Appendix XIV, p. 185.

Although panic disorder rarely resolves without medical intervention, it can be treated in primary care. To learn about panic disorder, you can follow the diagnosis, treatment, and management of our patient, Mrs. RM. You can progress through the practice case study from start to finish, or you can select your own learning path in the Practice Case Study Index, p. xxv. The choice is yours.

Clinical Presentation

Patients with panic attacks or panic disorder (PD) experience the following:[4]

TABLE 5.1 CHARACTERISTICS OF PANIC ATTACKS AND PANIC DISORDER

PANIC ATTACKS	PANIC DISORDER
A *panic attack* is a discrete period of sudden, intense fear or discomfort accompanied by 4 or more autonomic symptoms, such as palpitations, shortness of breath, sweating, and dizziness. Typically, the patient fears dying, losing control, having a heart attack, or "going crazy." The feeling of panic often has a weird quality that is qualitatively different from ordinary fear. By definition, panic attacks peak within minutes.	Patients with *panic disorder* have recurrent, unexpected *panic attacks*, and at least 1 of the attacks has been followed by at least 1 month or more of 1 of the following: • Fear of additional attacks (fear of where, when, and how the next panic attack may occur) • Worry about the implications of the attacks • A significant change in behavior related to the attacks ***Note:*** Patients with panic disorder have *unexpected* ("out of the blue") panic attacks rather than panic attacks caused by a situational trigger.

Panic attack criteria can be found in Appendix XIII, p. 184.

Because panic disorder with or without agoraphobia involves anxiety about and avoidance of particular situations, it can be confused with social anxiety disorder and specific phobia. Panic disorder and agoraphobia can be differentiated from social anxiety disorder and specific phobia by what the patient fears and the types of situations feared (see Table 5.2).

TABLE 5.2 DIFFERENTIATING PANIC DISORDER WITH OR WITHOUT AGORAPHOBIA FROM OTHER DISORDERS

	PANIC DISORDER WITH OR WITHOUT AGORAPHOBIA	SOCIAL ANXIETY DISORDER AND SPECIFIC PHOBIA
What the Patient Fears	The patient fears having an unexpected panic attack in a particular situation.	The patient fears a particular situation itself.
Type of Situation Feared	With panic disorder, the person fears the fear itself (i.e., having a panic attack). When panic disorder is associated with agoraphobia, the person fears places, situations, or events from which *escape* or getting help might be difficult in the event of a panic attack (e.g., situations in which having an attack might be humiliating), or panic-like, or other incapacitating or embarrassing symptoms (e.g., fear of falling or incontinence in the elderly).	With social anxiety disorder, the patient fears particular social situations or performing (e.g., because they may say or do things that might be, or be perceived by them to be, humiliating). With specific phobia, the patient fears a particular thing or situation (e.g., dogs, spiders).

The symptoms cause significant distress or impairment in social, occupational, or other important areas of functioning.[5]

Prevalence

The lifetime prevalence of panic disorder is approximately 2–6% of the general population.[6, 7] Comorbidity with other disorders including anxiety is common:

- Major depressive disorder occurs in 50–65% of individuals with panic disorder.

- Agoraphobia occurs in approximately 33% of all individuals with panic disorder.
- Alcohol use disorder occurs in approximately 20% of all individuals with panic disorder.

Panic disorder is diagnosed 2.5 times more often in women than in men. Age of onset is typically between late adolescence and the mid-30s.[8]

Panic Disorder Case Study: Meet Mrs. RM

Mrs. RM is a 29-year-old mother of a 5-year-old girl. She is a school teacher with no past history of heart or lung disease. Visibly anxious and upset, she presents to your office with the following symptoms:

- Episodes of chest pain, racing heartbeat, and difficulty breathing.
- During these episodes, she feels faint, feels like she's choking, and thinks she's having a heart attack.
- These episodes come "out of the blue."
- She worries about having heart problems.

> » What should you do?
> » What are your options?

ASSESSMENT: SCREENING AND PROVISIONAL DIAGNOSIS

Mrs. RM and her family are well known to you. You have been seeing Mrs. RM for annual physicals since she was 15 years old. She is in excellent health and there are no risk factors for cardiopulmonary disease. However, you do a cursory physical exam and some investigative workup to rule out underlying non-psychiatric medical conditions. These reveal no abnormalities.

Note: Some medical conditions and/or factors can present with anxiety symptoms, but rarely to the point of a complete disorder. Refer to Chapter 2, p. 16, for further information on factors to consider when assessing anxiety symptoms, or go directly to Factors to Consider When Assessing Anxiety Symptoms (Appendix I, p. 155).

If you are pressed for time and there is no safety risk or clinical judgment of urgency, you can tell Mrs. RM that you understand her suffering and will help, but you need her to schedule an appointment to give you the time to assess her properly. Ask her to return should her condition get worse in the meantime. This is a very important step, particularly if time is an issue. It only takes 1–2 minutes and reassures her that even if you don't have time to spend with her this visit, you are concerned about her and want to take the time to address her complaints properly She will feel heard and relieved that someone will help. This lessens her distress while gaining her trust.

Screening for Anxiety and Related Disorders

> » How do you screen for common anxiety and related disorders?
> » How do you screen for common comorbid mental disorders?
> » What is the provisional diagnosis?

TOOLS FOR ASSESSMENT

Refer to the "Provisional Diagnosis" section of Chapter 2, p. 17, for information on screening for anxiety and related disorders and comorbid conditions, or go directly to the Patient Self-Report Screening Tool for Mental Illnesses (Appendix VI, p. 161). Physicians can subsequently review responses with patients to verify accuracy.

You can also review the "Anxiety and Related Disorders Types and Subtypes" section of Chapter 2, p. 17, which includes a useful tool to help differentiate anxiety disorders, or go directly to Differentiating Anxiety Disorders, Obsessive-Compulsive, and Trauma- and Stressor-Related Disorders (Appendix II, p. 156).

Provisional Diagnosis

Mrs. RM proceeds to tell you the following: "Roughly once a week, I get these awful episodes that last about 30 minutes. I feel like I'm about to die, I'm short of breath, I'm nauseous, my heart starts pounding, and I feel dizzy. It's really awful. And these episodes come for no reason—I can't tell what brings them on."

You suspect that Mrs. RM is suffering from panic attacks, perhaps to the point of panic disorder. To orient your provisional diagnosis and clarify further, you administer the Patient Self-Report Screening Tool for Mental Illnesses (Appendix VI, p. 161). In response to section 3 and 4 of the tool, Mrs. RM tells you the following:

Have you had an unprovoked ("out of the blue") attack or spell during which you suddenly felt anxious, frightened, uncomfortable, or uneasy, even in situations most people would not feel this way?	"Yes, that is exactly right. They come all of a sudden, without warning!"
Are the attacks of fear or panic so intense you have to do something to stop them, or are they so physically distressing you thought you might collapse or die?	"Yes, Doctor. I feel like I'm about to die."

Do these attacks peak quickly within minutes? Can you describe what happens when you get these attacks? Do you experience at least 4 of the following: palpitations, chest pains, chills, sweating, dizziness, hot flashes, or difficulty breathing during these spells?	"I get these awful episodes. Oh, they peak very quickly—within a few minutes—and then gradually go away. They last about 30 minutes. I'm short of breath, I'm nauseous, my heart starts pounding, and I feel dizzy."
How often do you get these attacks?	She tells you they happen roughly once a week.
After an attack, do you worry for at least 1 month about having another attack?	She tells you that for the last 3 months, she has been afraid of having another episode. She is afraid of the physical symptoms and of losing control. During these episodes, she has an overwhelming, intense fear that she's about to die.
Are the attacks brought on by any triggers, such as social situations?	She denies any social or specific trigger, saying she loves hosting dinner parties and has no problem speaking in public.
Does this fear of having attacks prevent you from doing certain things or interfere with your life; for example, do you avoid the "panic" triggers (going to the mall or crowded places)?	"Well, I definitely prefer to stay at home these days, but when I do go out, if I take my cellphone, usually I can stay and get through the attacks unless I am in crowded places. Does that count? Come to think of it, the fear of having another attack really stresses me—I would say that counts as 'interfering with my life.' I have to leave the place maybe about 30% of the time."

Mrs. RM's responses indicate that her attacks have the intense fear and the physical and cognitive symptoms typical of panic attacks. The attacks are both recurrent and unexpected, and her response to the question "Does this interfere with your life?" indicates that her anxiety has crossed the threshold for distress to "interference with functioning." Her answers suggest panic disorder. On further questioning, Mrs. RM tells you that her aunt suffered from panic attacks that required treatment with medication. She tells you that "talk therapy" did not work for her aunt.

You advise Mrs. RM of your suspicions and schedule an appointment in 2 weeks to investigate further.

CONFIRMING THE DIAGNOSIS

The next step is to confirm Mrs. RM's diagnosis. Keep in mind that panic disorder is commonly associated with agoraphobia.

The diagnosis of panic disorder is confirmed by using the DSM-5 criteria for panic disorder[9]

> » What factors must you consider to confirm Mrs. RM has panic disorder?
> » What instruments can be used to confirm the diagnosis?

(see Appendix XIV, p. 185). Physicians can also employ user-friendly tools adapted from the DSM-5 to recall diagnostic features:

The following scales are validated tools; however, they should be interpreted in conjunction with clinical judgment and a review of DSM-5 criteria.

- Patient self-report tool: the Panic Disorder Self-Report Scale (100% specificity, 89% sensitivity for panic disorder; validated against DSM-IV criteria only; the scale in this book is tailored to reflect DSM-5 criteria, but requires validation.)[10] (Appendix XV, p. 186).
- The Mini International Neuropsychiatric Interview (MINI) for panic disorder is a widely used physician-directed instrument (proprietary tool).[11]

In Mrs. RM's case, the DSM-5 supports your diagnosis of panic disorder:
- She has attacks during which she suddenly feels anxious, and she suffers 4 or more of the 13 cognitive or physical symptoms of a panic attack.
- The attacks peak within minutes.
- The attacks come on unexpectedly.
- Following a panic attack, she is afraid of having another attack for 1 month or more.
- The symptoms and distress interfere with her day-to-day functioning.

BASELINE ASSESSMENT

The next step is to conduct a baseline assessment. This will provide you and your patient with important information to tailor a treatment plan.

> » What should be included in a baseline assessment?
> » What tools are useful at baseline and follow-up visits?

Patient self-report tools are used in primary care for many medical conditions. These practical, time-efficient tools can be used in mental health assessments as well; however, responses should be interpreted by clinicians together with the DSM-5 criteria and clinical judgment. A careful assessment and rating of each of the following parameters will establish a baseline from which to measure treatment response:

- Suicide Assessment Questionnaire (Appendix III, p. 157)
- Panic disorder symptom severity. The following tools can be used to assess severity:
  - GAD-7 (sensitivity 74%, specificity 81%) (Appendix V, p. 160)
  - Panic Disorder Severity Scale Self-Report Form[12] (Appendix XVI, p. 190)
  - Severity Measure for Panic Disorder—Adult[13] (see note below)
- Comorbid conditions
- Somatic complaints; Symptom Assessment Checklist (Appendix VIII, p. 167)
- Functional impairment; Functional Impairment Assessment Scale (Appendix IX, p. 168)

You can also refer to the "Baseline Assessment" section of Chapter 2, p. 18.

Note: The Severity Measure for Panic Disorder—Adult can be downloaded directly from the APA site at http://www.psychiatry.org/psychiatrists/practice/dsm/dsm-5/online-assessment-measures. These measures can be reproduced without permission by researchers and clinicians for use with their patients. Rating information is provided as well.

Mrs. RM's Baseline Assessment

Mrs. RM describes fleeting suicidal thoughts, but she says she would never consider that option. "My daughter is my life, and I would never hurt her that way." The GAD-7 yields a score of 9 (mild). She rates sweating (3), tiredness (2), nausea (2), dizziness (2), stomach pains (2), and sleep problems (1), which she describes as waking up approximately 1 hour early in the morning, though she is able to get back to sleep if she stays in bed. The Functional Impairment Assessment Scale (Appendix IX, p. 168) reveals that she is not able to socialize like she used to due to her fear and rates her capacity at 70% of what her social life used to be when she felt well.

MANAGEMENT GUIDELINES

Now that you have confirmed the diagnosis of panic disorder and have a general idea of Mrs. RM's illness severity and how it affects her, you can begin to develop a care plan. Information collected to date will guide your management plan; however, the choice of treatment will depend on several factors, for example:[14, 15]

- Patient opinions about treatment
- Receptivity to counseling
- Receptivity to medication
- Severity of symptoms
- Comorbidity
- Previous response (or lack of response) to treatment
- Availability of resources in the community

Unlike other anxiety and related disorders, in panic disorder there is clear evidence of better outcomes with combination therapy than with psychotherapy or pharmacotherapy alone.[16, 17]

> You can also refer to Chapter 3: Management, p. 25. First-, second-, and third-line treatments for panic disorder are listed in Table 5.3.

Psychotherapy

Among non-pharmacological treatments, CBT is the therapy of choice—specifically *exposure therapy* (e.g., systematic desensitization) delivered individually or in groups. It should be considered alongside pharmacotherapy for all patients diagnosed with panic disorder as it has a higher efficacy and lower relapse rate than pharmacotherapy alone.[18] Therapy involves cognitive restructuring: countering anxious beliefs, exposure to fear symptoms or situations, addressing and eliminating or reducing anxiety-maintaining behaviors, and maintaining therapeutic gains, thereby reducing relapse. Other delivery formats, including Internet-based or telephone-guided CBT, can be effective and cost-efficient, in particular for patients who cannot or will not travel. There is some evidence to suggest that adding d-cycloserine enhances the therapeutic effects of psychotherapy.[19] Table 5.3 summarizes the psychotherapy and pharmacological treatments recommended for panic disorder.

Other approaches include:

- Psychoeducation
- Self-help manuals
- Breathing retraining

Patients should be advised to reduce excessive caffeine from their diets.

TABLE 5.3 PSYCHOTHERAPY AND PHARMACOTHERAPY RECOMMENDATIONS FOR PANIC DISORDER*

	PSYCHOTHERAPY	PHARMACOLOGICAL AGENT
First-line	CBT (usually 12–20 weekly sessions). Treatment via telephone/videoconferencing[20, 21] and Internet-based CBT (ICBT) are as effective as face-to-face CBT and may be cost-efficient options, particularly for agoraphobic patients unwilling to attend a clinic.[22, 23]	Citalopram, escitalopram, fluoxetine, fluvoxamine, paroxetine, paroxetine CR, sertraline, venlafaxine XR
Second-line	Acceptance and commitment therapy (ACT), although research is still in its infancy, shows promising results.[24] Psychodynamic therapy shows promise.[25] Applied relaxation self-help training over the Internet shows promise; however, randomized controlled trials have shown that the most severely ill patients fared less well.[26]	Alprazolam, clomipramine, clonazepam, diazepam, imipramine, lorazepam, mirtazapine, reboxetine
Third-line	Another option to consider when patients cannot leave the house is bibliotherapy.[27, 28, 29]	Bupropion SR, divalproex, duloxetine, gabapentin, levetiracetam, milnacipran, moclobemide, olanzapine, phenelzine, quetiapine, risperidone, tranylcypromine
Adjunctive therapy		**Second-line:** Alprazolam ODT used short term (<8 weeks including taper with initiation of antidepressant can lead to quicker relief), clonazepam **Third-line:** Aripiprazole, divalproex, olanzapine, pindolol, risperidone

CR = controlled release; ODT = orally disintegrating tablets; SR = sustained release; XR = extended release

With SSRIs, SNRIs, and TCAs, initial response (decrease in panic attacks, anticipatory anxiety, and avoidance) may be evident within 3–4 weeks.

It can take up to 8 weeks with at least 2 weeks at maximum dose for initial response. Wait 8 weeks to decide if change of treatment is warranted, unless symptoms are severe (not feasible to wait); decisions on management should be individualized for each patient.

At the maximum tolerated dose, full remission may take 6 months or longer.[30]

*Adapted from Katzman et al. (2014).[31]

Biological and Complementary and Alternative Medicine

More studies are needed for these types of treatments; however, according to expert consensus guidelines, some studies show that novel treatments such as noninvasive brain stimulation using a radioelectric asymmetric conveyor (REAC), repetitive transcranial magnetic stimulation (rTMS), and alternative therapies such as capnometry-assisted respiratory training, may be effective.[32] More information on these therapies can be found in the open-access publication by Katzman et al. at http://www.biomedcentral.com/1471-244X/14/S1/S1.

VISIT-BY-VISIT GUIDE: MILD PANIC DISORDER

Current Visit	At this point, you have determined that Mrs. RM has mild panic disorder as she reports that she has, on average, one 30-minute panic attack per week, and she worries about future attacks. There is no safety risk, and functional impairment is mild.
	She is quite receptive to pharmacotherapy because she admits that she doesn't have faith in psychotherapy. "Doctor," she tells you, "it didn't work for my aunt, and I really think I am very much like her." You attended a recent workshop on anxiety disorders and learned that combination therapy is more effective than either therapy alone. After negotiating with Mrs. RM, she understands the benefits of this management plan and agrees to give combination therapy a try. You decide to initiate first-line pharmacotherapy. After considering the possibilities, you choose citalopram 10 mg daily for 1 week to be increased to 20 mg for an additional week, plus alprazolam 0.5 mg 3 times daily. You arrange for a referral for CBT and schedule a follow-up appointment 2 weeks later.
Second Visit	Two weeks later, Mrs. RM returns reporting severe headaches (2) and nausea (2). She reveals that she continues to have, on average, 1 panic attack per week. Her functional impairment remains unchanged, and there is no safety risk.
	What is your next step? • Switch to another medication. • Reduce the citalopram to 5 mg daily. • Reduce the citalopram to 10 mg daily. • Increase the citalopram to 30 mg daily.
	You verify Mrs. RM's baseline data and see that headaches were not present before. She admits that the headaches have increased with the increase in the citalopram dose from 10 mg to 20 mg. This is consistent with the medication side effects. You explain that such side effects are common, tell her that they will subside soon, and ask if this is tolerable. She replies that the side effects are quite troublesome. You choose to reduce the citalopram dose to 10 mg daily and maintain this dose for another 1–2 weeks.
	You schedule an appointment for 2 weeks later.
Third Visit	Two weeks later (at 4 weeks of treatment), Mrs. RM returns. Although her panic attacks and functional impairment remain unchanged, the side effects she was experiencing have decreased substantially; she reports mild nausea only. As agreed at the last visit, she increased citalopram to 20 mg once the side effects subsided, which occurred after 1 week on 10 mg, and maintained alprazolam. You advise her to maintain the current dose for 2 more weeks. She explains that she is fine with this approach.
	You schedule an appointment for 2 weeks later.

Fourth Visit	Two weeks later (at 6 weeks of treatment), Mrs. RM returns with slight improvement on citalopram 20 mg daily.
	Note: The response time delay is not unusual. Patients with panic disorder usually start to show improvement within 6–8 weeks when treatment consists of psychosocial intervention or pharmacotherapy (non-benzodiazepine). Taking into account the week on a lower than minimum dose, a clinical response may only be evident in another 1–3 weeks. If there is no response by 8 weeks, reevaluate the diagnosis or consider a different treatment.
Fifth Visit	Two weeks later, Mrs. RM returns reporting she feels much improved. You ask her to maintain citalopram at a dose of 20 mg daily and explain that it is best to gradually withdraw alprazolam to prevent dependence. She tells you that the psychotherapy is really helping, too. You ask her to schedule an appointment for 4 weeks later.
Sixth Visit	Finally, Mrs. RM's symptoms subside; she reports no panic attacks in the previous 2 weeks and has minimal side effects. She feels much better and thanks you for helping her. She evaluates her functional capacity at 90% (minimal dysfunction).
	You emphasize to Mrs. RM the importance of continuing with the citalopram and the CBT therapy, reminding her that ongoing treatment is required in 20–40% of cases.
Maintenance Visits	**In Mrs. RM's case, how long should you continue therapy of 20 mg citalopram daily?** • 2 months • 4 months • 6 months • 12 months
	Maintenance therapy for at least 12 months after achieving a minimum response of 75–80% (assessed through illness severity and functional impairment) increases the odds of achieving and maintaining *functional* remission. Once full remission is achieved, discontinue therapy gradually over 2–6 months. Reinforce the importance of continuing with CBT strategies learned over the course of therapy.

VISIT-BY-VISIT GUIDE: MODERATE PANIC DISORDER

First Visit	Mrs. RM returns 9 months later. Unfortunately, even though she is taking citalopram, her symptoms have worsened. She now reports 4 panic attacks per week, each approximately 15–30 minutes in length. A functional impairment assessment reveals that she has missed no days of work, but social functioning is reduced (she rates functioning at 50%; moderate). She reports a newly developed fear of having an attack in a shopping mall, and she therefore avoids shopping malls altogether. She is able to socialize with her friends as long as they stay away from crowded places.
	You note that she has developed comorbid agoraphobia specifically pertaining to malls and being among crowds.
	You remind her that a combination of psychotherapy and pharmacotherapy is more effective than either therapy alone, and she agrees to CBT booster sessions. You decide to increase citalopram to the maximum dose of 40 mg per day.

Subsequent Visits	Over the course of the next 2 months, she improves gradually. Eventually, the panic attacks subside. Functional impairment assessment shows that the panic disorder is minimally problematic, as she rates her functional capacity (social/leisure domain) at 80%.
Maintenance Visits	You advise her to maintain the psychotherapy and pharmacotherapy combination for at least 2 years to prevent reoccurrence. You see her monthly at first. Within 4 months, she is in complete remission and able to socialize, as well as go to the mall. Follow-up appointments are scheduled accordingly.

VISIT-BY-VISIT GUIDE: SEVERE PANIC DISORDER

First Visit	Mrs. RM has been in full remission for 18 months. She has been using the CBT strategies and has been compliant with 40 mg of citalopram daily. She reports a reoccurrence and gradual increase in panic attacks in the last 4 weeks. "Doctor, I get 8 full-blown panic attacks per week." Upon further questioning, she tells you each attacks consists of the following:

- Accelerated heart rate

- Sweating

- Feeling of choking

- Chest pain

- Nausea

- Profound fear of death

You decide to review the following:

- Suicide Assessment Questionnaire (Appendix III, p. 157)

- Disorder illness severity

- Comorbidity with the Patient Self-Report Screening Tool for Mental Illnesses (Appendix VI, p. 161)

- Symptom Assessment Checklist (Appendix VIII, p. 167)

- Functional Impairment Assessment (Appendix IX, p. 168)

You ask her to rate the severity of the panic attacks from 1–10, with 10 being the most severe. She rates her severity at 10. She denies suicidal thoughts but adds that no one would want to live this way. On item 1 of the Patient Self Report Screening Tool for Mental Illnesses, you suspect comorbid depression; however, a further evaluation with the Patient Health Questionnaire-9 (Appendix VII, p. 165) determines that it does not meet the threshold for major depressive disorder. You do note, however, that she has comorbid agoraphobia.

Mrs. RM reports daily headaches, fatigue, and loss of concentration due to interrupted sleep most nights. You ask about her Internet use. At the workshop you attended, the speaker talked about Internet addiction[33] as a severity "red flag" among people who experience anxiety and related disorders, including panic disorder with or without agoraphobia. To your surprise, she says, "Yes, Doctor, I don't go out, and this is the only way I stay in contact with people." You suspect that prolonged use of the Internet may in part be responsible for the headaches.

She is now profoundly afraid of having a panic attack in a shopping mall, riding on a bus, or crossing a bridge. Consequently, she spends almost the entire day trapped in her home. On the Functional Impairment Assessment Scale (Appendix IX, p. 168), she indicates that she is unable to work or socialize (rates both at a capacity of 0%; extreme impairment).

Mrs. RM now has severe PD.

You discuss this with Mrs. RM, and you both agree to switch to another first-line medication—paroxetine 20 mg daily—as she asks you for "something that will calm me down." You ask her to see her psychotherapist for a few sessions to reinforce CBT skills, keeping in mind that psychodynamic psychotherapy and acceptance and commitment therapy (ACT), although research is still in its infancy, show promising results in terms of efficacy. You advise her that these can be alternative psychotherapy options should the current treatment plan not work for her. You schedule a follow-up appointment for 2 weeks later.

| **Subsequent Visits** | Two weeks later, there is no improvement. She is still unable to work (extreme impairment). You increase paroxetine every week by 10 mg to 60 mg daily. After an 8-week trial period, there is no significant improvement, and she reports headaches, nausea, and extreme fatigue related to lack of sleep. |

What is your next step?

- Switch to another first-line medication.
- Increase paroxetine to 80 mg daily.
- Switch to clomipramine.
- Add ACT or psychodynamic psychotherapy.

You feel that clomipramine may be a good option, a second-line therapy, as you have tried 2 first-line SSRIs. In addition, alprazolam 0.25 mg TID is prescribed. Clomipramine is initiated at a dose of 25 mg daily, gradually increasing as tolerated every 1–2 weeks (maximum dose is 300 mg daily). At 300 mg of clomipramine daily, there is partial improvement (50% response). You feel that acceptance and commitment therapy (ACT) could help, which she agrees to try.

Finally, after 3 months on this new treatment plan—ACT in addition to medication—her panic attacks begin to subside, and she is able to return to work and frequent malls and crowded places without worry. Her Internet use gradually decreases. Side effects are minimal. "I feel like myself again," she says. Mrs. RM stays in remission with clomipramine and ACT. Alprazolam is gradually decreased.

| **Maintenance Visits** | Given the severity of this episode, you choose to continue therapy for a minimum of 2–3 years with frequent monitoring. |

SUMMARY

You have completed a case study illustrating the screening, diagnosis, treatment, and management of PD. This case study is only a guide. Decision making should be individualized and based on clinical judgment. For an overview of the management guidelines, refer to the Panic Disorder Treatment Guide Summary (Appendix XVII, p. 194).

PANIC DISORDER KEY POINTS

- Panic disorder is a common, chronic, and often disabling condition.
- It can mimic a cardiopulmonary disorder.
- The panic attacks are recurrent and *unprovoked* (no identifiable trigger).
- The attacks peak within minutes and generally last less than 1 hour.
- The panic attacks are followed by 1 month or more of fear of having another attack.
- The disorder causes dysfunction in some area of the person's life (home, work, school, or relationships).
- Comorbid MDD is extremely common.
- Among non-pharmacological treatments, psychosocial intervention (including CBT-based therapy) is the first-line of therapy.
- ACT and psychodynamic psychotherapy show promising results.
- Among pharmacological treatments, SSRIs with or without benzodiazepines are the first line of therapy.
- Benzodiazepines should be withdrawn promptly to prevent dependency.
- Patients with Internet addiction raise a red flag.

NOTES

1 American Psychiatric Association. Diagnostic and statistical manual of mental disorders (DSM-5). 5th ed. Arlington, VA: American Psychiatric Association; 2013.

2 Gloster AT, Sonntag R, Hoyer J, Meyer AH, Heinze S, Ströhle A, Eifert G, Wittchen HU. Treating treatment-resistant patients with panic disorder and agoraphobia using psychotherapy: a randomized controlled switching trial. Psychother Psychosom. 2015; 84(2):100–109.

3 Psych Central [Internet]. [Place unknown]: Psych Central; 1995–2016. Bressert S. Agoraphobia symptoms; 2013 [cited 2015 Mar 9]. Available from: http://psychcentral.com/disorders/agoraphobia-symptoms/

4 American Psychiatric Association. Diagnostic and statistical manual of mental disorders (DSM-5). 5th ed. Arlington, VA: American Psychiatric Association; 2013.

5 Adapted from the American Psychiatric Association. Diagnostic and statistical manual of mental disorders (DSM-5). 5th ed. Arlington, VA: American Psychiatric Association; 2013.

6 Narrow WE. Age and gender considerations in psychiatric diagnosis: a research agenda for DSM-V. Arlington, VA: American Psychiatric Association; 2007.

7 National Institute of Mental Health [Internet]. Bethesda (MD): National Institute of Mental Health; n.d. Panic disorder among adults; n.d. [cited 2015 May 9]. Available from: http://www.nimh.nih.gov/health/statistics/prevalence/panic-disorder-among-adults.shtml

8 Sheikh J, Leskin G, Klein D. Gender differences in panic disorder: findings from the National Comorbidity Survey. Am J Psychiatry. 2002; 159(1):55–58.

9 American Psychiatric Association. Diagnostic and statistical manual of mental disorders (DSM-5). 5th ed. Arlington, VA: American Psychiatric Association; 2013.

10 Newman M, Holmes M, Zuellig A, Kachin K, Behar E, Strauss ME. The reliability and validity of the Panic Disorder Self-Report: a new diagnostic screening measure of panic disorder. Psychol Assess. 2006; 18(1):49–61. The Panic Disorder Self-Report scale is found in the appendices of this manuscript and can also be downloaded directly from http://www.psychologie.tu-dresden.de/i2/klinische/mitarbeiter/materialien/pdsr.pdf

11 Sheehan DV, Lecrubier Y, Sheehan KH, Amorim P, Janavs J, Weiller E, et al. The Mini-International Neuropsychiatric Interview (MINI): the development and validation of a structured diagnostic psychiatric interview for DSM-IV and ICD-10. J Clin Psychiatry. 1998; 59 Suppl 20:22–33.

12 Shear M, Brown T, Barlow D, Money R, Sholomskas D, Woods S, et al. Multicenter collaborative panic disorder severity scale. Am J Psychiatry. 1997; 154(11):1571–1575. The Panic Disorder Severity Scale–Self-Report Form, included in the appendices, has been reproduced with permission from the author. Clinicians can also download the scale directly from http://www.goodmedicine.org.uk/files/panic,%20assessment%20pdss.pdf

13 American Psychiatric Association [Internet]. Arlington (VA): American Psychiatric Association; 2013. Online assessment measures; c2013 [cited 2015 August 29]. Available from: http://www.psychiatry.org/psychiatrists/practice/dsm/dsm-5/online-assessment-measures. This measure can be accessed directly online and reproduced without permission by researchers and by clinicians for use with their patients.

14 Evans M, Bradwejn J, Dunn L, editors. Ontario guidelines for the treatment of anxiety disorders in primary care. 1st ed. Toronto: Queen's Printer of Ontario; 2000.

15 Kennedy SH, Lam RW, Parikh SV, Patten SB, Ravindran AV. Canadian Network for Mood and Anxiety Treatments (CANMAT) clinical guidelines for the management of major depressive disorder in adults. J Affect Disord. 2009; 117 Suppl 1:S1–S2.

16 Bandelow B, Seidler-Brandler U, Becker A, Wedekind D, Rüther E. Meta-analysis of randomized controlled comparisons of psychopharmacological and psychological treatments for anxiety disorders. World J Biol Psychiatry. 2007; 8(3):175–187.

17 Hofmann SG, Sawyer AT, Korte KJ, Smits JA. Is it beneficial to add pharmacotherapy to cognitive-behavioral therapy when treating anxiety disorders? A meta-analytic review. Int J Cogn Ther. 2009; 2(2):160–175.

18 American Psychiatric Association. Practice guidelines for the treatment of patients with panic disorder. 2nd ed. Washington, DC: American Psychiatric Association; 2009.

19 Otto MW, Tolin DF, Simon NM, Pearlson GD, Basden S, Meunier SA, et al. Efficacy of d-cycloserine for enhancing response to cognitive-behavior therapy for panic disorder. Biol Psychiatry. 2010; 67(4):365–370.

20 Lewis C, Pearce J, Bisson J. Efficacy, cost-effectiveness and acceptability of self-help interventions for anxiety disorders: systematic review. Br J Psychiatry. 2012; 200(1):15–21.

21 Titov N, Andrews G, Johnston L, Robinson E, Spence J. Transdiagnostic Internet treatment for anxiety disorders: a randomized controlled trial. Behav Res Ther. 2010; 48(9):890–899.

22 Swinson RP, Fergus KD, Cox BJ, Wickwire K. Efficacy of telephone-administered behavioral therapy for panic disorder with agoraphobia. Behav Res Ther. 1995; 33(4):465–469.

23 Bouchard S, Paquin B, Payeur R, Allard M, Rivard V, Fournier T, et al. Delivering cognitive-behavior therapy for panic disorder with agoraphobia in videoconference. Telemed J E Health. 2004; 10(1):13–25.

24 Gloster AT, Sonntag R, Hoyer J, Meyer AH, Heinze S, Ströhle A, et al. Treating treatment-resistant patients with panic disorder and agoraphobia using psychotherapy: a randomized controlled switching trial. Psychother Psychosom. 2015; 84(2):100–109.

25 Milrod B, Chambless DL, Gallop R, et al. Psychotherapies for panic disorder: a tale of two sites. J Clin Psychiatry [Internet]. 2015 Jun [cited 2015 Oct 10]. Available from: http://www.psychiatrist.com/jcp/article/Pages/2015/aheadofprint/14m09507.aspx

26 Carlbring P, Ekselius L, Andersson G. Treatment of panic disorder via the Internet: a randomized trial of CBT vs. applied relaxation. J Behav Ther Exp Psychiatry. 2003; 34(2):129–140.

27 Lewis C, Pearce J, Bisson J. Efficacy, cost-effectiveness and acceptability of self-help interventions for anxiety disorders: systematic review. Br J Psychiatry. 2012; 200(1):15–21.

28 Lucock M, Padgett K, Noble R, Westley A, Atha C, Horsefield C, Leach C. Controlled clinical trial of a self-help for anxiety intervention for patients waiting for psychological therapy. Behav Cogn Psychother. 2008; 36(5):541–551.

29 Lidren D, Watkins P, Gould R, Clum G, Asterino M, Tulloch H. A comparison of bibliotherapy and group therapy in the treatment of panic disorder. J Consult Clin Psychol. 1994; 62(4):865–869.

30 Lecrubier Y, Judge R. Long-term evaluation of paroxetine, clomipramine and placebo in panic disorder. Acta Psychiatr Scand. 1997; 95(2):153–160.

31 Adapted from Katzman MA, Bleau P, Blier P, Chokka P, Kjernisted K, Van Ameringen M, et al. Canadian clinical practice guidelines for the management of anxiety, posttraumatic stress and obsessive-compulsive disorders. BMC Psychiatry. 2014; 14 Suppl 1:S1. This is a PMC Free Article; copyright and licence information can be found at: http://www.ncbi.nlm.nih.gov/pmc/articles/PMC4120194/

32 Katzman MA, Bleau P, Blier P, Chokka P, Kjernisted K, Van Ameringen M, et al. Canadian clinical practice guidelines for the management of anxiety, posttraumatic stress and obsessive-compulsive disorders. BMC Psychiatry. 2014; 14 Suppl 1:S1.

33 Santos V, Nardi AE, King AL. Treatment of Internet addiction in patient with panic disorder and obsessive compulsive disorder: a case report. CNS Neurol Disord Drug Targets. 2015; 14(3):341–344.

6

Agoraphobia

Introduction

*A*goraphobia is a marked, unreasonable fear or anxiety about, or the avoidance of, places or situations from which escape might be difficult or in which help might not be available. Agoraphobia diagnosis within the context of panic disorder is no longer required. Both are now considered distinct disorders and are separate conditions in the DSM-5. This stems from the understanding that agoraphobia is no longer considered a complication of panic disorder.[1]

To learn about agoraphobia, you can follow the diagnosis, treatment, and management of our patient, Dr. GC. You can progress through the practice case study from start to finish, or you can select your own learning path in the Practice Case Study Index, p. xxv. The choice is yours.

Clinical Presentation

People with agoraphobia experience unreasonable anxiety about going to places or being in situations or events from which escape might be difficult or in which help may not be available in the event that they have a panic attack or experience panic-like or other incapacitating or embarrassing symptoms (e.g., elderly individuals may have a fear of falling or fear of incontinence) for the majority of days during a 6-month period.

The worry is difficult to control and is accompanied by a variety of associated symptoms, such as restlessness, fatigue, and muscle tension. The symptoms cause significant distress or impairment in social, occupational, or other important areas of functioning, and can lead to suicidal behavior.[2]

The individual experiences intense fear in response to or in anticipation of at least 2 of the following 5 scenarios:

1. Leaving the home alone
2. Being in open spaces (e.g., parking lots, marketplaces, bridges)
3. Being in enclosed spaces (e.g., shops, theaters, cinemas)
4. Being in a crowd or standing in line
5. Using public transportation (e.g., automobiles, buses, planes)

People express the following feelings:

- Helplessness
- Detachment from others
- Agitation
- Loss of control
- Sense of derealization

The diagnostic criteria for agoraphobia can be found in Appendix XVIII, p. 195.

People with agoraphobia often experience panic attacks and need the presence of a loved one (friend, partner, or family member) to be able to confront the situation; in severe situations, the person is housebound. Agoraphobia is often chronic; when patients discontinue their medication

- 25–50% relapse within 6 months
- 40–50% have residual symptoms after 3–6 years.[3]

Prevalence

The lifetime prevalence rate of agoraphobia without panic disorder is estimated at 0.8%.

The prevalence of agoraphobia in conjunction with panic disorder is 1.1%.[4] The average age of onset is 20 years of age, and agoraphobia is twice as common in women as in men.[5]

Agoraphobia is highly comorbid. The rate of occurrence of associated comorbid disorders will require further studies as limited information exists that evaluates agoraphobia as a distinct anxiety disorder. The best available evidence to date on the most common lifetime comorbidity includes:

- Panic disorder
- Major depressive disorder
- Substance use disorder

Agoraphobia Case Study: Meet Dr. GC

Dr. GC is a 55-year-old physician in a solo community practice. He is brought to you by his wife, also a physician, because she is concerned about his use of alcohol. They have both been your patients for 10 years now. Dr. GC is hesitant to talk with you and says that for more than 6 months, his wife has been trying to convince him to seek help for what she believes to be an addiction problem. He adds that she is exaggerating and doesn't know what she is talking about.

His wife says his health has been deteriorating, with weight loss, poor and agitated sleep, and an unstable mood that fluctuates from anxiety to episodes of depression. On weekends, he is restless, irritable, and verbally aggressive. He locks himself in his room for hours on end and refuses to socialize in any capacity unless he has a drink before leaving the house. He then will stop at a bar and have another within the hour. She suspects that he carries a flask as well. She reports that when she asks her husband about work, he becomes very guarded and simply responds that all is well. She has found empty "mickey" bottles of vodka in the house, as well as his office, yet he denies any particular abuse of alcohol. She also tells you that he has a heart condition. "If you remember," she says, "he was diagnosed as having ischemic heart disease, hypertriglyceridemia, and hypercholesterolemia, as well as peripheral vascular disease 5 years ago." His condition is stable on current medication, and he denies having chest pains.

Dr. GC looks quite uncomfortable, and says, "My wife is picky and won't leave me alone. "She exaggerates a lot."

He asks, "Is it bad to have a few drinks once in a while?"

> » What should you do?
> » What are your options?

ASSESSMENT: SCREENING AND PROVISIONAL DIAGNOSIS

You do a cursory review of Dr. GC's chart and notice that you had requested routine blood tests 9 months ago; however, he never went for the tests. You were investigating possible diabetes due to reports of fatigue, polyuria, polydipsia, and weakness, and wonder if he is hesitant about getting the tests done as they might uncover a liver affliction from alcohol abuse. Your gut feeling tells you that you need to conduct as much of the assessment as possible at this visit; otherwise, you will lose him as you feel he is unlikely to follow-up.

You tactfully ask him if he would prefer to talk to you alone first and then, with his permission, you will see his wife with or without him being present. He replies, "Yes." You tell him you want to help and you understand his concerns. He agrees to continue as he feels heard and relieved, and this lessens his distress. You tell his wife that you prefer to conduct this first assessment with him alone. With his permission, you will bring her back for questioning in future visits. She agrees.

You ask about his history, and he replies that when he was 22 years old, he experienced a sudden sense of feeling trapped at the mall. He noticed shortness of breath, flushed skin, weakness, and a feeling that things around him were not real. He attributed this to being quite nervous around exam time as he was completing his postgraduate studies in a pre-med program and knew the importance of getting high marks. This sense of distress never left him, and each time he went to a mall, he had to leave. He was fine for several years as he always went out with his buddy. In the past 10 years, he has noticed that his fear was not limited to malls, but has gradually begun to occur in different places as well, such as crossing a bridge, being in an elevator, or standing in line. He was able to take the edge off by having a drink before leaving the house. On further inquiry, he agreed that from time to time, he began to take 1 or 2 drinks of vodka per day at home, but he quickly added, "only a few drinks . . . I'm not an alcoholic." With surprising frankness, Dr. GC added that when he was in medical school, he took caffeine tablets, but only when studying for exams. You ask if he was taking alcohol when in medical school; his hesitant answer is "yes" but only on weekends with friends and in moderate amounts. He tells you that drinking alcohol is the only thing that cheers him up and allows him to be able to confront the different situations in which he experiences intense fear. When you ask him when he first remembers feeling these panicky feelings, he replies that he was always seen as a strange child, and people made fun of him to the point that he was bullied frequently. He developed these panicky feelings when bullies trapped him. He later noticed that in malls, he was afraid that he could not escape easily if the bullies showed up. He would never go to the mall without his friend. The panicky feelings continued into adulthood. The picture is becoming clearer as you suspect a primary anxiety disorder for which he self-medicates with alcohol.

Note: You can arrange for an investigative workup to rule out underlying non-psychiatric medical conditions as appropriate and schedule a follow-up appointment. Some non-psychiatric medical conditions or factors can present with anxiety symptoms, but rarely to the point of a complete disorder. Refer to Chapter 2, p. 16, for further information on factors to consider when assessing anxiety symptoms, or go directly to Factors to Consider When Assessing Anxiety Symptoms (Appendix I, p. 155).

Screening for Anxiety and Related Disorders
You suddenly become conscious of the time but are still keenly aware that Dr. GC should not

> » How do you screen for common anxiety and related disorders?
>
> » How do you screen for common comorbid mental disorders?
>
> » What is the provisional diagnosis?

leave the clinic at this time, so you ask him to fill in the self-report questionnaires while you tend to another patient. As you leave the room, you notice his facial expression—slight relief.

TOOLS FOR ASSESSMENT

Refer to the "Provisional Diagnosis" section of Chapter 2, p. 17, for information on screening for anxiety and related disorders and comorbid conditions, or go directly to the Patient Self-Report Screening Tool for Mental Illnesses (Appendix VI, p. 161). Physicians can subsequently review responses with patients to verify accuracy.

You can also review the "Anxiety and Related Disorders Types and Subtypes" section of Chapter 2, p. 17, which includes a useful tool to help differentiate anxiety disorders, or go directly to Differentiating Anxiety Disorders, Obsessive-Compulsive, and Trauma- and Stressor-Related Disorders (Appendix II, p. 156).

Provisional Diagnosis

Dr. GC provides the following answers to the questions in section 5 of the screening tool, which supports your suspicion that he may be suffering from primary agoraphobia.

Do you feel anxious or particularly uneasy in places or situations where you might find it difficult to leave or escape and where help might not be available (e.g., in a crowd, standing in line, when you are alone away from home or alone at home, or when crossing a bridge in a bus, train, or car)?	"I am very anxious when I feel I can't leave easily, for example, in a mall, crossing a bridge, being in an elevator, or standing in line." "Lately I feel anxious leaving the house, so I have a drink or two. I am okay at work, though, because I feel safe there."
Do you fear these situations so much that you avoid them, suffer through them, or need a companion to face them?	"I definitely need to be with my wife or a friend to go to the mall. I avoid elevators and bridges whenever I can."
Has this lasted more than 6 months for most days?	"As I said, it has been years, and it seems as though there are now more situations where I feel very anxious when I can't leave the place."
Is the anxiety out of proportion to the actual danger or threat in the situation?	"Definitely. It makes me physically ill, and although I know that there is likely no danger, I can't help it."

He finally breaks down. In tears, he admits that he has been abusing alcohol for more than 2 years but with a definite escalation in quantity in the past 6 months. At first he is reluctant to divulge his daily intake, but on further inquiry, he finally agrees that he needs help. Covering his face with his hands as if embarrassed, he blurts out, "I should be stronger. I should be able to go in these places. What is wrong with me?" He admits to not being truthful on the alcohol part of the questionnaire and says he is having about 1–3 drinks of vodka after work 2–3 times per week—never at work, he adds—and on weekends he may have as many as 6–8 drinks to calm down. The escalating increase in his intake recently has forced him to hide alcohol in several places around the house to avoid having to tell his wife. You reassure him that weakness plays no part in this. "Let's get you better. It looks as though you may have been suffering from agoraphobia for years, and alcohol helped you face the distress related to this." Relieved, he agrees to work on this with you.

CONFIRMING THE DIAGNOSIS

The next step is to confirm Dr. GC's diagnosis.

The diagnosis of agoraphobia is confirmed by using the DSM-5 criteria for agoraphobia[6] (see Appendix XVIII, p. 195). Physicians can employ user-friendly tools adapted from the DSM-5 to recall diagnostic features:

> » What factors must you consider to confirm that Dr. GC has agoraphobia?
> » What instruments can be used to confirm the diagnosis?

- Patient-directed tools include the Patient-Directed Agoraphobia Self-Report Tool (Appendix XIX, p. 196).
- Physician-directed validated tools include the Mini International Neuropsychiatric Interview (MINI) for agoraphobia, which is a widely used instrument (proprietary tool).[7]

Validated self-report diagnostic aids will require further studies, as limited information exists evaluating agoraphobia as a distinct anxiety disorder.

Dr. GC satisfies the DSM-5 criterion for agoraphobia:

- He is anxious in situations from which escape is difficult.
- He experiences fear in at least 2 different types of situations.
- His anxiety is out of proportion to the threat.
- His symptoms have lasted longer than 6 months.
- There is substantial dysfunction (avoidance behavior, which can manifest as having to face situations with a companion or having a drink).

SCENARIOS INCLUDED IN AGORAPHOBIA DIAGNOSIS

To satisfy the diagnostic for agoraphobia, the individual must experience intense fear in response to or in anticipation of at least 2 of the following 5 scenarios:

1. Being outside of the home alone
2. Being in open spaces (e.g., parking lots, marketplaces, bridges)
3. Being in enclosed spaces (e.g., shops, theaters, cinemas)
4. Being in a crowd or standing in line
5. Using public transportation (e.g., automobiles, buses, planes)

BASELINE ASSESSMENT

The next step is to conduct a baseline assessment. This will provide you and your patient with important information to tailor a treatment plan specific to your patient.

| » What should be included in a baseline assessment?
» What tools are useful at baseline and follow-up visits? |

Patient self-report tools are used in primary care for many medical conditions. These practical, time-efficient tools can be used in mental health assessments as well; however, responses should be interpreted by clinicians using the DSM-5 criteria and clinical judgment. A careful assessment and rating of each of the following parameters will also establish a baseline from which to measure treatment response:

- Suicide Assessment Questionnaire (Appendix III, p. 157)
- Agoraphobia symptom severity: Severity Measure for Agoraphobia—Adult[8] (Appendix XX, p. 197)
- Comorbid conditions
- Somatic complaints; Symptom Assessment Checklist (Appendix VIII, p. 167)
- Functional impairment; Functional Impairment Assessment Scale (Appendix IX, p. 168)

You can also refer to the "Baseline Assessment" section of Chapter 2, p. 18.

Note: The Severity Measure for Agoraphobia—Adult is included in Appendix XX, p. 197. Permission to reprint or copy the scale has been granted by the American Psychiatric Association (APA). The scale with rating information can also be downloaded directly from the APA site at http://www.psychiatry.org/psychiatrists/practice/dsm/dsm-5/online-assessment-measures. These measures can be reproduced without permission by researchers and by clinicians for use with their patients.

Dr. GC's Baseline Assessment

Dr. GC admits that he does have fleeting suicidal thoughts. You ask if he has a suicide plan, and he replies that he does not. You assess the risk of suicide as low, and you both agree that should the thoughts increase or should he have any impulses to end his life, he will call you immediately. The Severity Measure for Agoraphobia—Adult yields a score of 1 (mild). He reports chest pains (2), fatigue (1), nervousness (2), and dizziness (2), and he says he feels unstable on his feet when he thinks of going to a mall. He admits taking a drink of vodka before he goes there, which calms him. He also explains that he feels anxious when crossing a bridge, being in an elevator, or standing in line, but he can handle those situations by talking to himself. The Functional Impairment Assessment Scale reveals that his performance at work is 100%, but he describes his ability for recreational activities as diminished because he has to take a drink and go with a companion. If he didn't, he would rate his ability for recreational activities at 70%.

He further reveals that his father, also a doctor, suffered from the same thing and described himself as claustrophobic; however, he remembers that other than going to his office, which was in the home, his father did not go out much.

You reiterate the importance of conducting an investigative workup to rule out underlying non-psychiatric conditions, which he agrees to get done. Dr. GC's blood tests return with liver function and fasting glucose results in the upper-normal range. Further cardiovascular investigation reveals no abnormalities. You are considering alcohol use disorder. You ask Dr. GC if he would feel comfortable with you talking to his wife just to get her input. You explain to him that it would just be a general inquiry. He agrees. She confirms what he has already told you.

MANAGEMENT GUIDELINES
Now that you have confirmed the diagnosis of agoraphobia and have a general idea of Dr. GC's illness severity and how it affects him, you begin to develop a care plan. Information collected to date will guide your management plan; however, the choice of treatment will depend on several factors; for example:[9, 10]

- Patient opinions about treatment
- Receptivity to counseling
- Receptivity to medication
- Severity of symptoms
- Comorbidity
- Previous response (or lack of response) to treatment
- Availability of resources in the community

As with panic disorder, combination therapy with CBT plus pharmacotherapy appears to be more effective than either therapy alone.[11, 12, 13, 14] Paroxetine, sertraline, citalopram, and escitalopram show the most consistent results. Paroxetine, the most widely studied, shows the highest efficacy *specifically when combined with CBT*, and reduces panic attacks—panic attacks worsen both agoraphobic behavior in panic disorder and remission rates in agoraphobia. Fluvoxamine, fluoxetine, and imipramine may have limited efficacy.[15] Table 6.1 summarizes the psychotherapy and pharmacological agents recommended for the treatment of agoraphobia.

AGORAPHOBIA AS A DISTINCT DISORDER
Studies on the management of agoraphobia as a distinct disorder are lacking. Recommendations are based on a meta-analysis of randomized controlled trials that include patients with agoraphobia associated with panic disorders. Specific criteria for treatment with CBT, pharmacotherapy, or both are difficult to establish. As new information becomes available, evidence-based management guidelines for agoraphobia will be updated in future editions.

You can also refer to Chapter 3: Management, p. 25. First-, second-, and third-line treatments for agoraphobia are listed in Table 6.1.

TABLE 6.1 PSYCHOTHERAPY AND PHARMACOTHERAPY RECOMMENDATIONS FOR AGORAPHOBIA*[16]

	PSYCHOTHERAPY	PHARMACOLOGICAL AGENT
First-line	CBT (usually 12–20 weekly sessions), in particular virtual exposure therapy (WRET).[17, 18, 19, 20] D-cycloserine may increase the effectiveness of CBT;[22, 23] further studies are warranted. Treatment via telephone/video-conferencing[24, 25] and Internet-based CBT (ICBT) are as effective as face-to-face CBT and may be cost-efficient options, particularly for agoraphobic patients unwilling to attend a clinic.[26, 27]	Paroxetine, paroxetine CR, sertraline, citalopram, escitalopram, fluoxetine, fluvoxamine, venlafaxine XR[21]
Second-line	Acceptance and commitment therapy (ACT), although research is still in its infancy, shows promising results.[28] Psychodynamic therapy shows promise.[29] Applied relaxation training shows promise; however, randomized controlled trials have shown that the most severely ill patients fared less well.[30]	Clomipramine most effective; imipramine may have limited efficacy Alprazolam, clonazepam, diazepam, lorazepam, mirtazapine, reboxetine
Third-line	Another option to consider when patients cannot leave the house is bibliotherapy.[31, 32, 33]	Bupropion SR, divalproex, duloxetine, gabapentin, levetiracetam, milnacipran, moclobemide, olanzapine, phenelzine, quetiapine, risperidone, tranylcypromine
Adjunctive therapy		**Second-line:** Alprazolam ODT used short term (<8 weeks including taper with the initiation of an antidepressant can lead to quicker relief), clonazepam **Third-line:** Aripiprazole, divalproex, olanzapine, pindolol, risperidone

CR = controlled release; ODT = orally disintegrating tablets; SR = sustained release; XR = extended release

*Adapted from Katzman et al. (2014).[34]

Biological and Complementary and Alternative Medicine

More studies are needed regarding these therapies; however, according to Katzman et al., some studies have shown that novel treatments such as noninvasive brain stimulation using a radioelectric asymmetric conveyor (REAC), repetitive transcranial magnetic stimulation (rTMS), and alternative therapies such as capnometry-assisted respiratory training can be effective.[35, 36]

TMS

Transcranial magnetic stimulation (TMS) is a noninvasive treatment consisting of stimulating some regions of the brain. A magnetic field generator placed near the head sends small electrical currents into a particular region of the brain, penetrating up to 5 cm.

Capnometry-assisted respiratory training has been evaluated in panic disorder plus agoraphobia.[37] Cannabinoid receptors are the focus of future research as the receptor modulation has been linked to improved efficacy of exposure-based therapy.[38]

VISIT-BY-VISIT GUIDE: MILD AGORAPHOBIA

Dr. GC expresses a strong preference for medication but is not averse to psychotherapy.

You both decide on the combination of medication and CBT. Dr. GC has a long-standing illness with a risk of substance use, and although the agoraphobia is mild, you feel that exposure therapy plus medication may be more effective than a single therapy in this case.

You are well aware that paroxetine shows the highest efficacy rates with agoraphobia; however, citalopram, escitalopram, and sertraline have less potential for drug-drug interaction as well as fewer complications in chronic disease. Due to Dr. GC's

> What treatment should you consider out of the choices provided below?
> » Pharmacotherapy alone
> » A combination of psychotherapy and pharmacotherapy
> » Exercise and self-management strategies
> » Insist on psychotherapy due to the fact that Dr. GC's severity is mild

history of cardiovascular disease, you initiate sertraline 50 mg to be increased to 100 mg after 2 weeks and make a referral to a psychotherapist for CBT. The therapist includes virtual exposure therapy as part of the treatment. This combination works really well.

After 4 weeks, Dr. GC returns, feeling slightly better. Although he still will not frequent malls without a companion, he reports feeling a bit more relaxed. The Severity Measure for Agoraphobia—Adult still yields a score of 1 (mild). He reports chest pains (1), fatigue (0), and nervousness (1). He does not feel the need to take a drink of vodka before he goes to the mall, which he says is quite wonderful. You ask him to increase the sertraline dose to 150 mg daily, and after 4 more weeks, he is in full remission. His score on the Severity Measure for Agoraphobia—Adult is (0), and he is able to go to the mall on his own. He has had 8 weekly psychotherapy sessions but will continue for 4 more sessions to solidify the gains. You ask to see him monthly, initially for 6 months, to monitor his alcohol intake, which he states he doesn't need at all. The combination is continued for a minimum of 12 months. You discuss with him that 6–24-month follow-up studies show that combination therapy is superior as long as the treatment is maintained.[39, 40] He agrees to your recommendation for frequent monitoring over the next year, and you will reassess withdrawing medication no sooner than 12 months from now.

VISIT-BY-VISIT GUIDE: MODERATE AGORAPHOBIA

First Visit   Two years after his last visit, Dr. GC comes in for a checkup. He did not keep the follow-up appointment beyond 12 months of maintenance therapy; however, he did refill his prescription for sertraline, which he takes at a daily dose of 150 mg. His appearance is different—you notice that his clothing is disheveled and his hands shake slightly. He looks at you as if embarrassed. You go through the physical and ask about his drinking. He admits without hesitation this time that he is drinking daily as he cannot leave the house unless he does.

You reassess the diagnosis and comorbidity, asking Dr. GC to complete the Patient Self-Report Screening Tool for Mental Illnesses (Appendix VI, p. 161). Your assessment once again is consistent with agoraphobia, plus he is experiencing panic attacks and further questioning suggests alcohol use disorder.

The Severity Measure for Agoraphobia—Adult (Appendix XX, p. 197) yields a score of 2.5 (moderate to severe). He reports chest pains (2), fatigue (2), nervousness (3), and sleep problems (2). He mentions that, for example, crossing a bridge, being in an elevator, or standing in line triggered panic attacks, so he began drinking daily to face these situations. In the last few weeks, panic attacks have occurred even when he's had a drink.

He rates functional impairment at moderate to borderline severe, as he reports having missed 3 days of work in the last week. In addition, he rates his ability to socialize at 50% because he experiences panic attacks in many situations. Clinical judgment tells you that he may be more impaired than reported as he needs to drink daily to function.

What is your next step?

- Switch to another medication.
- Add a second first-line drug.
- Add acupuncture.
- Increase dose, titrating every 2 weeks.

Dr. GC is not on the maximum dose of sertraline. The next step would be to titrate the drug until remission or the maximum dose is achieved, unless he experiences intolerable side effects. You increase the dose to 200 mg daily with follow-up 2 weeks later. You explain that you will make a referral to an addiction specialist, and he agrees.

At 200 mg daily (the maximum dose for sertraline), Dr. GC responds slightly. The Severity Measure for Agoraphobia—Adult (Appendix XX, p. 197) yields a score of 2 (moderate). He reports chest pains (2), fatigue (2), nervousness (2), and sleep problems (1). He has noticed a reduction in panic attacks of 50% when crossing a bridge, being in an elevator, or standing in line.

You ask him to see the psychotherapist for booster sessions. The psychotherapist adds applied relaxation training.

You schedule a follow-up appointment in 2 weeks.

Subsequent Visits	After 2 weeks, Dr. GC returns and reports that he is feeling better. You both agree to continue on the same treatment regime, and you will see him monthly.
Maintenance Visits	You advise him to continue his pharmacotherapy for at least 2 years, at which point he will be reassessed. With the help of the addiction specialist, he is gradually able to completely abstain from alcohol. You schedule follow-up sessions for 2 years as you are aware that the greatest chance of relapse for alcohol use disorder occurs within that time frame. You also ensure regular monitoring by a specialist for the alcohol use disorder to prevent relapse. To reduce the risk of relapse, you discuss the importance of optimum functional recovery and optimum quality of life as the goal.

VISIT-BY-VISIT GUIDE: SEVERE AGORAPHOBIA

First Visit	After 5 years, Dr. GC's wife again visits your office with her husband. She is visibly distraught. Although he has abstained from alcohol, she tells you that he refuses to leave the house. You see that he is sweating and fidgeting uncontrollably. He doesn't want to stay in your office, but both you and his wife convince him to stay. He worries all the time now that he is caught in a situation where escape is not possible. He reports having panic attacks to the point of disorder just thinking about it.

Dr. AG has been compliant on sertraline 200 mg daily, and he tells you that before discharge, the psychotherapist taught him strategies to maintain the treatment gains, which he has been performing faithfully. You reevaluate the diagnosis and comorbidity using the Patient Self-Report Screening Tool for Mental Illnesses (Appendix VI, p. 161). His answers are consistent with agoraphobia and panic disorder. He reports fleeting thoughts of suicide because he feels life is not worth living. The Severity Measure for Agoraphobia—Adult (Appendix XX, p. 197) yields a score of 4 (extreme). He reports chest pains (3), fatigue (3), nervousness (3), and sleep problems (3). He describes his symptoms as an intense fear when crossing a bridge, being in an elevator, standing in line, or going to the mall. What is new in the last 6 months is the addition of fear when he takes any form of public transportation. He will not leave the house.

He tells you, "I feel helpless. There is nothing I can do to get better." He is not interested in anything and feels detached from others, including his family. He denies taking any alcohol, and his wife confirms that he has been abstinent, but he admits that alcohol use is very tempting.

	During functional impairment assessment, he reports that he has been on complete medical leave from work for the last 6 months. You realize that his condition is very serious and that if you don't do something soon, he will deteriorate and/or begin abusing alcohol again. You decide to refer him to an intensive in-house treatment program for 6 weeks. Once discharged, outpatient follow-up with a multidisciplinary treatment team (including psychiatry) has been arranged. You ask him to see you regularly as well.
Subsequent Visits	He returns to see you 1 month after discharge and tells you, "That treatment saved my life. I just didn't realize how far gone I was." He reports substantial improvement. He was discharged from the in-house treatment program on citalopram at maximum dose and with a recommendation to continue for life, which he agrees to.
Maintenance Visits	At his 4-month follow-up appointment, Dr. GC states that he feels much better and is at his previous level of functioning. He tells you that he is no longer scared of his downward spiral and feels he has regained control. He still gets anxious feelings but has learned what they mean and not to be afraid of them. You begin to plan his gradual return to work in 1 month's time to help him regain his sense of purpose and pride. He has also regained his will to socialize.

Due to Dr. GC's relapse and his long-standing agoraphobia, plus comorbid panic disorder and alcohol use disorder, maintaining pharmacotherapy for a minimum of 24 months and possibly indefinitely, along with psychotherapy booster sessions and frequent monitoring, is a good option. Also note that in-house programs are very effective in refractory disorders (e.g., panic, agoraphobia, PTSD, and alcohol use disorder, to name a few).

SUMMARY
You have completed a case study illustrating the screening, diagnosis, treatment, and management of agoraphobia. This case study is only a guide. Decision making should be individualized and based on clinical judgment.

AGORAPHOBIA KEY POINTS
- Patients have marked fear or anxiety about places, situations, or events from which "escape" may be difficult or in which help may not be available in the event that the individual has a panic attack or panic-like or other incapacitating or embarrassing symptoms.
- The patient experiences fear in at least 2 different types of situations.
- Fear is present for the majority of days during a 6-month period.
- The patient experiences associated symptoms, such as restlessness, fatigue, and muscle tension.
- Agoraphobia can trigger panic attacks.
- Agoraphobia causes significant distress or impairment in social, occupational, or other important areas of functioning.
- It is often chronic; when patients with agoraphobia discontinue their medication
  - 25–50% relapse within 6 months
  - 40–50% have residual symptoms after 3–6 years.

- CBT or therapy based on CBT principles, particularly exposure therapy, are first-line non-pharmacological treatments.
- SSRI and SNRIs are first-line pharmacological treatments.

NOTES

1 Psych Central [Internet]. [Place unknown]: Psych Central; 1995–2016. Bressert S. Agoraphobia symptoms; 2013 [cited 2015 Mar 9]. Available from: http://psychcentral.com/disorders/agoraphobia-symptoms/

2 American Psychiatric Association. Diagnostic and statistical manual of mental disorders (DSM-5). 5th ed. Arlington, VA: American Psychiatric Association; 2013.

3 Mavissakalian M, Perel J. Duration of imipramine therapy and relapse in panic disorder with agoraphobia. J Clin Psychopharmacol. 2002; 22(3):294–299.

4 UpToDate [Internet]. [Place unknown]: Wolters Kluwer; n.d. McCabe RE. Agoraphobia in adults: epidemiology, pathogenesis, clinical manifestations, course, and diagnosis; 2014 Dec 12 [cited 2015 Mar 10]. Available from: http://www.uptodate.com/contents/agoraphobia-in-adults-epidemiology-pathogenesis-clinical-manifestations-course-and-diagnosis

5 Magee W, Eaton W, Wittchen H, Mcgonagle K, Kessler R. Agoraphobia, simple phobia, and social phobia in the National Comorbidity Survey. Arch Gen Psychiatry. 1996; 53(2):159–168.

6 American Psychiatric Association. Diagnostic and statistical manual of mental disorders (DSM-5). 5th ed. Arlington, VA: American Psychiatric Association; 2013.

7 Sheehan, DV, Lecrubier Y, Sheehan KH, Amorim P, Janavs J, Weiller E, et al. The Mini-International Neuropsychiatric Interview (MINI): the development and validation of a structured diagnostic psychiatric interview for DSM-IV and ICD-10. J Clin Psychiatry. 1998; 59 Suppl 20:22–33.

8 American Psychiatric Association, Online assessment measures [Internet]. Arlington (VA): American Psychiatric Association; c2015. Severity Measure for Agoraphobia—Adult; 2013 [cited 2015 Jul 10]. Available from: http://www.psychiatry.org/psychiatrists/practice/dsm/dsm-5/online-assessment-measures

9 Evans M, Bradwejn J, Dunn L, editors. Ontario guidelines for the treatment of anxiety disorders in primary care. 1st ed. Toronto: Queen's Printer of Ontario; 2000.

10 Kennedy SH, Lam RW, Parikh SV, Patten SB, Ravindran AV. Canadian Network for Mood and Anxiety Treatments (CANMAT) clinical guidelines for the management of major depressive disorder in adults. J Affect Disord. 2009; 117 Suppl 1:S1–S2.

11 Sánchez-Meca J, Rosa-Alcázar AI, Marín-Martínez F, Gómez-Conesa A. Psychological treatment of panic disorder with or without agoraphobia: a meta-analysis. Clin Psychol Rev. 2010; 30(1):37–50.

12 Van Apeldoorn FJ, Van Hout WJ, Timmerman ME, Mersch PP, den Boer JA. Rate of improvement during and across three treatments for panic disorder with or without agoraphobia: cognitive behavioral therapy, selective serotonin reuptake inhibitor or both combined. J Affect Disord. 2013; 150(2):313–319.

13 Katzman MA, Bleau P, Blier P, Chokka P, Kjernisted K, Van Ameringen M, et al. Canadian clinical practice guidelines for the management of anxiety, posttraumatic stress and obsessive-compulsive disorders. BMC Psychiatry. 2014; 14 Suppl 1:S1.

14 Quero S, Pérez-Ara M, Bretón-López J, García-Palacios A, Baños R, Botella C. Acceptability of virtual reality interoceptive exposure for the treatment of panic disorder with agoraphobia. Brit J Guid Couns. 2014; 42(2):123–137.

15 Perna G, Daccò S, Menotti R, Caldirola D. Antianxiety medications for the treatment of complex agoraphobia: pharmacological interventions for a behavioral condition. Neuropsychiatr Dis Treat. 2011; 7:621–637.

16 Perna G, Daccò S, Menotti R, Caldirola D. Antianxiety medications for the treatment of complex agoraphobia: pharmacological interventions for a behavioral condition. Neuropsychiatr Dis Treat. 2011; 7:621–637.

17 Vincelli F, Anolli L, Bouchard S, Wiederhold BK, Zurloni V, Riva G. Experiential cognitive therapy in the treatment of panic disorders with agoraphobia: a controlled study. Cyberpsychol Behav. 2003; 6:321–328.

18 Meyerbröker K, Emmelkamp P. Virtual reality exposure therapy in anxiety disorders: a systematic review of process-and-outcome studies. Depress Anxiety. 2010; 27(10):933–944.

19 Malbos E, Rapee RM, Kavakli M. A controlled study of agoraphobia and the independent effect of virtual reality exposure therapy. Aust N Z J Psychiatry. 2013; 47(2):160–168.

20 Pitti C, Peñate W, de la Fuente J, Bethencourt J, Roca-Sánchez M, Acosta L, et al. The combined use of virtual reality exposure in the treatment of agoraphobia. Actas Esp Psiquiatr. 2015; 43(4):133–141.

21 Bandelow B, Domschke K, Baldwin DS. Panic disorder and agoraphobia. 1st ed. Oxford, UK; New York, NY: Oxford University Press; 2014.

22 Ressler K, Rothbaum B, Tannenbaum L, Anderson P, Graap K, Zimand E, et al. Cognitive enhancers as

adjuncts to psychotherapy: use of d-cycloserine in phobic individuals to facilitate extinction of fear. Arch Gen Psychiatry. 2004; 61(11):1136–1144.

23 Ressler K, Rothbaum B, Tannenbaum L, Anderson P, Graap K, Zimand E, et al. Cognitive enhancers as adjuncts to psychotherapy: use of d-cycloserine in phobic individuals to facilitate extinction of fear. Arch Gen Psychiatry. 2004; 61(11):1136–1144.

24 Lewis C, Pearce J, Bisson J. Efficacy, cost-effectiveness and acceptability of self-help interventions for anxiety disorders: systematic review. Br J Psychiatry. 2012; 200(1):15–21.

25 Titov N, Andrews G, Johnston L, Robinson E, Spence J. Transdiagnostic Internet treatment for anxiety disorders: a randomized controlled trial. Behavr Res Ther. 2010; 48(9):890–899.

26 Swinson RP, Fergus KD, Cox BJ, Wickwire K. Efficacy of telephone-administered behavioral therapy for panic disorder with agoraphobia. Behav Res Ther. 1995; 33(4):465–469.

27 Bouchard S, Paquin B, Payeur R, Allard M, Rivard V, Fournier T, et al. Delivering cognitive-behavior therapy for panic disorder with agoraphobia in videoconference. Telemed J E Health. 2004; 10(1):13–25.

28 Gloster AT, Sonntag R, Hoyer J, Meyer AH, Heinze S, Ströhle A, Eifert G, Wittchen HU. Treating treatment-resistant patients with panic disorder and agoraphobia using psychotherapy: a randomized controlled switching trial. Psychother Psychosom. 2015; 84(2):100–109.

29 Milrod B, Chambless DL, Gallop R, et al. Psychotherapies for panic disorder: a tale of two sites. J Clin Psychiatry [Internet]. 2015 Jun [cited 2015 Oct 10]. Available from: http://www.psychiatrist.com/jcp/article/Pages/2015/aheadofprint/14m09507.aspx

30 National Health Service Choices [Internet]. United Kingdom: National Health Service; c2015. Agoraphobia—treatment options; n.d. [cited 2015 Sep 16]. Available from: http://www.nhs.uk/conditions/agoraphobia/pages/treatmentoptions.aspx

31 Lewis C, Pearce J, Bisson J. Efficacy, cost-effectiveness and acceptability of self-help interventions for anxiety disorders: systematic review. Br J Psychiatry. 2012; 200(1):15–21.

32 Lucock M, Padgett K, Noble R, Westley A, Atha C, Horsefield C, Leach C. Controlled clinical trial of a self-help for anxiety intervention for patients waiting for psychological therapy. Behav Cogn Psychother. 2008; 36(5):541–551.

33 Lidren D, Watkins P, Gould R, Clum G, Asterino M, Tulloch H. A comparison of bibliotherapy and group therapy in the treatment of panic disorder. J Consult Clin Psychol. 1994; 62(4):865–869.

34 Adapted from Katzman MA, Bleau P, Blier P, Chokka P, Kjernisted K, Van Ameringen M, et al. Canadian clinical practice guidelines for the management of anxiety, posttraumatic stress and obsessive-compulsive disorders. BMC Psychiatry. 2014; 14 Suppl 1:S1. This is a PMC Free Article; copyright and licence information can be found at: http://www.ncbi.nlm.nih.gov/pmc/articles/PMC4120194/

35 Katzman MA, Bleau P, Blier P, Chokka P, Kjernisted K, Van Ameringen M, et al. Canadian clinical practice guidelines for the management of anxiety, posttraumatic stress and obsessive-compulsive disorders. BMC Psychiatry. 2014; 14 Suppl 1:S1.

36 Mannu P, Rinaldi S, Fontani V, Castagna A, Margotti M. Noninvasive brain stimulation by radioelectric asymmetric conveyor in the treatment of agoraphobia: open-label, naturalistic study. Patient Prefer Adherence. 2011; 5:575–580.

37 Meuret A, Rosenfield D, Seidel A, Bhaskara L, Hofmann S, La Greca AM. Respiratory and cognitive mediators of treatment change in panic disorder: evidence for intervention specificity. J Consult Clin Psychol. 2010; 78(5):691–704.

38 Chhatwal JP, Davis M, Maguschak KA, Ressler KJ. Enhancing cannabinoid neurotransmission augments the extinction of conditioned fear. Neuropsychopharmacology. 2004; 30(3):516–524.

39 Furukawa T, Watanabe N, Churchill R. Psychotherapy plus antidepressant for panic disorder with or without agoraphobia: systematic review. Br J Psychiatry. 2006; 188:305–312.

40 Furukawa T, Watanabe N, Churchill R. Combined psychotherapy plus antidepressants for panic disorder with or without agoraphobia. Cochrane Database Syst Rev. 2007; (1):CD004364.

7

Social Anxiety Disorder

Introduction

The overriding feature of social anxiety disorder or social phobia is intense and out-of-proportion fear of negative evaluation by others. When confronting situations that involve social interaction or performance in front of others, patients with social anxiety disorder either avoid these situations or suffer through them with intense fear and autonomic arousal.[1]

To learn about social anxiety disorder, you can follow the diagnosis, treatment, and management of our patient, Ms. SA. You can progress through the practice case study from start to finish, or you can select your own learning path in the Practice Case Study Index, p. xxv. The choice is yours.

Clinical Presentation

The essential feature of social anxiety disorder is the distinctive anxiety. For these patients, social interaction or performance in front of others produces physical, cognitive, and behavioral signs and symptoms. Examples of *social interaction* situations include the following:

- Parties
- Dating
- Meeting new people
- Conversation with peers
- Asking a teacher for help

- Speaking to a boss or supervisor at work
- Asking a sales clerk for help
- Asking a stranger for directions

Examples of *performance* situations include:

- Public speaking
- Writing in front of others
- Eating in front of others
- Playing an instrument in front of others
- Playing a sport in front of others
- Entering a room that has people in it
- Using a public toilet

If the fear is restricted to speaking or performing in public, specify "performance only" (Table 7.1).

By definition, a patient with social anxiety disorder experiences fear that is out of proportion to the actual threat posed by the social or performance situation. The fear is present for most days for 6 months or more.[3]

TABLE 7.1 CHARACTERISTICS OF SOCIAL ANXIETY DISORDER, PERFORMANCE ONLY

Represents a distinct subset of social anxiety disorder in terms of etiology, age at onset, physiologic response, and treatment response.[2]	Fear is not familial.
	Fewer childhood characteristics of shyness or behavioral inhibition.
	Later onset (mean age is 16.9).
	Conditioning is more important in its development.
	Stronger psychophysiological responses (e.g., increased heart rate).
	Attribution of fear to panic attacks (i.e., fear of the physiological response) more than to negative evaluation.
	Treatment response is the same as for typical social anxiety disorder: CBT and medication.
	Beta-blockers have been shown to be effective in this group (musicians, performing artists, people taking exams).

Social Anxiety Disorder versus Nonpathological Anxiety

To differentiate social anxiety disorder from nonpathological (normal) anxiety, remember that social anxiety disorder worries have the following characteristics:

- The anxiety is out of proportion to the actual threat posed by the social or performance situations.
- The anxiety is difficult to control.
- The worries are accompanied by certain associated symptoms in varying degrees, such as restlessness, fatigue, muscle tension, and panic attacks.
- Perhaps most importantly, social anxiety disorder worries cause significant distress or functional impairment.

The diagnostic criteria for social anxiety disorder can be found in Appendix XXI, p. 199.

Prevalence

Social anxiety disorder, also known as social phobia, is the most common anxiety disorder, with a lifetime prevalence of up to 13%.[4] It is the third most common psychiatric disorder, after depression and alcohol use disorder. Specific phobia and agoraphobia are the most common comorbid disorders:[5]

- Specific phobia occurs in up to 59% of individuals with social anxiety disorder.
- Agoraphobia occurs in 27.6% of individuals with social anxiety disorder.

Social anxiety disorder often leads to depression and alcohol use disorder.[6] Many patients will turn to alcohol or sedative drugs to relieve their anxiety. Social anxiety disorder is diagnosed roughly as often in women as in men. The disorder typically starts in adolescence at around 12 years of age.[7, 8] Only 5% of patients with social anxiety disorder seek medical help for it; therefore, you will usually diagnose social anxiety disorder over the course of investigating a patient for other reasons.

Social Anxiety Disorder Case Study: Meet Ms. SA

Ms. SA, a 28-year-old female university professor, comes into your office and says she's been drinking too much alcohol lately. She says the alcohol occasionally causes her to slur her words. She would like some help with reducing her drinking. She also says that for the past few years, she has felt "tense" most of the time.

You ask her how much she drinks. She says she starts out determined to have only 1 drink, but she usually has 2 or 3 every time she socializes. She also describes being very sad and having lost enjoyment in usually pleasurable activities.

You then ask her why she's been drinking so much lately. She says that she got her PhD and started a new job as a university professor 1 year ago. She is invited to events where she feels she has to be on her best game because if she says something stupid or unintelligent, the rest of the group, who she refers to as "distinguished colleagues," will see her as a fraud; she worries that they will not see her as credible. Drinking helps her relax.

Ms. SA says she has become progressively more anxious since her promotion. Speaking in front of her students in her previous job as a schoolteacher caused no problems; however, in this new position, she is expected to converse at regular work functions in front of her peers. "They will think I am stupid," she says. It appears as though Ms. SA is afraid of being humiliated in public. Your initial thought was that Ms. SA's presentation was that of primary depression with secondary alcohol use disorder (as self-medication); however, you begin to suspect a primary diagnosis of social anxiety disorder with possible secondary depression and substance use disorder.

When you ask about her childhood, she responds, "It started when I was a teenager. Just talking to other people made me anxious. When I was invited to parties, I felt that people laughed at me. I am so clumsy, I spill food all over, and people always commented about that. I was so uncomfortable. I was very self-conscious eating in front of people, which I found stressful. Then, slowly, talking in groups made me shaky. Crowded settings gave me a headache, and I had to force myself to engage in the conversation. It caused me such uneasiness, sometimes panic.

"In the last year, I hid it well, Doctor. I would always have a few drinks at parties, but then the next morning, I would remember the embarrassing things I did or said because I really let loose. Aww, I feel so embarrassed."

> » What should you do?
> » What are your options?

ASSESSMENT: SCREENING AND PROVISIONAL DIAGNOSIS

Ms. SA is a new patient to you. On examination, you see a well-groomed, immaculately dressed woman. Careful questioning reveals that she denies suicidal thoughts. She doesn't know if there were psychiatric illnesses in her family. She is not close with them because her father is an alcoholic, and she left home as soon as she turned 18. She is a non-smoker and denies any street or over-the-counter drug use. You feel that there is no immediate safety risk, so you explain that you will help her get to the bottom of her concerns.

If you are pressed for time and there is no safety risk or clinical judgment of urgency, you can tell her you understand her suffering and will help, but that you need her to schedule an appointment that will give you the time to assess her properly. Ask her to return should her condition get worse in the meantime. This is a very important step, particularly if time is an issue. It takes 1–2 minutes and reassures her that even if you don't have time to spend with her this visit, you are concerned about her and want to take the time to address her complaints properly. She feels heard and relieved that someone will help. This lessens her distress while gaining her trust.

> **Note:** You can arrange for an investigative workup to rule out underlying non-psychiatric medical conditions as appropriate and schedule a follow-up appointment. Some non-psychiatric medical conditions or factors can present with anxiety symptoms, but rarely to the point of a complete disorder. Refer to Chapter 2, p. 16, for further information on factors to consider when assessing anxiety symptoms, or go directly to Factors to Consider When Assessing Anxiety Symptoms (Appendix I, p. 155).

Screening for Anxiety and Related Disorders

Ms. SA's investigative workup is unremarkable; therefore, you are considering an anxiety or related disorder at this point.

> » How do you screen for common anxiety and related disorders?
> » How do you screen for common comorbid mental disorders?
> » What is the provisional diagnosis?

TOOLS FOR ASSESSMENT

Refer to the "Provisional Diagnosis" section of Chapter 2, p. 17, for information on screening for anxiety and related disorders and comorbid conditions, or go directly to the Patient Self-Report Screening Tool for Mental Illnesses (Appendix VI, p. 161). Physicians can subsequently review responses with patients to verify accuracy.

You can also review the "Anxiety and Related Disorders: Types and Subtypes" section of Chapter 2, p. 17, which includes a useful tool to help differentiate anxiety disorders, or go directly to Differentiating Anxiety Disorders, Obsessive-Compulsive, and Trauma- and Stressor-Related Disorders (Appendix II, p. 156).

Provisional Diagnosis

Ms. SA provides the following answers to the questions in section 6 of the screening tool, which supports your suspicion that she may be suffering from social anxiety disorder:

Do unfamiliar social situations cause you to feel anxious, distressed, or panicky?	"Yes, even as a child. I have been been shy for as long as I can remember. My mother was also extremely shy."
Are you fearful of being humiliated or embarrassed in social situations or when you are performing, such as speaking in public, being watched, or eating?	"Absolutely. I don't think that my fear is unreasonable, Doctor. I really will do something stupid or embarrassing and people will see me as not credible. I feel like a fraud."
Are you uncomfortable or embarrassed at being the center of attention?	"I can't stand being the center of attention, particularly the center of attention among a large group of people."
Do you blush, sweat, and/or tremble when speaking in public or in social situations such as eating or writing?	"Yes, I have had panic attacks many times, but mostly my hands shake and my voice trembles. I feel that my thoughts are very disjointed, and I can't get the words out to say what I want to say."

What types of social situations make you feel anxious or panicky (giving a speech, introducing yourself, talking in groups, eating in public, walking into a gathering of unfamiliar people, having someone watching you do things such as writing)?	She says she gets anxious when talking in front of a group, speaking up at meetings or talks, being the center of attention in a large group (e.g., going to work functions and being asked to respond to many questions). "I am the new girl, so everyone is asking so many questions."
Are there things that you avoid or activities that you cannot or will not do because of your worries or your fears?	"As a university professor, I cannot avoid public speaking, but I really suffer." "I do not miss work; however, lately I find myself reaching for a drink of alcohol to relax before a presentation. This is the only way I can face going up there, but I am scared that people are noticing."

You ask her to rate her distress level out of 10. She states that her distress level is around 4 out of 10. Based on her responses, the fact that the duration of her symptoms has been longer than 6 months, and your clinical judgment that the anxiety is out of proportion to the actual danger or threat in the situation, you make a preliminary diagnosis of social anxiety disorder, with the specifier "performance only."

The change in criteria in the DSM-5 allows the health professional to judge whether or not the anxiety is out of proportion to the actual danger, as it is not uncommon for people to believe that their fear is not unreasonable or excessive (DSM-IV criteria).

CONFIRMING THE DIAGNOSIS

The next step is to confirm Ms. SA's diagnosis.

The diagnosis of social anxiety disorder is confirmed by using the DSM-5 criteria for social anxiety disorder[9] (see Appendix XXI, p. 199). Physicians can employ user-friendly tools adapted from the DSM-5 to recall diagnostic features:

> » What factors must you consider to confirm that Ms. SA has social anxiety disorder?
> » What instruments can be used to confirm the diagnosis?

- Patient self-directed tools: Social Phobia Diagnostic Questionnaire (SPDQ)[10] (Appendix XXII, p. 200)
- Physician-directed validated tool: the Mini International Neuropsychiatric Interview (MINI) for Social Anxiety Disorder is also a widely used instrument (proprietary tool).[11]

The SPDQ is a self-report tool validated against the DSM-IV criteria as a screening, diagnostic, and severity-monitoring tool. It measures excessive anxiety in social situations, fear of embarrassment or humiliation, and avoidance. It contains a list of questions on the severity of anxiety or fear in specific situations and the degree to which people avoid these situations (questions 4–23). To reflect the DSM-5 criteria, the author added the following clinician assessment follow-up questions (30–32):

30. Is social fear out of proportion to the actual threat posed by the social situation and to the sociocultural context? (The DSM-5 has deleted the requirement that the person feels the fear

is excessive or unreasonable—question 30 requires a clinician's assessment of question 26 of the scale.
31. Have these symptoms been present for 6 months or more?
32. Is the fear better explained by another psychiatric or medical condition or substance (a drug of abuse, a medication)?

The following provides relevant scoring information:

A. The Provisional Diagnosis Legend (can be used to recall DSM-5 criteria; requires validation through research):
   1. Are questions 1, 2, (24 or 25), 30, 31 coded "Yes"? (Note: Either 24 or 25 must be coded "Yes.")
   2. Is question 3 coded "Yes" or question 28 ≥4?
   3. Is question 27 ≥4?
   4. Is question 32 coded "No"?

Positive answers to questions in the above Provisional Diagnosis Legend are consistent with a diagnosis of social anxiety disorder. Consider further evaluation and review with the DSM-5 criteria.

B. Total Cut-off Score Legend:

Note: Screening and detection for social anxiety disorder "Total Cut-off Scores" below have been validated with DSM-IV criteria only.[12] Nonetheless, the tool can be of value to clinicians as a guide until a validated tool in keeping with DSM-5 criteria is available, as most criteria remain unchanged. **If this tool is used, clinicians should note that question 26 "Would you say your social fear is excessive or unreasonable?" is no longer a valid criterion. Question 30 above reflects the DSM-5 criteria and should be used instead of 26 in creating the "Total Score."**

- Screening for social anxiety disorder: Total Score >7.38 (85% specificity, 82% sensitivity)
- Detecting social anxiety disorder: Total Score >12.13 (94% specificity, 47% sensitivity)

To create a total score for the SPDQ, use the following:

1. All "Yes" answers for items 1, 2, 3, 24, 25, 26 are coded 1; "No" answers are coded 0.
2. Only items in the "a" column from 4a to 23a are summed and divided by 4.
3. Items 27 and 28 are summed and divided by 2.

Note: To create a total score, all "Yes" answers were coded as 1 and all "No" answers as 0 as in, for example, items (1) Nervous or fearful of social situations? (2) Overly worried that you may embarrass yourself? (3) Do you try to avoid social situations? (24) Experience fear each time? (25) Fear come on as soon as you encounter the situation? (26) Is social fear out of proportion to the actual threat posed by the social situation and to the sociocultural context? Additional items (i.e., 4a, 5a, 6a, 7a, 8a, 9a,10a, 11a, 12a, 13a, 14a, 15a, 16a, 17a, 18a, 19a, 20a, 21a, 22a, 23a) were each divided by 4, whereas distress and interference items (i.e., 27 and 28) were divided by 2 and these numbers were added to the total. Avoidance scores (4–23, b columns) and item 29 are not factored into the total score; avoidance scores were not found to add anything to the scoring.

In Ms. SA's case, the DSM-5 supports your diagnosis of social anxiety disorder:

- Ms. SA has marked fear about social situations, in which she suddenly feels anxious.
- She has marked fear about being embarrassed or humiliated in performance situations.
- Performance situations almost always provoke fear or anxiety.
- She avoids or endures performance situations with marked distress.
- The fear is out of proportion to the actual threat posed by the social situation.
- The fear duration is ≥6 months.
- Her symptoms cause significant distress or functional impairment.
- There are 2 specifiers: performance only, and panic attacks.

BASELINE ASSESSMENT

The next step is to conduct a baseline assessment. This will provide you and your patient with important information to tailor a treatment plan specific to your patient.

Patient self-report tools are used in primary care for many medical conditions. These practical, time-efficient tools can be used in mental health assessments as well; however, responses should be interpreted by clinicians together with the DSM-5 criteria and clinical judgment. A careful assessment and rating of each of the following parameters will also establish a baseline from which to measure treatment response:

> » What should be included in a baseline assessment?
>
> » What tools are useful at baseline and follow-up visits?

- Suicide Assessment Questionnaire (Appendix III, p. 157)
- Social anxiety disorder symptom severity; the following tools can be used to assess severity:
  – Social Phobia Inventory (SPIN) (Appendix XXIII, p. 203)
  – Severity Measure for Social Anxiety Disorder (Social Phobia)—Adult[13] (see note below)
  – GAD-7 (sensitivity 72%, specificity 80%) (Appendix V, p. 160)
- Comorbid conditions
- Somatic complaints; Symptom Assessment Checklist (Appendix VIII, p. 167)
- Functional impairment; Functional Impairment Assessment Scale (Appendix IX, p. 168)

You can also refer to the "Baseline Assessment" section of Chapter 2, p. 18.

Note: The Severity Measure for Social Anxiety Disorder (Social Phobia)—Adult can be downloaded directly from the APA site at http://www.psychiatry.org/psychiatrists/practice/dsm/dsm-5/online-assessment-measures. These measures can be reproduced without permission by researchers and by clinicians for use with their patients. Rating information is provided as well.

The Social Phobia Inventory (SPIN)[14] is a short, simple, validated patient self-report tool specifically developed for social anxiety disorder and can be used to screen for the presence of this disorder. It yields a total score of 0–68. A score of ≥19 and associated dysfunction (work, home, social) suggests a diagnosis of social anxiety disorder and can be reviewed against the

DSM-5 criteria. The SPIN is particularly useful in assessing and monitoring the severity of social anxiety disorder:[15]

<20 = none or very mild
21–30 = mild
31–40 = moderate
41–50 = severe
>51 = very severe

Three subscales provide further information concerning the dimensions of fear, avoidance, and physical symptoms as follows:

- Fear: 1, 3, 5, 10, 14, 15 (range 0–24)
- Avoidance: 4, 6, 8, 9, 11, 12, 16 (range 0–28)
- Physical symptoms: 2, 7, 13, 17 (range 0–16)

Ms. SA's Baseline Assessment
Ms. SA denies any suicidal thoughts. She has a SPIN score of 23 (mild) and reports tiredness (3) due to worries of having panic attacks, shaking, etcetera when performing in front of her peers, which interferes with her sleep (2), which she describes as not being able to fall asleep, and nervousness (3). The Functional Impairment Assessment Scale (Appendix IX, p. 168) reveals that her performance at work is not affected except when she needs to speak up in meetings. She is able to get her message across even if her voice trembles and her heart pounds. She is able to calm down by doing deep-breathing exercises. Ms. SA explains how she suffers inside when she speaks up or is about to speak up in meetings. She rates her performance at work at 90% because, for the moment, she feels more or less familiar with her current group, so she performs well; however, she knows that if the team changes, her performance could drastically change.

MANAGEMENT GUIDELINES
Now that you have confirmed the diagnosis of social anxiety disorder and have a general idea of the illness severity and how it affects Ms. SA, you begin to develop a care plan. Information collected to date will guide your management plan; however, the choice of treatment will depend on several factors, for example:[16, 17]

- Patient opinions about treatment
- Receptivity to counseling
- Receptivity to medication
- Severity of symptoms
- Comorbidity
- Previous response (or lack of response) to treatment
- Availability of resources in the community

You can also refer to Chapter 3: Management, p. 25. First-, second-, and third-line treatments for social anxiety disorder are listed in Table 7.2.

Psychotherapy

Studies suggest that pharmacotherapy with CBT in group or individual formats, in particular when exposure therapy is included, is more effective than pharmacotherapy alone in maintaining gains achieved, and remains effective for up to 5 years.[18] Internet-based CBT (ICBT) studies show promising results and may be the only option when access to therapy is a barrier.

Although more studies are needed, preliminary findings suggest that short-term dosing of d-cycloserine can enhance exposure therapy for social anxiety disorder.[19, 20] Mindfulness-based therapy can also be useful.[21, 22] Exercise and self-management strategies should be offered to all receptive patients.[23] Table 7.2 summarizes the psychotherapy and pharmacological agents recommended for the treatment of social anxiety disorder; Table 7.3 lists medications for the treatment of performance anxiety.

TABLE 7.2 PSYCHOTHERAPY AND PHARMACOTHERAPY RECOMMENDATIONS FOR SOCIAL ANXIETY DISORDER**

	PSYCHOTHERAPY	PHARMACOLOGICAL AGENT
First-line	CBT, in particular with exposure therapy (12–20 weekly sessions). Individual, group, or Internet-based CBT (ICBT). **Note:** D-cycloserine can enhance exposure therapy for social anxiety disorder.	Escitalopram, fluvoxamine, fluvoxamine CR, paroxetine, paroxetine CR, pregabalin effective at higher dose of 600 mg/day only (not lower doses), sertraline, venlafaxine XR
Second-line		Alprazolam, bromazepam, citalopram, clonazepam, gabapentin, phenelzine
Third-line		Atomoxetine, bupropion SR, clomipramine, divalproex, duloxetine, fluoxetine, mirtazapine, moclobemide, olanzapine, selegiline, tiagabine, topiramate
Adjunctive therapy	Mindfulness-based therapy Exercise	More research is required to determine if beta-blockers are effective as monotherapy or an add-on to first-line drug (e.g., SSRIs or SNRIs) therapy in performance social anxiety disorder.* Evidence to date suggests that add-on therapy is optimal. **Third-line:** Aripiprazole, buspirone, paroxetine, risperidone

CR = controlled release; XL or XR = extended release; SR = sustained release

*Beta-blockers have been successfully used in clinical practice for performance situations such as public speaking.

Note: Although there is limited evidence for the use of citalopram in social anxiety disorder, it is likely as effective as the other SSRIs; in contrast, there are negative trials for fluoxetine in social anxiety disorder, suggesting it may be less effective than other SSRIs.

**Adapted from Katzman et al. (2014).[24]

TABLE 7.3 MEDICATIONS USED TO TREAT PERFORMANCE ANXIETY*

MEDICATION	TYPICAL DOSAGE
Propranolol	10–40 mg
Nadolol	20–120 mg
Atenolol	50–100 mg

* Beta-blockers are off-label use

Note: These medications can relieve autonomic and somatic symptoms such as tachycardia, tremors, and stuttering when used in low doses. Propranolol 10 mg about 1 hour before performance is the most common dose; test dose before live performance to ensure tolerability.

Evaluate the patient's medical history and cardiovascular status (contraindications include heart failure, bradycardia, breathing difficulties, and hypotension).

Biological Therapies

Neuro-psycho-physical optimization–radioelectric asymmetric conveyor (NPPO-REAC), a brain-stimulation technique, was as effective as sertraline for the treatment of social anxiety disorder (Level 3 evidence).[25]

VISIT-BY-VISIT GUIDE: MILD SOCIAL ANXIETY DISORDER

Ms. SA feels tells you that she would prefer psychotherapy.

Ms. SA has a SPIN score of 23 (mild); she is receptive to psychotherapy. You are keenly aware of the risk of alcohol use escalating, in particular with the family history of alcohol use disorder. You also consider the possibility of a family history of social anxiety disorder, namely as a primary cause of her father's resultant alcohol use disorder. You negotiate frequent monitoring with Ms. SA, to which she agrees, and decide that CBT is a good option at this time.

After 2 months of CBT, Ms. SA returns, feeling much better. She no longer needs to drink at functions. Her SPIN score is 10 (remission). You see her monthly at first, and then according to her needs.

> What treatment should you consider out of the choices provided below?
> » Pharmacotherapy alone
> » Psychosocial intervention plus pharmacotherapy
> » Exercise and self-management strategies
> » Insist on psychotherapy due to the fact that the social anxiety disorder severity is mild

VISIT-BY-VISIT GUIDE: MODERATE SOCIAL ANXIETY DISORDER

First Visit — Two years later, Ms. SA returns, visibly tense. Using the CBT techniques she learned, she has been able to perform reasonably well in public situations for the past 2 years. However, a few weeks ago, she had to give a major lecture in front of her colleagues. After the lecture, when she was on stage answering questions, one of her colleagues pointed out a major flaw in her talk. Profoundly embarrassed—both personally and professionally—she suffered a massive panic attack, complete with palpitations, sweating, dizziness, nausea, and the same awful hot, tingling sensation that she experienced 2 years ago.

Her self-confidence devastated, she is once again terrified of any sort of performance in front of large groups. The symptoms are worse now than when she first saw you. A few days ago, in the middle of giving a lecture, she suffered a panic attack so severe that she had to leave the room and cancel the class. Furthermore, she is now afraid in more situations than before; she is now terrified of performing in front of small groups and of going on a first date.

Ms. SA is fighting the urge to resume drinking, but the stress is enormous, and she is desperate for your help.

You reassess comorbidity using the Patient Self-Report Screening Tool for Mental Illnesses (Appendix VI, p. 161), which indicates social anxiety disorder; however, there is an element of sadness and loss of interest in the things she used to enjoy, though not to the point of clinical depression.

Note: The PHQ-9 self-report scale is a useful tool for primary care practitioners to diagnose, assess, and monitor depression.[26]

Her SPIN score has risen to 38 (high end of moderate). The Functional Impairment Assessment Scale (Appendix IX, p. 168) is rated at 50% in social/leisure situations (moderate) due to the fact that she is irritable, which causes conflict with her friends. She attributes this to the distress caused by the anxiety.

You ask her to see the psychotherapist again to reinforce the CBT techniques she is currently using and to help her with exposure exercises to deal with her new fears. In addition to the ongoing CBT therapy, you decide to initiate first-line pharmacotherapy. After considering the possible pharmacological therapies, you prescribe paroxetine as she is having panic attacks (paroxetine reduces panic attacks) and reports being quite anxious. Paroxetine is initiated at 10 mg daily for 3 days, then 20 mg daily.

You schedule an appointment for 2 weeks later. You also advise her to consider mindfulness strategies, which have shown some efficacy in social anxiety disorder.

Subsequent Visits

You conduct the following assessments:

- Suicide Assessment Questionnaire (Appendix III, p. 157)
- SPIN (Appendix XXIII, p. 203)
- Symptom Assessment Checklist (Appendix VIII, p. 167)
- Functional Impairment Assessment Scale (Appendix IX, p. 168)

To keep Ms. SA on the lowest possible effective dose, you maintain 20 mg paroxetine daily for 4 weeks, with a follow-up appointment in 2 weeks. Side effects are minimal. Unfortunately, her social anxiety disorder symptoms persist unabated. She reports that she finds giving lectures and speaking in small groups more intimidating than before, but her anxiety about going on dates remains the same.

She is quite distressed; therefore, clinically you feel that waiting another 2 weeks to assess response is not feasible in this case and choose to increase paroxetine by 20 mg every 2 weeks as tolerated up to the maximum dosage of 60 mg daily.

Note: *Experts suggest that if there is partial or non-response at 6 weeks, increase dose. In this case, the patient is quite distressed and waiting another 2 weeks may not be feasible.*[27]

At the maximum dosage of 60 mg daily in addition to CBT and mindfulness, Ms. SA responds (SPIN score 22), but not to the point of complete remission. You feel a trial of propranolol may halt the progression as it appears to be specific to performance situations. You initiate propranolol at 10 mg to be taken 1 hour before anxiety-provoking performance situations and increase to 20 mg within 2 weeks.

You reassess 4 weeks later, at which time her SPIN score is 12 (complete remission). She tells you, "Propranolol is a life saver. I was so caught up in perceiving myself to be weak if they saw me shake and tremble, I couldn't function. The combination is working for me."

Maintenance Visits You plan see her once a month for the first 3 months, and then every 3 months for at least 1 year. You conduct the following assessments on a monthly basis as required:

- Suicide Assessment Questionnaire (Appendix III, p. 157)
- SPIN (Appendix XXIII, p. 203)
- Symptom Assessment Checklist (Appendix VIII, p. 167)
- Functional Impairment Assessment Scale (Appendix IX, p. 168)

VISIT-BY-VISIT GUIDE: SEVERE SOCIAL ANXIETY DISORDER

First Visit Unfortunately, 6 months after remission, Ms. SA's condition deteriorates—this time for no apparent reason. As before, she is terrified of performing in front of large groups, performing in front of small groups, and interacting with strangers.

Now, however, she is also afraid of simply being in a public place, even if she is not the center of attention. She worries about having to use the washroom or eating in a restaurant, so she stays home most days. She has, on average, 4 drinks a day to help her get through the day. Her SPIN score has risen precipitously to 64 (very severe). Once again, you reassess comorbidity using the Patient Self-Report Screening Tool for Mental Illnesses (Appendix VI, p. 161), which indicates that she now has comorbid depression—her PHQ-9 score is 25 (severe)—and agoraphobia. She reports headaches (3), fatigue (3), nervousness (3), confusion, abdominal pain (2), and sleep problems (3). Her functional impairment is severe (rated at 20% capacity at work and for social activities). She is on sick leave, and she will only leave the house briefly to run errands, immediately returning home and avoiding any encounter with familiar individuals.

As previously, you advise her to initiate the CBT strategies she learned and to see her psychotherapist to learn new techniques to deal with the new fears. You ask her to practice mindfulness as well as continue propranolol, which you increase to 40 mg before exposure to anxiety-provoking performance situations.

With respect to medication, many options are acceptable, including switching to another first-line therapy. You decide to use another first-line therapy, SNRI, prescribing venlafaxine 37.5 mg BID for 3 days, then switching to venlafaxine XR 75 mg daily. You plan to maintain venlafaxine at that dose for 2 weeks.

Subsequent Visits	When she returns after 2 weeks, side effects are minimal, but her symptoms have not resolved. The SPIN yields a score of 65 (severe, upper limit).
	You decide to increase the venlafaxine XR to 150 mg daily. In 2 weeks, she responds. Her SPIN score is now at 55; however, she is still quite symptomatic. You gradually increase the venlafaxine dose to the maximum of 225 mg daily and advise her to continue with CBT strategies, mindfulness techniques, and the propranolol. Fortunately, she is in remission after 6 weeks on this regimen.
Maintenance Visits	**For how long should you continue her therapy?**
	Remember:
	• Ms. SA has had social anxiety disorder since adolescence.
	• Her social anxiety disorder was extreme.
	• Her father, and also possibly her mother, may have had undiagnosed social anxiety disorder.
	Due to the long-standing social anxiety disorder, it is recommended that medication is continued for at least 12 months and up to 24 months. There is evidence that psychotherapy can maintain treatment gains long term.[28] Keep in mind that treatment needs to be individualized for each patient, accompanied by close monitoring.
	For these reasons, you plan to see her monthly for 3 months, then every 3 months for at least 1 year. The medication is tapered gradually after 1 year of maintenance therapy, but you strongly recommend that she continue with CBT and mindfulness exercises. You monitor her for a minimum of 3 years, reassessing her at least once a year.

SUMMARY

You have completed a case study illustrating the screening, diagnosis, treatment, and management of social anxiety disorder. This case study is only a guide. Decision making should be individualized and based on clinical judgment. For an overview of the management guidelines, refer to Social Anxiety Disorder Treatment Guide Summary (Appendix XXIV, p. 205).

SOCIAL ANXIETY DISORDER KEY POINTS

- Social anxiety disorder is the most common anxiety disorder, with a lifetime prevalence of approximately 13%.
- In social or performance situations, patients have a fear of scrutiny and negative evaluation that is out of proportion to the situation.
- Performance social anxiety disorder represents a distinct subset of social anxiety disorder in terms of etiology, age at onset, physiologic response, and treatment response.
- The fear causes significant functional impairment or marked distress.
- Patients try to avoid the feared situations.
- Among non-pharmacological treatments, CBT-based principles are the first line of therapy, specifically exposure therapy.
- Among pharmacological treatments, SSRIs and SNRIs are the first line of therapy.

NOTES

1 American Psychiatric Association. Diagnostic and statistical manual of mental disorders (DSM-5). 5th ed. Arlington, VA: American Psychiatric Association; 2013.

2 Bögels S, Alden L, Beidel D, Clark L, Pine D, Stein M, Voncken M. Social anxiety disorder: questions and answers for the DSM-V. Depress Anxiety. 2010; 27(2):168–189.

3 American Psychiatric Association. Diagnostic and statistical manual of mental disorders (DSM-5). 5th ed. Arlington, VA: American Psychiatric Association; 2013.

4 Kessler R, Berglund P, Demler O, Jin R, Merikangas K, Walters E. Lifetime prevalence and age-of-onset distributions of DSM-IV disorders in the National Comorbidity Survey Replication. Arch Gen Psychiatry. 2005; 62(6):593–602.

5 Nutt DJ, Ballenger JC. Anxiety disorders. Malden, MA: Wiley-Blackwell; 2003.

6 Schneier FR, Foose TE, Hasin DS, Heimberg RG, Liu SM, Grant BF, Blanco C. Social anxiety disorder and alcohol use disorder co-morbidity in the National Epidemiologic Survey on Alcohol and Related Conditions. Psychol Med. 2010; 40(6):977–988.

7 Narrow WE, First MB, Sirovatka PJ, Regier DA, editors. Age and gender considerations in psychiatric diagnosis: a research agenda for DSM-V. Arlington, VA: American Psychiatric Association; 2007.

8 Beesdo K, Bittner A, Pine D, Stein M, Höfler M, Lieb R, Wittchen H. Incidence of social anxiety disorder and the consistent risk for secondary depression in the first three decades of life. Arch Gen Psychiatry. 2007; 64(8):903–912.

9 American Psychiatric Association. Diagnostic and statistical manual of mental disorders (DSM-5). 5th ed. Arlington, VA: American Psychiatric Association; 2013.

10 Newman MG, Kachin KE, Zuellig AR, Constantino MJ, Cashman L. The social phobia diagnostic questionnaire: preliminary validation of a new self-report diagnostic measure of social phobia. Psychol Med. 2003; 33(4):623–635.

11 Sheehan DV, Lecrubier Y, Sheehan KH, Amorim P, Janavs J, Weiller E, et al. The Mini-International Neuropsychiatric Interview (MINI): the development and validation of a structured diagnostic psychiatric interview for DSM-IV and ICD-10. J Clin Psychiatry. 1998; 59 Suppl 20:22–33.

12 Newman MG, Kachin KE, Zuellig AR, Constantino MJ, Cashman L. The social phobia diagnostic questionnaire: preliminary validation of a new self-report diagnostic measure of social phobia. Psychol Med. 2003; 33(4):623–635. Social Phobia

Diagnostic Questionnaire (SPDQ) measure and scoring can be accessed at https://sites.google.com/site/michellegnewmanphd/summary. The scale is also included in Appendix XXII and can be reproduced with the author's permission.

13 American Psychiatric Association [Internet]. Arlington (VA): American Psychiatric Association; 2013. Online assessment measures; c2013 [cited 2015 August 29]. Available from: http://www.psychiatry.org/psychiatrists/practice/dsm/dsm-5/online-assessment-measures

14 Connor K, Davidson J, Churchill L, Sherwood A, Foa E, Weisler R. Psychometric properties of the Social Phobia Inventory (SPIN). New self-rating scale. Br J Psychiatry. 2000; 176:379–386.

15 Antony MM, Coons MJ, McCabe RE, Ashbaugh A, Swinson RP. Psychometric properties of the social phobia inventory: further evaluation. Behav Res Ther. 2006; 44(8):1177–1185.

16 Evans M, Bradwejn J, Dunn L, editors. Ontario guidelines for the treatment of anxiety disorders in primary care. 1st ed. Toronto: Queen's Printer of Ontario; 2000.

17 Kennedy SH, Lam RW, Parikh SV, Patten SB, Ravindran AV. Canadian Network for Mood and Anxiety Treatments (CANMAT) clinical guidelines for the management of major depressive disorder in adults. J Affect Disord. 2009; 117 Suppl 1:S1–S2.

18 Hedman E, Furmark T, Carlbring P, Ljótsson B, Rück C, Lindefors N, Andersson G. A 5-year follow-up of Internet-based cognitive behavior therapy for social anxiety disorder. J Med Internet Res. 2011; 13(2):e39.

19 Hofmann S, Meuret A, Smits J, Simon N, Pollack M, Eisenmenger K, et al. Augmentation of exposure therapy with d-cycloserine for social anxiety disorder. Arch Gen Psychiatry. 2006; 63(3):298–304.

20 Bontempo A, Panza K, Bloch M. D-cycloserine augmentation of behavioral therapy for the treatment of anxiety disorders: a meta-analysis. J Clin Psychiatry. 2012; 73(4):533–537.

21 Koszycki D, Benger M, Shlik J, Bradwejn J. Randomized trial of a meditation-based stress reduction program and cognitive behavior therapy in generalized social anxiety disorder. Behav Res Ther. 2007; 45(10):2518–2526.

22 Hofmann S, Sawyer A, Witt A, Oh D, La Greca AM. The effect of mindfulness-based therapy on anxiety and depression: a meta-analytic review. J Consult Clin Psychol. 2010; 78(2):169–183.

23 Haug T, Blomhoff S, Hellström K, Holme I, Humble M, Madsbu H, Wold J. Exposure therapy and sertraline in social phobia: 1-year follow-up of a randomised controlled trial. Br J Psychiatry. 2003; 182:312–318.

24 Adapted from Katzman MA, Bleau P, Blier P, Chokka P, Kjernisted K, Van Ameringen M, et al. Canadian

clinical practice guidelines for the management
of anxiety, posttraumatic stress and obsessive-
compulsive disorders. BMC Psychiatry. 2014; 14
Suppl 1:S1. This is a PMC Free Article; copyright and
licence information can be found at: http://www.ncbi.
nlm.nih.gov/pmc/articles/PMC4120194/

25 Fontani V, Mannu P, Castagna A, Rinald, S. Social
anxiety disorder: radio electric asymmetric conveyor
brain stimulation versus sertraline. Patient Prefer
Adherence. 2011; 5:581–586.

26 Spitzer R, Kroenke K, Williams J. Validation and
utility of a self-report version of PRIME-MD: the

PHQ primary care study. Primary Care Evaluation
of Mental Disorders. Patient Health Questionnaire.
JAMA. 1999; 282(18):1737–1744.

27 Stein M, Fyer A, Davidson J, Pollack M, Wiita B.
Fluvoxamine treatment of social phobia (social
anxiety disorder): a double-blind, placebo-controlled
study. Am J Psychiatry. 1999; 156(5):756–760.

28 Katzman MA, Bleau P, Blier P, Chokka P, Kjernisted
K, Van Ameringen M, et al. Canadian clinical
practice guidelines for the management of anxiety,
posttraumatic stress and obsessive-compulsive
disorders. BMC Psychiatry. 2014; 14 Suppl 1:S1.

SECTION III
Obsessive-Compulsive and Related Disorders

Obsessive-compulsive disorder (OCD) was classified in the "Anxiety Disorders" chapter in the DSM-IV. In the DSM-5, a new chapter has been created: "Obsessive-Compulsive and Related Disorders." The decision to create this new chapter was based on commonalities in clinical features, biology, and treatment approaches among these disorders. It is felt that this change will improve accuracy of diagnosis and effectiveness of treatments. The obsessive-compulsive and related disorders spectrum includes the following:

- Obsessive-compulsive disorder
- Body dysmorphic disorder (BDD)
- Hoarding disorder
- Trichotillomania (hair-pulling disorder)
- Excoriation (skin-picking disorder)
- Substance/medication-induced obsessive-compulsive and related disorder
- Obsessive-compulsive and related disorder due to another medical condition
- Other specified obsessive-compulsive and related disorder
- Unspecified obsessive-compulsive and related disorder

This section will focus on the screening, assessment, and management of obsessive-compulsive disorder.

8

Obsessive-Compulsive Disorder

Introduction

In OCD, people are troubled by unwanted thoughts. The distress is substantial, as they worry that they will act on these thoughts (violent intrusive thoughts) or that something bad will happen if they don't embark on certain rituals. Detection is often delayed as these patients are profoundly embarrassed by their symptoms. To learn about OCD, you can follow the diagnosis, treatment, and management of our patient, Mr. DH. You can progress through the practice case study from start to finish, or you can select your own learning path in the Practice Case Study Index, p. xxv. The choice is yours.

Clinical Presentation

Patients with OCD have obsessions and/or compulsions that are time-consuming (>1 hour/day) or cause marked distress or significant impairment.

Obsessions are recurrent and persistent ideas, thoughts, urges, or images that are experienced as intrusive and unwanted and cause marked anxiety or distress. The patient tries to neutralize, suppress, or ignore these obsessions with some other thought or action.

Compulsions are repetitive, purposeful, and intentional behaviors (e.g., hand washing) or mental acts (e.g., praying, counting) that are performed to neutralize or suppress obsessions, or according to rules that must be applied rigidly. Compulsions do not give pleasure. Rather, they are typically performed to relieve the anxiety caused by obsessions.

Specifiers:
1. Insight—Degree of insight as to the reality of OCD beliefs:

   - Good or fair insight (i.e., definitely or probably not true)
   - Poor insight (i.e., probably true)
   - Absent insight/delusional beliefs (i.e., completely convinced beliefs are true)

2. "Tic-related" OCD

Novel treatment approaches are emerging that could significantly impact prognosis. However, to date, OCD is rarely completely curable, but comprehensive treatment usually results in considerable improvement and return to normal life.

Differentiating from Other Disorders

Because OCD involves compulsions, it can be confused with depression, generalized anxiety, and tic disorder. If the content of the obsession or compulsion is restricted

TABLE 8.1 DIFFERENTIATION OF OBSESSIVE-COMPULSIVE DISORDER FROM OTHER DISORDERS

COMMON DISORDERS VS. OCD	
Tic disorder vs. OCD	Unlike tics, compulsions are voluntary.
Depression ruminations vs. OCD	In depressive ruminations, thoughts are not intrusive; no true compulsions.
	Unlike depressive thoughts, obsessions are experienced as intrusive and unwanted and cause marked anxiety or distress.
GAD vs. OCD	In GAD, worries are not intrusive.
	Unlike the worries associated with GAD, obsessions are not simply worries about real-life problems that are out of proportion to the actual danger or threat in the situation.
Body dysmorphic disorder vs. OCD	Obsessions are related with imagined, exaggerated defects in appearance.

to another disorder (e.g., preoccupation with physical appearance in the presence of body dysmorphic disorder), then the patient does not meet the DSM-5 criteria for OCD. Use Table 8.1 to differentiate obsessive-compulsive disorder from depression, generalized anxiety, and tic disorder.

> The diagnostic criteria for OCD can be found in Appendix XXV, p. 207.

Prevalence

The lifetime prevalence of OCD is approximately 2.3% of the general population.[1] Approximately 60–90% of OCD patients have lifetime comorbidity. The most common comorbid conditions are[2, 3]

- Major depression (67.2%)
- Impulse control disorder (up to 55.9%)
- Substance use disorder (38.6%)
- Social anxiety disorder (27.6%)
- Panic disorder (18.4%)
- Specific phobia (18.1%)
- Dysthymia (7.8%)
- Bipolar disorder (2.7%)

The male:female ratio is 1:1, and age of onset is typically in the late teens. The typical delay in diagnosis is 5–10 years due to feelings of shame, secrecy, and lack of recognition by health professionals.

Obsessive-Compulsive Disorder Case Study: Meet Mr. DH

Mr. DH, a 35-year-old vice-principal of a nearby rural elementary school, presents to you with the following symptoms:
- He is always "stressed out," restless, and tense, more so lately.
- He is always tired.
- He gets frequent headaches.
- He has difficulty getting to work on time and gets into trouble as a result.
- He has difficulty concentrating.
- He thinks his blood pressure might be high.

Mr. DH tells you he has always been relatively healthy. He has no pertinent family history. He says he has always been anxious, even as a child. Lately, however, his anxiety is getting worse. He doesn't want to go to work because he has trouble concentrating. He worries a lot and has difficulty controlling his worries. Mr. DH has been seeing you for 2 years; he frequently laughed about his stress at work but never really focused on it. Now he wants to talk about his stress more seriously.

Your first impression is that Mr. DH is overworked and procrastinates in the morning to the point of being late.

His physical examination is unremarkable; a neurological exam is normal. His blood pressure is slightly high at 145/90. For the past 4 years, he has been taking Ativan s/l PRN, recently increased to 1 mg TID in the last 2 months due to anxiety. He tells you that the medication is not working; he does feel better at times, but then the symptoms invariably get worse in a waxing and waning pattern. "I am tired of this, Doctor. Please help me."

> » What should you do?
> » What are your options?

ASSESSMENT: SCREENING AND PROVISIONAL DIAGNOSIS

If you are pressed for time and there is no safety risk or clinical judgment of urgency, you can tell Mr. DH you understand his suffering and will help him, but you need him to schedule an appointment when you have time to assess him properly. Ask him to return should his condition get worse in the meantime. This is a very important step, particularly if time is an issue. It only takes 1–2 minutes and reassures him that even if you don't have time to spend with him this visit, you are concerned about him and want to take the time to address his complaints properly. He feels heard and relieved that someone will help. This lessens his distress while gaining his trust.

Note: You can arrange for an investigative workup to rule out underlying non-psychiatric medical conditions as appropriate and schedule a follow-up appointment. Some medical conditions and/or factors can present with anxiety symptoms, but rarely to the point of a complete disorder. Refer to Chapter 2, p. 16, for further information on factors to consider when assessing anxiety symptoms, or go directly to Factors to Consider When Assessing Anxiety Symptoms (Appendix I, p. 155).

Because you are short of time and you know Mr. DH well and feel confident that nothing requires urgent attention, you decide to give him the the Patient Self-Report Screening Tool for Mental Illnesses (Appendix VI, p. 161) to complete at home and bring back at the next visit. You also send him for bloodwork to rule out any underlying conditions.

Screening for Anxiety and Related Disorders

> » How do you screen for common anxiety and related disorders?
> » How do you screen for common comorbid mental disorders?
> » What is the provisional diagnosis?

TOOLS FOR ASSESSMENT

Refer to the "Provisional Diagnosis" section of Chapter 2, p. 17, for information on screening for anxiety and related disorders and comorbid conditions, or go directly to the Patient Self-Report Screening Tool for Mental Illnesses (Appendix VI, p. 161). Physicians can subsequently review responses with patients to verify accuracy.

You can also review the "Anxiety and Related Disorders: Types and Subtypes" section of Chapter 2, p. 17, which includes a useful tool to help differentiate anxiety disorders, or go directly to Differentiating Anxiety Disorders, Obsessive-Compulsive, and Trauma- and Stressor-Related Disorders (Appendix II, p. 156).

Provisional Diagnosis

Mr. DH's blood tests return normal and further investigation reveals no abnormalities. He returns the completed Patient Self-Report Screening Tool for Mental Illnesses, which to your surprise uncovers new information possibly missed since he first reported being stressed. You are now considering an anxiety or related disorder, keeping in mind that depressive disorders are comorbid 60% of the time. You review answers specifically to the questions in section 7 of the screening tool, which helps narrow the provisional diagnosis.

ASK MR. DH OCD SCREENING QUESTIONS TO SEE IF HE MATCHES THE OCD PROFILE.	MR. DH ANSWERS "YES" TO ALL THE QUESTIONS.	HIS ANSWERS SUGGEST OCD.
Are you experiencing intrusive or repetitive thoughts, images, or urges that you cannot stop, for example, thoughts of dirt, germs, or violent or disturbing sexual thoughts?	"Yeah, my thoughts keep popping in and I can't stop them. At one level, I know my hands are perfectly clean; on another level, I can't be completely sure." He elaborates that he does not want these thoughts and that they make him very anxious as well. The thoughts have become more frequent over the past 8 months.	By this point in your examination, it's pretty clear that Mr. DH has an obsession. His thoughts that he is unclean • are recurrent, persistent • are intrusive • cause marked distress • are not simply worries about real-life problems.

You proceed with the remaining OCD screening questions.

Do these thoughts cause you to do things repeatedly or compulsively, such as excessive washing or checking until it feels right?	"Yes, it comes and goes. I sometimes have to wash my hands on average 25 times a day because if I don't, I think that I will be full of germs, but more often than not, the thoughts interfere more so in the morning."	He attempts to neutralize the thoughts with an action (washing his hands). This response indicates that he has a compulsion—he washes his hands • repetitively • in response to an obsession (i.e., his thought that he is in some way unclean) • to relieve anxiety and feel clean excessively.

Do you believe that this will actually happen; e.g., if you do not keep washing your hands repeatedly, you will be full of germs or your hands will not be clean?	"I know that there is probably no reason to worry about catching germs, but like I said, I can't stop."	With this response, Mr. DH satisfies the criterion of good or fair insight as he recognizes that the beliefs are probably not true.
Do these thoughts interfere with your normal routine at home, work, school, or socially?	"The thoughts and the hand washing are interfering with my life somewhat. I can't leave the house for at least 1 hour, so lately I have been getting up earlier to go to work." "This makes me tired, so concentration is affected and my chronic lateness is impacting both my work and my marriage because I take my frustration out on my spouse, which is making me depressed."	This response indicates his anxiety has crossed well over the threshold of "significant distress or interference with functioning."

You further explore the lateness getting to work; he takes a deep breath, looks at the floor, pauses, and quietly reiterates the unsurprising fact that he has recurrent and annoying thoughts that he is somehow unclean. When you ask him about these thoughts, he reveals that he can usually ignore them. However, they persist, distract him, and affect his concentration. When he gives in to them and washes his hands—on average 25 times a day—he then feels calmer, but the resultant hand washing makes him chronically late.

He is particularly discouraged lately because the thoughts have gotten more intense, exacerbating both the concentration and lateness problems. It becomes obvious that Mr. DH worries only about the effect that his concentration and lateness problems will have on his job and his marriage. When questioned about whether he remembers having these thoughts in childhood, he says yes, they probably started when he was a teenager, but he really didn't think much of them and was able to "forget about them" just by going out with his friends or watching TV.

You further explore the presence of tics. He denies having any at the present time but remembers experiencing tics when he was around 10 years old, when they lasted around 4 months. His family is well known to you, and you are aware that his mother also suffers from chronic OCD and is currently under a psychiatrist's care. Based on this information, you make a preliminary diagnosis of OCD.

CONFIRMING THE DIAGNOSIS

The next step is to confirm Mr. DH's diagnosis.

The diagnosis of OCD is confirmed by using the DSM-5 criteria for obsessive-compulsive disorder[4] (see Appendix XXV, p. 207). Physicians can employ user-friendly tools adapted from the DSM-5 to recall diagnostic features:

> » What factors must you consider to confirm Mr. DH has OCD?
>
> » What instruments can be used to confirm the diagnosis?

- Patient-directed tools: the Brief Obsessive-Compulsive Scale (BOCS)[5] (Appendix XXVI, p. 209)
- Physician-directed validated tool: the Mini International Neuropsychiatric Interview (MINI) for OCD is also a widely used instrument (proprietary tool)[6]

The BOCS is a short version of the Yale-Brown Obsessive-Compulsive Scale (Y-BOC), a commonly used tool for diagnosis; however, the Y-BOC is possibly too time-consuming for a busy primary care office.[7] The BOCS is a 15-item symptom checklist that includes 5 subscales (Symmetry, Forbidden Thoughts, Contamination, Magical Thoughts, and Dysmorphic Thoughts) followed by a 6-item severity scale (range 0–24). Endorsement of 2 or more items in the checklist or a mean score of 1.5 or above on the severity scale suggests OCD.

With the use of self-report tools, clinicians should review responses and compare with the DSM-5 diagnostic criteria, as studies show inconsistencies between patients' self-report versus clinician-administered measures.[8] Making a diagnosis based on the rating scores alone can lead to over-diagnosis. For example, the DSM-5 criteria require that obsessions or compulsions be time-consuming (e.g., take >1 hour/day). If there is endorsement of 2 or more items in the "checklist section," but they are minimally time-consuming (<1 hour per day), this would not be consistent with a diagnosis of OCD. Furthermore, the BOCS has been validated for the DSM-IV criteria only. For example Item 14. Somatic Obsessions: preoccupation with appearance criteria is more in keeping with dysmorphic disorder body. Nonetheless, the tool can be of value to clinicians as a guide, until such time a validated tool in keeping with DSM-5 criteria is available as most criteria remain unchanged. If this tool is used, clinicians should note that in the DSM-5, the word "impulse" (which appears in this original scale) has been replaced with the word "urge" to describe obsessions more accurately, and the word "inappropriate" when referring to obsessions has been replaced with the word "unwanted" (the meaning of "inappropriate" can vary with culture, gender, age, and other factors).

In Mr. DH's case, the DSM-5 supports your diagnosis of OCD. By definition, OCD involves recurrent obsessions or compulsions that are time-consuming (taking >1 hour/day) or cause marked distress or significant impairment. Mr. DH appears to have both an obsession (recurrent thoughts that he is unclean) and a compulsion (repetitive hand washing):

- He has recurrent thoughts and urges that are intrusive, distressing, and unwanted.
- The urges are repetitive even when he tries to get rid of them.
- He washes his hands repeatedly and excessively to reduce the anxiety.
- His obsessions and/or compulsions interfere with his life.
- He has good insight because he knows that the obsessions are probably not true.
- He is not experiencing tics.

PATIENT INSIGHT

Patient's degree of insight as to the reality of his or her OCD beliefs:

- Good or fair insight (i.e., the beliefs are definitely or probably not true)
- Poor insight (i.e., the beliefs are probably true)
- Absent insight/delusional beliefs (i.e., completely convinced the beliefs are true)

BASELINE ASSESSMENT

The next step is to conduct a baseline assessment. This will provide you and your patient with important information to tailor a treatment plan specific to your patient.

Patient self-report tools are used in primary care for many medical conditions. These practical, time-efficient tools can be used in mental health assessments as well; however, responses should be interpreted by clinicians together with the DSM-5 criteria and clinical judgment. A careful assessment and rating of each of the following parameters will also establish a baseline from which to measure treatment response:

> » What should be included in a baseline assessment?
>
> » What tools are useful at baseline and follow-up visits?

- Suicide Assessment Questionnaire (Appendix III, p. 157)
- Symptom severity
  - Level 2—Repetitive Thoughts and Behaviors—Adult (Appendix XXVII, p. 215)
  - Six-item severity section of the BOCS (p. 213)
- Comorbid conditions
- Somatic complaints; Symptom Assessment Checklist (Appendix VIII, p. 167)
- Functional impairment; Functional Impairment Assessment Scale (Appendix IX, p. 168)

You can also refer to the "Baseline Assessment" section of Chapter 2, p. 18.

Note: The Level 2—Repetitive Thoughts and Behaviors—Adult scale can be copied from Appendix XXVII, p. 215, or downloaded directly from the APA site at http://www.psychiatry.org/psychiatrists/practice/dsm/dsm-5/online-assessment-measures, under Level 2 Cross-Cutting Symptom Measures.

Another validated self-report tool helpful for primary care settings is the Obsessive Compulsive Inventory (OCI).[9] The OCI can be accessed and completed online by patients. The online form auto-populates 7 subscales: Washing, Checking, Doubting, Ordering, Obsessing (i.e., having obsessional thoughts), Hoarding, and Mental Neutralizing. It also auto-populates Mean OCI distress and a Mean OCI Total score. There is an option for patients to print the completed form, which also prints scoring information at the end of the document, so the completed OCI can be brought to clinicians.[10]

Approximately 60–90% of OCD patients have comorbidity, so it's a good idea to use a tool that screens for depression and anxiety disorders in general. Depression and alcohol use disorder are 2 common comorbid conditions with OCD.

Mr. DH's Baseline Assessment

The Repetitive Thoughts and Behaviors—Adult scale yields a score of 1 (mild OCD). Mr. DH denies suicidal thoughts. He is experiencing headaches (2), nervousness (3), sleep problems (3), and concentration problems (3). The Patient Self Report Screening Tool for Mental Illnesses indicates possible comorbid conditions:

- Generalized anxiety disorder
- Depression

He worries about losing his job or getting into trouble at work because he is frequently late for work by 1 hour or more. However, given his situation, his worries are not simply worries about real-life problems that are out of proportion to the actual danger or threat in the situation; therefore, he does not meet the criteria for GAD. As you discuss his depressive symptoms, you learn that he is not as interested in his hobbies as usual and that his wife has found him crying a couple of times. The PHQ-9 assessment scale for depression yields a result of mild depression.

Is Mr. DH's obsessive-compulsive disorder primary or secondary?

Mr. DH reports that his low mood and loss of interest in his hobbies started well after his obsessions and compulsions. Therefore, his depression is secondary to his OCD. He denies suicidal thoughts and scores his functioning at 70% at home and work.

MANAGEMENT GUIDELINES

Now that you have confirmed the diagnosis of OCD and have a general idea of illness severity and how it affects Mr. DH, you begin to develop a care plan. Information collected to date will guide your management plan; however, the choice of treatment will depend on several factors, for example [11, 12]:

- Patient's opinions about treatment
- Receptivity to counseling
- Receptivity to medication
- Severity of symptoms
- Comorbidity
- Previous response (or lack of response) to treatment
- Availability of resources in the community

Psychoeducation is key, particularly for OCD. Patients are convinced that something is really wrong with them, they are a bad person, or they are extremely weird, and they are very embarrassed by their symptoms. Explaining to them that these thoughts are not who they are—the thoughts are intrusive and not voluntary—is very important, particularly if a patient is experiencing disturbing or violent sexual thoughts. This causes them extreme distress and tremendous worry that they will act out these thoughts and harm someone or themselves (perceived threat). They feel responsible to try to prevent harm from happening, which drives them to carry out their safety-seeking behavior—the compulsions. Bringing importance to these thoughts increases the frequency and severity of them. Compulsions temporarily reduce the anxiety, but it gets worse over the long run, which in turn increases the anxiety and depression. Helping patients understand that the usual reason these thoughts have such a huge impact is not "this is who the person is or what he or she wants to do," but the obsessions and the anxiety related to them are in direct conflict with a person's own convictions and beliefs.

Getting this message across early in the illness may relieve some distress as patients can see that the unwanted thoughts are not their wish, and they can begin to accept living with these thoughts. Treatment becomes more effective as the thoughts become unimportant and begin to subside or fade away. Explain that in periods of stress, the symptoms can reoccur or worsen, but the patient should remember that the thoughts are unwanted and "not who they are." Patients should acknowledge the dysfunctional thoughts, accept them (basis of ACT therapy), and then focus on the day's tasks.

It is important to inform patients of a delay in treatment response with OCD and therefore encourage adherence to treatment. The treatment goal is for patients to spend less than 1 hour per day on obsessive-compulsive behaviors with minimal dysfunction with daily activities.[13]

> You can also refer to Chapter 3: Management, p. 25. First-, second-, and third-line treatments for OCD are listed in Table 8.2.

Psychotherapy
Among non-pharmacological treatments, CBT is the first line of therapy and has emerged as a solid treatment.[14]

The most effective strategy is exposure/response prevention. Exposure targets the patient's obsessions, while response prevention targets the patient's compulsions. Exposure/response prevention with an experienced psychotherapist should be included in every patient's therapy. Patients learn to confront the feared situation, as well as to avoid performing the compulsions. It can take 6–12 sessions for response, and an average of 15–20 sessions of weekly outpatient CBT or 3 weeks of daily CBT is required for a good response.[15] If successful, consider monthly booster sessions for 3–6 months. Long-term effects have been shown to last up to 5 years. D-cycloserine add-on to CBT shows enhancement to therapy response in some studies.[16] Explain to patients that it is hard work, but in the long run, the treatment will lessen the fear.[17] If patients have difficulty attending a treatment center, ICBT could be a good solution.

Other non-pharmacological therapies currently being studied could be useful when added to CBT (see Table 8.2).[18, 19, 20, 21, 22]

Pharmacology
First-line medications for OCD—SSRIs—are much more effective than second-line medications. Fluvoxamine is widely considered the medication of choice. Clomipramine is also as effective as a second-line medication due to tolerability and safety. Many patients will not notice substantial improvement until 4–6 weeks after a medication is started. Titration is individualized. If a patient worries about side effects, maintain the current dose for 4 weeks. If little or no response is seen after 4 weeks, increase the dose every 1–2 weeks as tolerated until the target dose, or lowest efficacious dose, is reached. You can also titrate the dose upwards within the first month if appropriate, in particular if there is a reoccurrence of OCD episodes and you are familiar with

TABLE 8.2 PSYCHOTHERAPY AND PHARMACOTHERAPY RECOMMENDATIONS FOR OBSESSIVE-COMPULSIVE DISORDER

	PSYCHOTHERAPY	PHARMACOLOGICAL AGENT				
First-line	CBT, particularly with exposure therapy and response prevention (15–20 weekly sessions) Individual, group, or Internet-based CBT (ICBT) for patients who have difficulty attending a clinic	Fluvoxamine	Fluoxetine	Sertraline	Paroxetine	Escitalopram
		TARGET DOSE				
		200 mg	40–60 mg	150–200 mg	40–60 mg	20 mg
Second-line	Acceptance and commitment therapy (ACT) (accepting dysfunctional thoughts) Cognitive therapy (altering dysfunctional beliefs regarding intrusive thoughts)	Citalopram, clomipramine, mirtazapine, venlafaxine XR				
Third-line		IV citalopram, IV clomipramine, duloxetine, phenelzine, tramadol, tranylcypromine				
Adjunctive therapy	Mindfulness-based Organizational training	**First-line:** aripiprazole, risperidone **Second-line:** memantine, quetiapine, topiramate **Third-line:** amisulpride, celecoxib, citalopram, granisetron, haloperidol, IV ketamine, mirtazapine, N-acetylcysteine, olanzapine, ondansetron, pindolol, pregabalin, riluzole, ziprasidone				

IV = intravenous; XR = extended release

Target dose is based on evidence-based guidelines.

Note: Antipsychotics as adjunctive therapy may be considered in treatment-resistant OCD, particularly in patients with tics, as comorbid tic disorder is a commonly cited predictor for treatment response to antipsychotics.[23, 24]

Maximum doses can be found in Pharmacological Therapies (Appendix X, p. 170).

Adapted from Katzman et al (2014).[25]

how your patient responds to medication. The target dose or lowest effective dose for response is typically higher with OCD, and there is a delayed onset of response, which can be up to 8 weeks for onset of symptom relief. Once the target dose or lowest effective dose is reached, improvement is usually seen over the next 4–8 weeks.[26] If there is no further improvement, titrate upwards (as tolerated) to the maximum or maximum tolerated dose. An adequate drug trial is a minimum of 10–12 weeks, as full response can take up to 12 weeks or more (including 4–6 weeks on the maximum tolerated dose). You may need to try several medications as many patients (40–68%) will not initially respond to a given drug trial.[27] Try two SSRIs before switching to a second-line medication or adding adjunctive medication.

COMBINATION THERAPY

For mild cases of OCD, cases of prepubertal OCD, and OCD during pregnancy—except in particularly severe cases—start with CBT alone. For more severe cases of adolescent and adult OCD, you should generally start with CBT plus SSRIs. In other words, the likelihood that you should include medication in a patient's starting therapy increases with

- the severity of the OCD
- the age of the patient.

Biological Therapies

Repetitive transcranial magnetic stimulation (rTMS) is a controversial, noninvasive treatment that consists of stimulating some regions of the brain. A magnetic field generator placed near the patient's head sends small electrical currents to a particular region of the brain, penetrating up to 5 cm. rTMS may be effective in some treatment-resistant patients as add-on treatment, particularly if comorbid depressive symptoms are present.[28]

Deep-brain stimulation can be effective. This recently FDA-approved treatment for use in severe chronic cases involves implanting a battery-operated neurostimulator to deliver electrical impulses to specific areas of the brain (much like a pacemaker). Several very small studies have suggested that deep-brain stimulation may improve symptoms and functionality in up to two-thirds of patients with highly treatment-refractory OCD. As a last resort, capsulotomy has been used.[29, 30, 31]

Complementary and Alternative Medicine

More research is needed into complementary and alternative medical treatments. The preparations are non-standardized and research is sparse, so it is difficult to recommend these therapies.

Maintenance

Although it is appropriate to maintain medication at a lower dose, the Expert Consensus Guideline Series recommends higher doses.[32] Maintenance treatment is often prescribed long-term (>12 months) and should be considered up to 24 months. Continue medication for 1–2 years before tapering.[33] Discontinue dosage very slowly. If symptoms reoccur on taper, increase medication to the previous effective dose. Some patients require life-long pharmacotherapy. There are high rates of relapse unless medication is combined with behavioral strategies.

VISIT-BY-VISIT GUIDE: MILD OBSESSIVE-COMPULSIVE DISORDER

Although many options are acceptable, the recommended initial treatment for mild OCD in an adult is CBT alone. Remember, Mr. DH has a Repetitive Thoughts and Behaviors—Adult score of 1 (mild). He is willing to try CBT.

After 3 months of CBT alone, including exposure/response prevention therapy, Mr. DH's depression and OCD symptoms have diminished substantially. Although he is by no means completely cured, his Repetitive Thoughts and Behaviors—Adult score has fallen from 1 to 0, he does not meet the DSM-5 criteria for OCD, and he is back to normal functioning (in remission). Most people require on average 13–20 sessions for full benefits. The

> **What treatment should you consider out of the choices provided below?**
> » CBT alone
> » Pharmacotherapy alone
> » CBT plus pharmacotherapy
> » Exercise and self-management strategies

exposure/response prevention therapy has taught Mr. DH better ways to deal with his obsessive thoughts. He thanks you very much for your help. You see him monthly for the next 3 months and consider periodic booster sessions of CBT with exposure and response prevention.[34]

VISIT-BY-VISIT GUIDE: MODERATE OBSESSIVE-COMPULSIVE DISORDER

First Visit   Mr. DH returns 6 months later. Unfortunately, even though he regularly practices CBT strategies, his obsessions and compulsions are worse than when he first saw you. The Level 2—Repetitive Thoughts and Behaviors—Adult (Appendix XXVII, p. 215) score has risen to 2 (moderate OCD). He now admits to washing his hands up to 100 times a day, spanned over most hours of the day. He admits to spending more than 2 hours on compulsions. He tells you that he shaves his sideburns repeatedly on each side because he just can't get them even. It takes him 1 1/2 hours trying to get them even until he finally gets frustrated and leaves for work. His chronic lateness has gotten even worse, and he is in trouble with his boss. He adamantly denies suicidal thoughts.

You ask Mr. DH to complete the Symptom Assessment Checklist, the Patient Self-Report Screening Tool for Mental Illnesses (Appendix VI, p. 161) and the Functional Impairment Assessment Scale while you see another patient.

You review his responses. He is experiencing headaches (3), nervousness (3), sleep problems (3), and concentration problems (3). The Patient Self-Report Screening Tool for Mental Illnesses (Appendix VI, p. 161) indicates comorbid depression with a PHQ-9 score of 15 (moderately severe depression). Functioning at work and home are rated around 45%. Your clinical workup indicates no new findings since you last saw him.

You encourage Mr. DH to see a CBT therapist for a few booster sessions to reinforce CBT techniques; however, you feel in this case that acceptance and commitment therapy (ACT) could help Mr. DH accept and learn to live with the intrusive thoughts. A new psychotherapist with these management skills just moved into the community, so you arrange for a consultation. After considering the possible pharmacological therapies, you start him on fluvoxamine 50 mg daily.

There is evidence that OCD requires higher mean doses than other anxiety disorders and that Mr. DH's OCD has already risen to a moderate level. In addition, he has comorbid depressive disorder. Luckily, you know that depressive symptoms improve in parallel with OCD. You advise him to increase the dose of fluvoxamine to 100 mg daily in 1–2 weeks. He responds minimally.

How long could you maintain on the minimum effective dose?

Usually improvement is seen over 4–8 weeks after symptom relief, but after 1 week on this dose, he is distraught and quite upset with his symptoms; therefore, you titrate the dose to 200 mg daily (target dose). He responds after 2 weeks on this dose. You schedule follow-up appointments every 2 weeks.

Subsequent Visits
After 10 weeks on 200 mg, side effects are minimal. The Level 2—Repetitive Thoughts and Behaviors—Adult (Appendix XXVII, p. 215) score is 1 (mild OCD), and he still spends >1 hour washing his hands. Functioning at work and home is still affected as he rates his functioning level around 30%. (Remember the treatment goal is spending <1 hour/day on obsessions-compulsions and minimal interference with daily living.)

You then choose to titrate the dose to a maximum of 300 mg daily and maintain this for 4 more weeks. At 14 weeks, there is no evidence of additional improvement. You can expect this sort of partial or non-response. Up to 60% of OCD patients do not respond to a complete trial of an SSRI.

What is your next step?

- Continue the same medication for another 4 weeks.
- Switch to another first-line SSRI.
- Add adjunctive therapy.
- Switch to clomipramine.

You decide to switch to another first-line SSRI: sertraline 50 mg daily, increased to 150 mg daily within 2 weeks. Adjunctive therapy would be a good option as well. Due to the family history (mother's diagnosis of OCD), you titrate quickly to a maximum dosage of 200 mg daily. Again, side effects are minimal.

Finally, at this maximum dosage of sertraline 200 mg daily and ACT therapy, Mr. DH's symptoms subside. He is in complete remission and functioning at work and home rises to 80–90%, then gradually to 100%.

Maintenance Visits
You see him monthly for 6 months and then as clinically warranted. You continue monitoring for a minimum of 1 year, considering drug taper only at that time.

VISIT-BY-VISIT GUIDE: SEVERE OBSESSIVE-COMPULSIVE DISORDER

First Visit
Nine months later, Mr. DH heads downhill again. The Level 2—Repetitive Thoughts and Behaviors—Adult (Appendix XXVII, p. 215) score is 4 (severe). He now yields to almost all of his urges to wash his hands. He has intrusive, repetitive thoughts that his children's health will deteriorate unless he counts from 1 to 100 in his head, over and over again. He's had to take a medical leave from his job because his obsessions and compulsions interfere substantially with work. He tells you that in total, the obsessions and compulsions take him away from his daily activities for at least 8–10 hours every day. Furthermore, he is extremely distressed by this because now his childhood tics have reappeared.

Mr. DH is practicing CBT and ACT techniques and is at the maximum dosage of sertraline 200 mg daily. You have already tried fluvoxamine. What is your next step?

- Switch to another SSRI.
- Add adjunctive medication.
- Switch to clomipramine.
- Add clomipramine.

At this point in time in Mr. DH's management, initiating a psychiatric referral should be considered, while taking the next step in management guidelines until the referral. You tell him to see his psychotherapist to learn the CBT techniques appropriate for new symptoms and reinforce the ACT strategies.

You choose to add aripiprazole, because you have already tried CBT, ACT, and two SSRIs. There is a family history of chronic OCD, plus he is now experiencing tics, an indicator that OCD associated with tics tends to respond better when augmenting an SSRI with an atypical antipsychotic.[35] Mr. DH has no contraindications to aripripazol. You add adjunctive aripiprazole at 2 mg daily, which you increase to 5 mg per day within 1 week (the mean effective dose is around 10–15 mg/day).[36, 37]

You schedule an appointment in 2 weeks and ask him to complete the Symptom Assessment Checklist, The Patient Self-Report Screening Tool for Mental Illnesses (Appendix VI, p. 161), and the Functional Impairment Assessment Scale (Appendix IX, p. 168) the night before the appointment. You review his responses. He is still experiencing headaches (3), nervousness (3), sleep problems (3), and concentration problems (3), and now has diarrhea (3). The Patient Self-Report Screening Tool for Mental Illnesses (Appendix VI, p. 161) indicates comorbid depression with a PHQ-9 score of 23 (severe depression). His functioning at work is rated at 0% (not working) and 25% at home. You decide to maintain this treatment and see him in 2 more weeks.

Subsequent Visits	On this treatment, Mr. DH's side effects are tolerable. Functional capacity at work remains at 0% (still not back at work) and 20% at home. You increase aripiprazole as tolerated every 2 weeks until you reach 10 mg daily. After a 4-week hold at this level, Mr. DH finally responds on sertraline and 10 mg of aripiprazole daily. Intrusive thoughts about his children's health decrease, and his Level 2—Repetitive Thoughts and Behaviors—Adult (Appendix XXVII, p. 215) score falls to 1 (mild). Functioning at work and home gradually rises to 70–80%. He is back at work on a gradual return-to-work program, slowly increasing the number of hours and days. His mood is elevated, and his anxiety is significantly lower. The aripiprazole gives him mild headaches and dizziness—side effects that he tolerates happily. Luckily, he receives notice of an appointment with the psychiatrist in 4 weeks.
Maintenance Visits	Given the extreme severity of his symptoms, you decide to follow him for at least 2–3 years in collaboration with psychiatry.

SUMMARY

You have completed a case study illustrating the screening, diagnosis, treatment, and management of OCD. This case study is only a guide. Decision making should be individualized and based on clinical judgment. For an overview of the management guidelines, refer to OCD Treatment Guide Summary (Appendix XXVIII, p. 218).

OCD KEY POINTS

- Obsessive-compulsive disorder is a chronic and often disabling condition.
- Obsessions are recurrent and persistent ideas, thoughts, urges, or images that are not simply worries that are out of proportion to real-life problems.
- Compulsions are repetitive, purposeful, and intentional behaviors or mental acts that are performed to neutralize or suppress obsessions or according to rules that must be applied rigidly.
- Approximately 60–90% of patients with OCD have a lifetime comorbid condition (mood, anxiety disorders, and alcohol use disorder are common).
- For mild cases and for cases of prepubertal OCD, start with CBT alone.
- For more severe cases of adolescent and adult OCD, generally start with CBT plus an SSRI; fluvoxamine has historically been widely considered the medication of choice, although current recommendations include other evidence-based drugs.
- OCD usually requires higher dosages of medications than depression or other anxiety disorders.
- The onset of clinical response is commonly delayed up to 8 weeks, even with both counseling and pharmacotherapy.
- The adequate treatment trial for psychotherapy is 12–15 weeks.
- Unlike most other anxiety disorders, for which an adequate medication trial for response is typically 6–8 weeks, an adequate medication trial for OCD can be 10–12 weeks or longer depending on individual circumstances (with a minimum 4 weeks on the maximum tolerated dose).
- For a first episode, consider continuing medication for 1–2 to years before tapering.

NOTES

1 Kessler RC, Chiu WT, Demler O, Walters EE. Prevalence, severity, and comorbidity of twelve-month DSM-IV disorders in the National Comorbidity Survey Replication (NCS-R). Arch Gen Psychiatry [Internet]. 2005 [cited 2015 March 27]; 62(6):617–627. Available from: http://doi.org/10.1001/archpsyc.62.6.617

2 Pinto A, Mancebo M, Eisen J, Pagano M, Rasmussen S. The Brown Longitudinal Obsessive Compulsive Study: clinical features and symptoms of the sample at intake. J Clin Psychiatry. 2006; 67(5):703–711.

3 Ruscio AM, Stein DJ, Chiu WT, Kessler RC. The epidemiology of obsessive-compulsive disorder in the National Comorbidity Survey Replication. Mol Psychiatry [Internet]. 2010 [cited 2015 March 27]; 15(1):53–63. Available from: http://doi.org/10.1038/mp.2008.94

4 American Psychiatric Association. Diagnostic and statistical manual of mental disorders (DSM-5). 5th ed. Arlington, VA: American Psychiatric Association; 2013

5 Bejerot S, Edman G, Anckarsäter H, Berglund G, Gillberg C, Hofvander B, et al. The Brief Obsessive-Compulsive Scale (BOCS): a self-report scale for OCD and obsessive-compulsive related disorders. Nord J Psychiatry [Internet]. 2014 [cited 2015 March 27]; 68(8):549–559. Available from: http://dx.doi.org/10.3109/08039488.2014.884631

6 Sheehan, DV, Lecrubier Y, Sheehan KH, Amorim P, Janavs J, Weiller E, et al. The Mini-International Neuropsychiatric Interview (MINI): the development and validation of a structured diagnostic psychiatric interview for DSM-IV and ICD-10. J Clin Psychiatry. 1998; 59 Suppl 20:22–33.

7 Goodman WK, Price LH, Rasmussen SA, Mazure C, Fleischmann RL, Hill CL, et al. The Yale-Brown Obsessive Compulsive Scale. I. Development, use, and reliability. Arch Gen Psychiatry. 1989; 46(11):1006–1011.

8 Federici A, Summerfeldt LJ, Harrington JL, McCabe RE, Purdon CL, Rowa K, Antony MM. Consistency between self-report and clinician-administered versions of the Yale-Brown Obsessive-Compulsive Scale. J Anxiety Disord. 2010; 24(7):729–733.

9 Foa E, Huppert J, Leiberg S, Langner R, Kichic R, Hajcak G, et al. The Obsessive-Compulsive Inventory: development and validation of a short version. Psychol Assess. 2002; 14(4):485–496.

10 The Obsessive-Compulsive Inventory (OCI) can be downloaded from http://serene.me.uk/tests/oci.pdf [cited 8 March 2016].

11 Katzman MA, Bleau P, Blier P, Chokka P, Kjernisted K, Van Ameringen M, et al. Canadian clinical practice guidelines for the management of anxiety, posttraumatic stress and obsessive-compulsive disorders. BMC Psychiatry. 2014; 14 Suppl 1:S1.

12 Kennedy SH, Lam RW, Parikh SV, Patten SB, Ravindran AV. Canadian Network for Mood and Anxiety Treatments (CANMAT) clinical guidelines for the management of major depressive disorder in adults. J Affect Disord. 2009; 117 Suppl 1:S1–S2.

13 Koran L, Hanna G, Hollander E, Nestadt G, Simpson H. Practice guideline for the treatment of patients with obsessive-compulsive disorder. Am J Psychiatry [Internet]. 2007 [cited 2014 Nov 19]; 164(7 Suppl):5–53. Available from: http://psychiatryonline.org/pb/assets/raw/sitewide/practice_guidelines/guidelines/ocd.pdf

14 Simpson H, Foa E, Liebowitz M, Huppert J, Cahill S, Maher M, et al. Cognitive-behavioral therapy vs risperidone for augmenting serotonin reuptake inhibitors in obsessive-compulsive disorder: a randomized clinical trial. JAMA Psychiatry. 2013; 70(11):1190–1199.

15 Koran L, Hanna G, Hollander E, Nestadt G, Simpson H. Practice guideline for the treatment of patients with obsessive-compulsive disorder. Am J Psychiatry [Internet]. 2007 [cited 2014 Nov 19]; 164(7 Suppl):5–53. Available from: http://psychiatryonline.org/pb/assets/raw/sitewide/practice_guidelines/guidelines/ocd.pdf

16 Chasson GS, Buhlmann U, Tolin DF, Rao SR, Reese HE, Rowley T, et al. Need for speed: evaluating slopes of OCD recovery in behavior therapy enhanced with d-cycloserine. Behav Res Ther. 2010; 48(7):675–679.

17 Katzman MA, Bleau P, Blier P, Chokka P, Kjernisted K, Van Ameringen M, et al. Canadian clinical practice guidelines for the management of anxiety, posttraumatic stress and obsessive-compulsive disorders. BMC Psychiatry. 2014; 14 Suppl 1:S1.

18 Twohig, M. The application of acceptance and commitment therapy to obsessive-compulsive disorder. Cogn Behav Pract. 2009; 16(1):18–28.

19 Wilhelm S, Steketee G, Fama JM, Buhlmann U, Teachman BA, Golan E. Modular cognitive therapy for obsessive-compulsive disorder: a wait-list controlled trial. J Cogn Psychother. 2009; 23(4):294–305.

20 Walsh K, McDougle C. Psychotherapy and medication management strategies for obsessive-compulsive disorder. Neuropsychiatr Dis Treat. 2011; 7:485–494.

21 Buhlmann U, Deckersbach T, Engelhard I, Cook LM, Rauch SL, Kathmann N, et al. Cognitive retraining for organizational impairment in obsessive-compulsive disorder. Psychiatry Res. 2006; 144(2):109–116.

22 Fairfax H. The use of mindfulness in obsessive-compulsive disorder: suggestions for its application and integration in existing treatment. Clin Psychol Psychother. 2008; 15(1):53–59.

23 Bloch MII, Landeros-Weisenberger A, Kelmendi B, Coric V, Bracken MB, Leckman JF. A systematic review: antipsychotic augmentation with treatment refractory obsessive-compulsive disorder. Mol Psychiatry. 2006; 11(7):622–632.

24 Arumugham SS, Reddy JY. Augmentation strategies in obsessive-compulsive disorder. Expert Rev Neurother. 2013 [cited 2016 March 8]; 13(2):187–203. Available from: http://www.tandfonline.com/doi/full/10.1586/ern.12.160

25 Adapted from Katzman MA, Bleau P, Blier P, Chokka P, Kjernisted K, Van Ameringen M, et al. Canadian clinical practice guidelines for the management of anxiety, posttraumatic stress and obsessive-compulsive disorders. BMC Psychiatry. 2014; 14 Suppl 1:S1. This is a PMC Free Article; copyright and licence information can be found at: http://www.ncbi.nlm.nih.gov/pmc/articles/PMC4120194/

26 Koran L, Hanna G, Hollander E, Nestadt G, Simpson H. Practice guideline for the treatment of patients with obsessive-compulsive disorder. Am J Psychiatry [Internet]. 2007 [cited 2014 Nov 19]; 164(7 Suppl):5–53. Available from: http://psychiatryonline.org/pb/assets/raw/sitewide/practice_guidelines/guidelines/ocd.pdf

27 Walsh K, McDougle C. Psychotherapy and medication management strategies for obsessive-compulsive disorder. Neuropsychiatr Dis Treat. 2011; 7:485–494.

28 Berlim MT, Neufeld NH, Van den Eynde F. Repetitive transcranial magnetic stimulation (rTMS) for obsessive-compulsive disorder (OCD): an exploratory meta-analysis of randomized and sham-controlled trials. J Psychiatr Res. 2013; 47(8):999–1006.

29 Greenberg BD, Gabriels LA, Malone DA, Rezai AR, Friehs GM, Okun MS, et al. Deep brain stimulation of the ventral internal capsule/ventral striatum for obsessive-compulsive disorder: worldwide experience. Mol Psychiatry 2008; 15(1):64–79.

30 Goodman WK, Foote KD, Greenberg BD, Ricciuti N, Bauer R, Ward H, et al. Deep brain stimulation for intractable obsessive compulsive disorder: pilot study using a blinded, staggered-onset design. Biol Psychiatry. 2010; 67(6):535–542.

31 Walsh K, McDougle C. Psychotherapy and medication management strategies for obsessive-compulsive disorder. Neuropsychiatr Dis Treat. 2011; 7:485–494.

32 Pittenger C, Kelmendi B, Bloch M, Krystal JH, Coric V. Clinical treatment of obsessive compulsive disorder. Psychiatry (Edgmont). 2005; 2(11):34–43.

33 Koran L, Hanna G, Hollander E, Nestadt G, Simpson H. Practice guideline for the treatment of patients

with obsessive-compulsive disorder. Am J Psychiatry [Internet]. 2007 [cited 2014 Nov 19]; 164(7 Suppl):5–53. Available from: http://psychiatryonline.org/pb/assets/raw/sitewide/practice_guidelines/guidelines/ocd.pdf

34 Koran L, Hanna G, Hollander E, Nestadt G, Simpson H. Practice guideline for the treatment of patients with obsessive-compulsive disorder. Am J Psychiatry [Internet]. 2007 [cited 2014 Nov 19]; 164(7 Suppl):5–53. Available from: http://psychiatryonline.org/pb/assets/raw/sitewide/practice_guidelines/guidelines/ocd.pdf

35 Arumugham SS, Reddy JY. Augmentation strategies in obsessive-compulsive disorder. Expert Rev Neurother.

2013 [cited 2016 March 8]; 13(2):187–203. Available from: http://www.tandfonline.com/doi/full/10.1586/ern.12.160

36 Muscatello M, Bruno A, Pandolfo G, Micò U, Scimeca G, Romeo V, et al. Effect of aripiprazole augmentation of serotonin reuptake inhibitors or clomipramine in treatment-resistant obsessive-compulsive disorder: a double-blind, placebo-controlled study. J Clin Psychopharmacol. 2011; 31(2):174–179.

37 Veale D, Miles S, Smallcombe N, Ghezai H, Goldacre B, Hodsoll J. Atypical antipsychotic augmentation in SSRI treatment refractory obsessive-compulsive disorder: a systematic review and meta-analysis. BMC Psychiatry. 2014; 14:317.

SECTION IV
Trauma- and Stressor-Related Disorders

The DSM-5 has a new chapter: "Trauma- and Stressor-Related Disorders." The decision to create this new chapter is based on commonalities in clinical features, biology, and treatment approaches for these disorders. Exposure to a traumatic or stressful event is required as a diagnostic criterion. People with disorders included in this chapter do not necessarily experience fear, so they do not truly fit in the "Anxiety" chapter. It is felt that this change will improve accuracy of diagnosis and effectiveness of treatments. The order of disorders listed in this new DSM-5 chapter is reflective of developmental perspective. It includes the following:

- Reactive attachment disorder
- Disinhibited social engagement disorder
- Posttraumatic Stress Disorder
- Acute stress disorder (ASD)
- Adjustment disorders
- Other specified trauma- and stressor-related disorders
- Unspecified trauma- and stressor-related disorders

In this section of *The Primary Care Toolkit*, we will review 2 common disorders seen in primary care: PTSD and adjustment disorder.

9

Posttraumatic Stress Disorder

Introduction

Posttraumatic stress disorder (PTSD) is a set of distinctive symptoms that develop after a patient experiences or witnesses an extreme traumatic stressor. Patients will often present in primary care with vague physical complaints or pain, and the diagnosis can be overlooked. Consider referral early to a dual diagnosis treatment program if substance use disorder is present and screen for suicidality; as many as 1 in 5 patients may attempt suicide.[1] To learn about PTSD, you can follow the diagnosis, treatment, and management of our patient, Mrs. BD. You can progress through the practice case study from start to finish, or you can select your own learning path in the Practice Case Study Index, p. xxv. The choice is yours.

Clinical Presentation

PTSD involves the following:

- A stressor
- Symptoms
- Duration of symptoms
- Distress or impairment of functioning

Stressor

A patient with PTSD

- has experienced or witnessed a traumatic event that involved actual or threatened death or serious injury, or sexual violence
- responded to the traumatic event with intense fear, helplessness, or horror.

The stressors are typically extreme and life-threatening and may include the following:

- Witnessing a violent or accidental, actual or threatened death of a loved one

- Witnessing or experiencing a serious accident (automotive, marine, industrial)
- Witnessing or experiencing a natural or human-made disaster
- Experiencing a violent personal assault (including sexual assault)

> Divorce and losing one's job are not PTSD stressors.

Symptoms

As a result of this trauma, the patient develops 4 distinctive symptom domains:[2]

- Re-experiences the traumatic event (memories, distressing dreams, flashbacks) and has psychological or physiological distress at reminders of the trauma
- Avoids stimuli associated with the trauma (memories, places)

- Becomes numb—the patient cannot recall important aspects of the trauma, shows diminished interest in activities that used to be pleasurable, and has feelings of detachment or estrangement from others, persistent negative beliefs, distorted blame, and negative emotional mood
- Manifests increased arousal

Duration and Distress/Impairment of Functioning

To meet the criteria for PTSD, symptoms must last for more than 1 month and cause significant distress or impairment of functioning. These symptoms can start months or even years after the traumatic stressor.

There are 2 specifiers:

- Dissociation (depersonalization or derealization)
- Delayed expression (full criteria are not met until at least 6 months after the event)

PTSD can be confused with other disorders due to having a stressor as a trigger or symptom presentation. To differentiate PTSD from acute stress disorder and depression, use Table 9.1.

The diagnostic criteria for PTSD can be found in Appendix XXIX, p. 219.

Prevalence

With a lifetime prevalence of 6.4 to 9.2%, PTSD is a common disorder.[3] It is difficult to cure completely:[4]

- 30% of patients recover completely
- 40% continue to have mild symptoms
- 20% continue to have moderate symptoms
- 10% remain unchanged or become worse

PTSD is diagnosed more often in veterans, rape victims, and first responders (police, emergency medical personnel). Largely because of the nature of the precipitating stressors, it is more common in younger people. However, it can occur at any age. It has been estimated that 75% of patients with PTSD will have at least 1 other mental disorder during their lifetime. Lifetime comorbidity includes[5] the following:

- Alcohol use disorder (41.8%)
- Specific phobia (37.3%)
- Major depression (35.2%)
- GAD (27.9%)
- Panic disorder with agoraphobia (24.2%)
- Agoraphobia (19%)

TABLE 9.1 DIFFERENTIATION BETWEEN POSTTRAUMATIC STRESS DISORDER AND OTHER DISORDERS

ACUTE STRESS DISORDER	DEPRESSION	ADJUSTMENT DISORDER
Mostly the same requirement for trauma and criteria as PTSD (trauma survivors in acute phase).	Symptoms can include numbing, social avoidance, concentration impairment, and irritability; however, in depression	Stressor involves a major life event but not to the point that meets the criteria for PTSD (threatened death or serious injury, witnessing a death, etc.).
Symptoms or distress lasts longer than 3 days and less than 1 month.	• there is no temporal association with a past traumatic event as described above • the presentation does not include the 4 distinctive symptom clusters of PTSD.	Begins within 3 months of the onset of stressors and terminates within 6 months of the end of stressors.

Posttraumatic Stress Disorder Case Study: Meet Mrs. BD

Mrs. BD is a new patient, a 38-year-old mother of 2 young children ages 4 and 7, who just moved from up north. She works as a nurse and presents to you with the following symptoms, which she has had for 16 months:

- Strong feelings of anxiety
- Racing heart
- Difficulty concentrating
- Insomnia
- Substantial increase in muscle and joint pain in the last 3 months

These symptoms have intensified in the last month, particularly the insomnia. She has been drinking about 1 glass of wine per day. Drinking helps her relax. On questioning, Mrs. BD tells you she has osteoarthritis of the lower spine and hypothyroidism. She takes ibuprofen 400 mg TID, pantoprazole 40 mg BID, and synthroid 0.125 mg OD. You inquire about any changes in her life, her marriage, her children, or physical activities that might explain the increase in muscle and joint pain. She tells you, "Not really, but about 18 months ago," she begins to cry, "I was involved in a serious car accident on an icy highway" [head-on collision]. She explains further, "I was driving, with my husband in the passenger seat. I feel sick to my stomach . . . my husband was killed in that accident. This is the reason I moved here. I needed to get away from the memories. I still think about that awful day." She also describes the following further symptoms:

- Nightmares involving themes of driving and/or a lack of control
- Fatigue
- Forgetfulness

She elaborates that she reported symptoms of sadness and loss of interest to her previous doctor but did not tell him about the accident. He treated her for depression with paroxetine, which she discontinued due to intolerable side effects. You suspect that this may have something to do with the onset of symptoms in recent months. She tells you that she smokes half a pack of cigarettes per day. The family history is unremarkable for psychiatric illnesses. You are a few hours behind in your work schedule, making it difficult to conduct a thorough investigation.

> » What should you do?
> » What are your options?

ASSESSMENT: SCREENING AND PROVISIONAL DIAGNOSIS

If you are pressed for time and there is no safety risk or clinical judgment of urgency, you can tell her you understand her suffering and will help, but you need her to schedule an appointment when you have time to assess her properly. Ask her to return should her condition get worse in the meantime. This is a very important step, particularly if time is an issue. This takes 1–2 minutes and reassures her that even if you don't have time to spend with her this visit, you are concerned about her and want to take the time to address her complaints properly. She feels heard and relieved that someone will help. This lessens her distress while gaining her trust.

Note: You can arrange for an investigative workup to rule out underlying non-psychiatric medical conditions as appropriate and schedule a follow-up appointment. Some medical conditions and/or factors can present with anxiety symptoms, but rarely to the point of a complete disorder. Refer to Chapter 2, p. 16, for further information on factors to consider when assessing anxiety symptoms, or go directly to Factors to Consider When Assessing Anxiety Symptoms (Appendix I, p. 155).

Because you do not know this patient very well, you assess her for suicidal risk, and she replies, "Absolutely not. My children lost their father—they will not lose their mother." You feel confident that although it is important to investigate her condition as soon as possible, she does not require urgent attention. You are considering an anxiety or related disorder, keeping in mind that depressive disorders are comorbid 60% of the time.

You ask Mrs. BD her to complete a screening questionnaire—the Patient Self-Report Screening Tool for Mental Illnesses (Appendix VI, p. 161)—at home for your review at the next visit. Mrs. BD tells you she had an annual checkup 6 months ago, therefore additional bloodwork is unnecessary. You send for her medical file.

Screening for Anxiety and Related Disorders

> » How do you screen for common anxiety and related disorders?
> » How do you screen for common comorbid mental disorders?
> » What is the provisional diagnosis?

TOOLS FOR ASSESSMENT

Refer to the "Provisional Diagnosis" section of Chapter 2, p. 17, for information on screening for anxiety and related disorders and comorbid conditions, or go directly to the Patient Self-Report Screening Tool for Mental Illnesses (Appendix VI, p. 161). Physicians can subsequently review responses with patients to verify accuracy.

You can also review the "Anxiety and Related Disorders: Types and Subtypes" section of Chapter 2, p. 17, which includes a useful tool to help differentiate anxiety disorders, or go directly to Differentiating Anxiety Disorders, Obsessive-Compulsive, and Trauma- and Stressor-Related Disorders (Appendix II, p. 156).

Provisional Diagnosis

At the follow-up visit, she hands you the completed Patient Self-Report Screening Tool for Mental Illnesses, which suggests a diagnosis of PTSD. You review her medical file, which provides no additional information other than what she's already told you. According to the test results, she is euthyroid and the back pain is stable on ibuprofen.

Mrs. BD provides the following clarification to questions answered positively in section 8 of the screening tool, which supports your suspicion that she may be suffering from PTSD:

Have you experienced, witnessed, or had to deal with an extremely traumatic event that included actual or threatened death or serious injury to you or someone else?	She has already told you about the accident that killed her husband.

Are you having anxiety symptoms related to a past traumatic event?	"The pain started after the accident. Come to think about it, the arthritis pain was under control and I had no pain until then. I am very anxious, of course."
Are you having recurrent recollections of the events; for example, memories, flashbacks, or dreams?	"Yes, I have flashbacks of the accident."
Are you re-experiencing the event in a distressing way (such as nightmares, intense recollections, or physical reactions and reminders of the trauma)?	"Yes, I have nightmares involving driving and losing control of the car. I see my husband in my dreams, and I wake up in a sweat and my heart is pounding so fast."
Do you avoid stimuli associated with the trauma (memories, places)?	"Lately, I have been avoiding the highway where I had the accident. I also am extremely protective of my children, not letting them play with their friends as much. I can't help it." She breaks down crying, "I don't know what I would do if I lost them, too. A glass of wine every night calms me. I can get through the day as I know I will feel better after work with a drink. I am so tired at work."
Do you feel emotionally numb or emotionally detached from your loved ones, or have you lost interest in activities that you used to enjoy?	"Yes, I do. I lost interest in anything I enjoyed. I can't even feel sorrow over the loss of my husband."
Have you been jumpy or agitated?	"Yes, very irritable, and I startle so easily. I feel I can't relax. That's why I drink."
Does this interfere with your life?	"Does this interfere with my life? I can still function, but I feel it has turned my life upside down!"

A history of a traumatic event that involved threatened death or serious injury, witnessing the death of her husband, and "Yes" answers to all 4 key distinctive symptom domains suggest a diagnosis of PTSD:

- Re-experiences the traumatic event
- Avoids stimuli associated with the trauma
- Has become emotionally numb/detached
- Experiences increased arousal

In the ensuing discussion, you learn the following:

- Mrs. BD feels guilty that she survived and her husband did not.
- She feels guilty that she can't feel sorrow over his death.
- She feels "alone and isolated," even though friends call and drop by.
- Her emotions are restricted; she says she feels "like a zombie."
- She avoids driving unless she absolutely has to.
- Her concentration is diminished, causing her to forget things at work. She makes errors recently.

Her symptoms have clearly crossed the threshold of "significant distress to interference with functioning." Based on her responses, you make a preliminary diagnosis of PTSD.

The Patient Self-Report Screening Tool for Mental Illnesses also suggests a possibility of the following:

- Clinical depression
- Panic disorder

When you review the answers to questions with her, you determine that she is not experiencing panic attacks, only frightening flashbacks. She tells you, "Flashbacks of the accident come without warning. I re-experience the knot in my stomach as I realize the crash is inevitable, and I hear the awful crunching sound of the impact." Because thinking about the accident can trigger flashbacks, she avoids thinking about it.

Her answers do, however, suggest a diagnosis of clinical depression. She says she has been "depressed" for the last 9 months. Whereas she used to read novels after dinner, she now just watches whatever is on TV until bedtime, when she tries, unsuccessfully, to fall asleep. "I'm usually cheerful, but this accident has left me emotionally numb. I can understand why I can't feel joy right now, but I can't feel sorrow, either. My husband has just died—what does it say about me and our relationship that I can't even feel genuine sorrow? I don't know what it means."

You acknowledge that it took strength to come in and see you. Confronting her problem is the right thing to do, even though it will require revisiting painful memories.

Is Mrs. BD's depression primary or secondary?
Mrs. BD's depression started after her PTSD, so her PTSD is primary.

CONFIRMING THE DIAGNOSIS
The next step is to confirm Mrs. BD's diagnosis.

The diagnosis of PTSD is confirmed by using the DSM-5 criteria for PTSD[6] (see Appendix XXIX, p. 219). Physicians can employ user-friendly tools adapted from the DSM-5 to recall diagnostic features:

> » What factors must you consider to confirm Mrs. BD has PTSD?
> » What instruments can be used to confirm the diagnosis?

- Patient-directed tools: PTSD Checklist for DSM-5 (PCL-5)[7] (Appendix XXX, p. 222).
- Physician-directed tools: the Mini International Neuropsychiatric Interview (MINI) for PTSD is also a widely used instrument (proprietary tool), but it is time-consuming to administer so may not be feasible for a busy primary care office.

The PCL-5 is a short, simple, validated 20-item self-report tool. It yields a score of 0–80. A total cut-off score of ≥38 appears to be reasonable for a positive screen for PTSD until further psychometric work is available.

Interpretation of the PCL-5 should be made by a clinician in conjunction with the DSM-5 criteria. A provisional diagnosis of PTSD can be made as follows:

PRESENCE OF CRITERION A OF THE DSM-5
A. Exposure to actual or threatened death, serious injury, or sexual violence in one (or more) of the following ways:
1. Directly experiencing the traumatic event(s).
2. Witnessing, in person, the event(s) as it occurred to others.

3. Learning that the traumatic event(s) occurred to a close family member or close friend. In cases of the actual or threatened death of a family member or friend, the event(s) must have been violent or accidental.
4. Experiencing repeated or extreme exposure to aversive details of the traumatic event(s) (e.g., first responders collecting human remains; police officers repeatedly exposed to details of child abuse).

Questions are positive if rated as 2 = "Moderately" or higher in at least:

- 1 B item (questions 1–5)
- 1 C item (questions 6–7)
- 2 D items (questions 8–14)
- 2 E items (questions 15–20)

In Ms. BD's case, the PCL-5 supports your diagnosis of PTSD:

- She experienced a serious car accident that killed her husband.
- She meets the criteria for the 4 symptom clusters with a minimum rating of 2 (moderately bothered) in:
- At least 1 B item (questions 1–5); she re-experiences the traumatic event through
  - flashbacks
  - nightmares
  - feeling very anxious when she thinks about or remembers the event
  - strong physical reactions.
- At least 1 C item (questions 6–7), avoidance, because she
  - avoids thinking about the event
  - avoids driving.
- At least 2 D items (questions 8–14), persistent negative alteration in cognition and mood, because she
  - feels "alone and isolated," even though friends call and drop by
  - feels "like a zombie," with no emotional highs or lows
  - feels guilty that she survived and her husband did not
  - feels guilty that she can't feel sorrow over his death
  - has lost interest in reading.
- At least 2 E items (questions 15–20), increased arousal, because she
  - has trouble falling asleep
  - is very irritable
  - startles easily
  - has difficulty concentrating at work.

You document a specifier of dissociative symptoms.

It is clear that her symptoms cause dysfunction: avoidance of the highway, irritability at home, and decreased concentration at work resulting in errors. In addition, Mrs. BD self-medicates with alcohol. Mrs. BD's PCL-5 score is 40.

BASELINE ASSESSMENT

The next step is to conduct a baseline assessment. This will provide you and your patient with important information to tailor a treatment plan specific to your patient.

Patient self-report tools are used in primary care for many medical conditions. These practical, time-efficient tools are also used in mental health assessments; however, responses should be interpreted by clinicians together with the DSM-5 criteria and clinical judgment. A careful assessment and rating of each of the following parameters will also establish a baseline from which to measure treatment response:

> » What should be included in a baseline assessment?
> » What tools are useful at baseline and follow-up visits?

- Suicide Assessment Questionnaire (Appendix III, p. 157)
- PTSD symptom severity
    - PTSD Checklist for DSM-5 (PCL-5) (Appendix XXX, p. 222)
    - Severity of Posttraumatic Stress Symptoms—Adult[8] (see note below)
    - GAD-7 (sensitivity 66%, specificity 81%) (Appendix V, p. 160)
- Comorbid conditions
- Somatic complaints; Symptom Assessment Checklist (Appendix VIII, p. 167)
- Functional impairment; Functional Impairment Assessment Scale (Appendix IX, p. 168)

> You can also refer to the "Baseline Assessment" section of Chapter 2, p. 18.

Note: The Severity of Posttraumatic Stress Symptoms—Adult scale provides cut-off scores of 0 (no illness), 1 (mild), 2 (moderate), 3 (severe), and 4 (extreme). The tool can be downloaded directly from the APA site at http://www.psychiatry.org/psychiatrists/practice/dsm/dsm-5/online-assessment-measures. These measures can be reproduced without permission by researchers and by clinicians for use with their patients. Rating information is provided as well.

The PCL-5 can be used to assess the severity of the illness and monitor treatment response. A total symptom severity score for the 20 items will range from 0 to 80. A 5–10 point change represents reliable change (i.e., not due to chance), whereas a 10–20 point change represents a clinically significant change. Therefore, a 5-point change is accepted as the minimum threshold for determining whether an individual has responded to treatment, and a 10-point change is the minimum threshold for determining whether the improvement is clinically meaningful. The PCL-5 has not to date been studied in terms of severity (i.e., no, mild, moderate, severe) cut-off scores.

Mrs. BD's Baseline Assessment

To reiterate, Mrs. BD denies any suicidal thoughts. The PCL-5 total score is 40. Baseline assessment indicates a positive screen for depression. You choose to administer the PHQ-9, which confirms mild depression. Her previous doctor treated her for depression with paroxetine, which she discontinued due to intolerable side effects. You choose to download and administer the Severity of Posttraumatic Stress Symptoms—Adult, which reveals a score of 1 (mild). Sleep is affected (3), as well as concentration (2), headache (1), tired (2), and tense (3). The Functional Impairment Assessment Scale (Appendix IX, p. 168) reveals that performance at work is not affected. She rates her ability to function at home and social life at 75% due to being overprotective of her children and having difficulty driving. She tells you that she is able to get to most places, though.

MANAGEMENT GUIDELINES

Now that you have confirmed the diagnosis of PTSD and have a general idea of illness severity and how it affects Mrs. BD, you begin to develop a care plan. Information collected to date will guide your management plan; however, the choice of treatment will depend on several factors, for example:[9, 10]

- Patient's opinions about treatment
- Receptivity to counseling
- Receptivity to medication
- Severity of symptoms
- Comorbidity
- Previous response (or lack of response) to treatment
- Availability of resources in the community

You can also refer to Chapter 3: Management, p. 25. First-, second-, and third-line treatments for PTSD are listed in Table 9.2.

Psychotherapy

Many non-pharmacological therapies are currently under investigation, with conflicting results. The strongest evidence to date supports the following non-pharmacological treatments: individual and group trauma-focused CBT (TF-CBT), particularly exposure therapy and eye movement desensitization and reprocessing (EMDR) as first-line psychotherapy (confronting anxiety triggers). Therapist-assisted, Internet-based CBT (ICBT) can also be effective for those unable or unwilling to attend clinics. Adjunctive anxiety (or stress) management (relaxation techniques) also has shown to be effective. When available, CBT should be included in every patient's therapy as studies show that therapeutic gains are maintained for up to 10 years.[11] TF-CBT with prolonged exposure can be helpful (e.g., for rape victims or combat veterans).[12] D-cycloserine does not seem to enhance the effects of exposure therapy.[13, 14, 15] Dialectable behavior has shown to be effective as pre-treatment to reduce self-harm behavior.[16] Marital counseling should be considered as improving family dynamics can improve recovery.[17] Virtual reality exposure is a promising treatment option for PTSD. It integrates real-time computer graphics and visual displays. Patients get a sense of being immersed in the virtual environments.[18]

Pharmacology

The evidence suggests that pharmacotherapy may be first line if the patient is receptive.[19] The first-line medications for PTSD are SSRIs and SNRIs (Table 9.2). The target dose for response is typically higher. Titrate dose as tolerated to reach the target dose (or minimum effective dose) and allow 4–6 weeks to assess drug response. If no response, titrate upwards (as tolerated) to the maximum dose. Where appropriate, allow a 6–8 week trial on the maximum tolerated dose to determine

TABLE 9.2 PSYCHOTHERAPY AND PHARMACOTHERAPY RECOMMENDATIONS FOR POSTTRAUMATIC STRESS DISORDER*

	PSYCHOTHERAPY	PHARMACOLOGICAL AGENT			
First-line	Individual and group CBT, trauma-focused CBT (TF-CBT)—particularly exposure therapy and eye movement desensitization and reprocessing (EMDR)	Fluoxetine	Paroxetine	Sertraline	Venlafaxine XR
		TARGET DOSE[20]			
		20–40 mg	20–50 mg	50–200 mg	50–150 mg
Second-line	Therapist-assisted, Internet-based CBT	Fluvoxamine, mirtazapine, phenelzine			
Third-line		Amitriptyline, aripiprazole, bupropion SR, buspirone, carbamazepine, desipramine, duloxetine, escitalopram, imipramine, lamotrigine, memantine, moclobemide, quetiapine, reboxetine, risperidone, tianeptine, topiramate, trazodone			
Adjunctive therapy	Adjunctive anxiety (or stress) management (applied relaxation training techniques) Marital counseling	**Second-line:** Eszopiclone, olanzapine, risperidone **Third-line:** Aripiprazole, clonidine, gabapentin, levetiracetam, pregabalin, quetiapine, reboxetine, tiagabine			

SR = sustained release; XR = extended release

Note: Target dose is based on evidence-based guidelines.

*Adapted from Katzman et al (2014).[21]

effectiveness. If the drug is not tolerated or there is no improvement on the treatment trial, consider switching to another first-line medication. First-line recommendation is to switch rather than add-on due to better tolerability and less potential for side effects. Add-on is also an option and is usually a second-line recommendation; however, it has advantages in patients who take a long time to respond to pharmacotherapy to keep them motivated to continue with the treatment plan, address side effects secondary to the current drug, or target residual symptoms. You may need to try several medications as many patients will not initially respond to certain drugs. Consider trying 2 first-line drugs (SSRIs/SNRIs), before switching to a second-line medication or adding adjunctive medication. Although the work of Katzman et al. lists atypical antipsychotics as second, third, and add-on therapy, Warner et al. recommend against this, stating that adverse effects outweigh benefits.

Prazosin can help with sleep disturbance caused by nightmares (average dose 10–13 mg/day; start at 1 mg Q HS and increase by 1 mg every 5–7 days; maximum dose 15 mg/day; consider period of use 6–8 weeks).[22, 23] Adjunctive propranolol in preventing physiological reactivity related to trauma shows conflicting results; however, it can be considered.[24, 25, 26] Naltrexone, an opioid antagonist used for the treatment of alcohol use disorder, can have synergistic effects when combined with prazosin in reducing alcohol craving and intake.[27] Fluphenazine and olanzepine may reduce re-experiencing trauma and psychotic symptoms.[28]

If a comorbid psychiatric disorder is present, in particular depression symptoms, consider starting with both CBT and pharmacotherapy. If substance use disorder is present, consider treatment centers that address both conditions. The management of comorbid conditions (e.g., pain or sleep management) should also be included as this can affect treatment response. Consider maintaining effective therapy for at least 1 year. Debriefing of the trauma victim is not necessarily helpful.[29]

Biological Therapies

More studies are needed; however, the following show promise:[30]

- Repetitive transcranial magnetic stimulation (rTMS) may be as effective as SSRIs as monotherapy. It also has shown to be effective as an add-on to SSRIs.
- Adjunctive ECT has been used in particular for refractory depression, which is often associated with PTSD.

Complementary and Alternative Medicine

Evidence is limited on the effectiveness of these types of therapies, although they are often used. Furthermore, some common botanicals and supplements prescribed with second-generation antidepressants can induce serotonin syndrome. Recent studies evaluating yoga and acupuncture as adjunctive therapy have shown beneficial effects, though more studies are needed.[31]

VISIT-BY-VISIT GUIDE: MILD POSTTRAUMATIC STRESS DISORDER

To reiterate, Mrs. BD has mild PTSD with secondary clinical depression.

Although all 3 threatment options are acceptable, in this case, you choose to initiate combination therapy: CBT with relaxation training techniques and pharmacotherapy for comorbid depression. As well, experience tells you that Mrs. BD may have minimized the severity of her symptoms. Fortunately, she is eager to do whatever it takes to make her symptoms stop as soon as possible. She

> What treatment should you consider out of the choices provided below?
> » CBT alone
> » Pharmacotherapy alone
> » CBT plus pharmacotherapy

is happy to start both CBT and pharmacotherapy. You consider the possible pharmacological therapies and start sertraline 50 mg daily. You are aware of the increased risk of upper GI bleed with SSRIs; however, she is on a proton pump inhibitor, so you advise her of the risk and symptoms to watch for and monitor her closely.

You schedule an appointment for 1 week later and ask her to complete the Severity of Posttraumatic Stress Symptoms—Adult, the Functional Impairment Assessment Scale, and the Symptom Assessment Checklist the night before the appointment.

After 1 week of CBT and sertraline 50 mg daily, there is little change. The Severity of Posttraumatic Stress Symptoms—Adult score remains unchanged at 1 (mild). She is feeling less alone and experiencing more emotional highs and lows. She is also sleeping a bit better. However, her flashbacks are more intense. On the Functional Impairment Assessment Scale, she rates functioning at 70% in the social and family categories and has missed no days of work (mild).

Although it is important to keep her on the lowest possible effective dose, experience tells you that higher doses are usually necessary to see a response in PTSD, in particular with alcohol use disorder and depression. You increase the sertraline to 150 mg daily and allow 4–6 weeks for response, seeing her every 2 weeks. Side effects are minimal, and somatic symptoms are unchanged. Sertraline is increased by 50 mg to the maximum dose of 200 mg. Finally, at 200 mg daily, her symptoms subside altogether. You encourage her to continue with CBT. For patients with PTSD, it is recommended that effective therapy is maintained for a minimum of 1 year. You see her monthly at first and then according to her needs.

VISIT-BY-VISIT GUIDE: MODERATE POSTTRAUMATIC STRESS DISORDER

First Visit	Four months later, Mrs. BD returns. Unfortunately, even with regular practice of CBT strategies and 200 mg of sertraline daily, her symptoms are worse. The Severity of Posttraumatic Stress Symptoms—Adult score has risen to 2 (moderate), with items mostly rated 2 (quite a bit bothered) and flashbacks rated at 3. She denies suicidal ideation. On the Functional Impairment Assessment Scale, the relationship functioning with her children is rated at 50%, and she has lost 2 days of work in the last week. In addition, sleep is affected (3), and she explains that her nightmares are awful and her concentration is diminished (2). She reports headache (1), tiredness (3), and tenseness (3). She has abstained from alcohol since she started sertraline.

You reassess comorbidity using the Patient Self-Report Screening Tool for Mental Illnesses (Appendix VI, p. 161) and PHQ-9 (Appendix VII, p. 165), which reconfirms comorbid clinical depression.

What treatment should you consider out of the choices provided below?

- Adjunctive therapy with olanzapine
- Switch to amitriptyline
- Switch to another first-line SSRI/SNRI
- Adjunctive prazosin

First-line recommendation is to switch to another first-line agent due to the lower potential for side effects and/or drug interactions; however, add-on is a good option if a patient takes a long time to respond (maintain the psychological gains) and keeps them motivated to continue treatment, addressing side effects secondary to the first antidepressant, or targeting residual symptoms. Factors such as a patient's past history, degree of response, side effects of the initial antidepressant, and the potential side effects of a new medication should be taken into account in the decision-making process.[32]

The patient has not responded to an adequate trial of SSRI, so you decide to switch to venlafaxine XR 75 mg daily, which you quickly increase to a target dose of 150 mg per day. With PTSD, as with OCD, the medication trial should be conducted at the average target dose. You advise her to go for booster sessions with the CBT therapist to reinforce techniques and add prazosin for nightmares with an initial dose of 1 mg, also gradually increased to 5 mg daily. You explain that prazosin will be maintained for 8 weeks.

Once the target dose is reached, you ask her to schedule a follow-up appointment in 2 weeks and to complete the Severity of Posttraumatic Stress Symptoms—Adult, the Functional Impairment Assessment Scale, and the Symptom Assessment Checklist the night before the appointment.

Subsequent Visits	After 2 weeks on 150 mg venlafaxine daily, she reports that side effects are minimal but symptoms remain unchanged. The Severity of Posttraumatic Stress Symptoms—Adult score is 2 (moderate). The Functional Impairment Assessment Scale reveals that the relationship with her children, which she rates at 40% (moderate), has deteriorated slightly. Functioning at work remains unchanged.
	You increase the dose to 225 mg daily, and finally the distressful symptoms subside at around 4 weeks on this regimen. She reports that she is no longer bothered by nightmares, her mood is lifting, and her relationship with her children is improving. Somatic symptoms present at baseline are gradually resolving. The Severity of Posttraumatic Stress Symptoms—Adult score is 1 (mild PTSD).
Maintenance Visits	You continue to monitor once a month for the first 3 months and then every 3 months for at least 1 year. There is gradual improvement in all areas until full remission is achieved.

VISIT-BY-VISIT GUIDE: SEVERE POSTTRAUMATIC STRESS DISORDER

First Visit	Unfortunately, 5 months after remission, Mrs. BD has a minor car accident. In addition to all her previous symptoms, she now

- avoids motor vehicles altogether

- has completely withdrawn from her circle of friends

- cannot have loving feelings towards her children

- lashes out in anger at her children and her friends

- tells you she feels detached from her body, saying, "I don't feel that things are real around me. It is as if I am in a dream."

She rates most symptoms as being positive and is extremely bothered by them; most are rated at 4 such that the Severity of Posttraumatic Stress Symptoms—Adult score has risen to 4 (extreme). She admits to fleeting suicidal thoughts; however, she is adamant that she would never consider killing herself. On the Functional Impairment Assessment Scale, she has taken a medical leave from work (extreme). She now drinks 3 glasses of wine per day. Given the severity of her symptoms and dissociative subtype, you initiate a referral to psychiatry.

You consider your options. You expect that Mrs. BD could benefit immensely from EMDR, so you find a psychotherapist that administers this form of treatment and maintain the venlafaxine XR at 225 mg daily.

You ask her to schedule an appointment in 2 weeks and complete the Severity of Posttraumatic Stress Symptoms—Adult, the Functional Impairment Assessment Scale (Appendix IX, p. 168), and the Symptom Assessment Checklist (Appendix VIII, p. 167) the night before the appointment.

Subsequent Visits	When she returns, Mrs. BD responds partially. She reports that she is still unable to drive, but flashbacks and dreams of the accident have minimally decreased. She is still very irritable. The Severity of Posttraumatic Stress Symptoms—Adult score improves slightly and is rated at 3. On the Functional Impairment Assessment Scale, she has returned to work but feels she is unproductive. Furthermore, the relationship with her children, which she rates at 30%, remains stressed.
	Fortunately, she sees the psychiatrist, who adjusts the medication and arranges for a consult at a day treatment program that deals with complex diagnoses: PTSD, alcohol use disorder, and depression. After 6 weeks of intense therapy, she improves substantially. The multidisciplinary team monitors her condition closely over the next year. Her symptoms subside to a mild level that she finds acceptable. A relapse prevention program is developed specifically for her as well.
Maintenance Visits	Given the extreme severity of her PTSD, in collaboration with the multidisciplinary team, maintenance therapy is continued for a minimum of 2 years, with consideration to extend based on a clinical assessment at that time.

Note: Day and in-house treatment programs can be effective in the management of treatment-resistant PTSD. In-house (and in some cases outpatient) treatment programs are usually not covered by publically funded provincial health care plans. However, most workplace insurance carriers will consider approving these treatments if the condition results in a disability severe enough to cause a long-term absence from the workplace, providing specific carrier policy criteria are met. This can be the case in many instances of long-term disability in the workplace, for which evidenced-based treatments are not covered by publically funded provincial health care plans.

SUMMARY

You have completed a case study illustrating the screening, diagnosis, treatment, and management of PTSD. This case study is only a guide. Decision making should be individualized and based on clinical judgment. For an overview of the management guidelines, refer to the PTSD Treatment Guide Summary (Appendix XXXI, p. 225).

PTSD KEY POINTS

- With a lifetime prevalence of 6.4 to 9.2%, PTSD is a common disorder.
- The patient has experienced or witnessed an extreme traumatic stressor.
- The patient has developed at least
  - One symptom of *re-experiencing*
  - One symptom of *avoidance*
  - Two persistent symptoms of *negative alteration* in cognition and mood
  - Two symptoms of *increased arousal*
- Depression and alcohol use disorder are common comorbid conditions.
- Among non-pharmacological treatments, CBT is the first line of therapy (particularly exposure therapy, adjunctive anxiety (stress) management, and EMDR).
- Among pharmacological treatments, SSRIs and SNRIs are the first line of therapy.
- A combination of CBT and pharmacotherapy appear to have longer-lasting benefits.

NOTES

1 Warner CH, Warner CM, Appenzeller GN, Hoge CW. Identifying and managing posttraumatic stress disorder. Am Fam Physician. 2013; 88(12):827–834.

2 American Psychiatric Association. Diagnostic and statistical manual of mental disorders (DSM-5). 5th ed. Arlington, VA: American Psychiatric Association; 2013

3 Kessler R, Berglund P, Demler O, Jin R, Merikangas K, Walters E. Lifetime prevalence and age-of-onset distributions of DSM-IV disorders in the National Comorbidity Survey Replication. Arch Gen Psychiatry. 2005; 62(6):593–602.

4 Sadock B, Sadock VA. Kaplan & Sadock's concise textbook of clinical psychiatry. 3rd ed. Philadelphia: Lippincott Williams & Wilkins; 2008.

5 Pietrzak RH, Goldstein RB, Southwick SM, Grant BF. Prevalence and Axis I comorbidity of full and partial posttraumatic stress disorder in the United States: results from Wave 2 of the National Epidemiologic Survey on Alcohol and Related Conditions. J Anxiety Disord. 2011; 25(3):456–465.

6 American Psychiatric Association. Diagnostic and statistical manual of mental disorders (DSM-5). 5th ed. Arlington, VA: American Psychiatric Association; 2013.

7 Weathers FW, Litz BT, Keane TM, Palmieri PA, Marx BP, Schnurr PP. The PTSD checklist for DSM-5 (PCL-5). U.S. Department of Veterans Affairs; 2013. Scale available from the National Center for PTSD at www.ptsd.va.gov.

8 American Psychiatric Association [Internet]. Arlington (VA): American Psychiatric Association; 2013. Online assessment measures; c2013 [cited 2015 August 29]. Available from: http://www.psychiatry.org/psychiatrists/practice/dsm/dsm-5/online-assessment-measures

9 Evans M, Bradwejn J, Dunn L, editors. Ontario guidelines for the management of anxiety disorders in primary care. 1st ed. Toronto: Queen's Printer of Ontario; 2000.

10 Kennedy SH, Lam RW, Parikh SV, Patten SB, Ravindran AV. Canadian Network for Mood and Anxiety Treatments (CANMAT) clinical guidelines for the management of major depressive disorder in adults. J Affect Disord. 2009; 117 Suppl 1:S1–S2.

11 Bisson J, Ehlers A, Matthews R, Pilling S, Richards D, Turner S. Psychological treatments for chronic post-traumatic stress disorder. Systematic review and meta-analysis. British J Psychiatry. 2007; 190:97–104.

12 Resick P, Nishith P, Weaver T, Astin M, Feuer C, Kendal PC. A comparison of cognitive-processing therapy with prolonged exposure and a waiting condition for the treatment of chronic posttraumatic stress disorder in female rape victims. J Consult Clin Psychol. 2002; 70(4):867–879.

13 De Kleine RA, Hendriks GJ, Kusters WJ, Broekman TG, van Minnen A. A randomized placebo-controlled trial of d-cycloserine to enhance exposure therapy for posttraumatic stress disorder. Biol Psychiatry. 2012; 71(11):962–968.

14 Hofmann S, Otto G, Pollack M, Smits W. D-cycloserine augmentation of cognitive behavioral therapy for anxiety disorders: an update. Curr Psychiatry Rep. 2015; 17(1):1–5.

15 Litz BT, Salters-Pedneault K, Steenkamp MM, Hermos JA, Bryant RA, Otto MW, Hofmann SG. A randomized placebo-controlled trial of d-cycloserine and exposure therapy for posttraumatic stress disorder. J Psychiatr Res. 2012; 46(9):1184–1190.

16 Katzman MA, Bleau P, Blier P, Chokka P, Kjernisted K, Van Ameringen M, et al. Canadian clinical practice guidelines for the management of anxiety, posttraumatic stress and obsessive-compulsive disorders. BMC Psychiatry. 2014; 14 Suppl 1:S1.

17 Monson C, Fredman S, Macdonald A, Pukay-Martin N, Resick P, Schnurr P. Effect of cognitive-behavioral couple therapy for PTSD: a randomized controlled trial. JAMA. 2012; 308(7):700–709.

18 Cukor J, Spitalnick J, Difede J, Rizzo A, Rothbaum BO. Emerging treatments for PTSD. Clin Psychol Rev. 2009; 29(8):715–726.

19 Warner CH, Warner CM, Appenzeller GN, Hoge CW. Identifying and managing posttraumatic stress disorder. Am Fam Physician. 2013; 88(12):827–834.

20 Warner CH, Warner CM, Appenzeller GN, Hoge CW. Identifying and managing posttraumatic stress disorder. Am Fam Physician. 2013; 88(12):827–834.

21 Adapted from Katzman MA, Bleau P, Blier P, Chokka P, Kjernisted K, Van Ameringen M, et al. Canadian clinical practice guidelines for the management of anxiety, posttraumatic stress and obsessive-compulsive disorders. BMC Psychiatry. 2014; 14 Suppl 1:S1. This is a PMC Free Article; copyright and licence information can be found at: http://www.ncbi.nlm.nih.gov/pmc/articles/PMC4120194/

22 Raskind MA, Peskind ER, Hoff DJ, Hart KL, Holmes HA, Warren D, et al. A parallel group placebo controlled study of prazosin for trauma nightmares and sleep disturbance in combat veterans with post-traumatic stress disorder. Biol Psychiatry. 2007; 61(8):928–934.

23 Steckler T, Risbrough V. Pharmacological treatment of PTSD—established and new approaches. Neuropharmacology. 2012; 62(2):617–627.

24 Pitman RK, Delahanty D. Driven pharmacologic approaches to acute trauma. CNS Spectr. 2005; 10(2):99–106.

25 Pitman RK, Sanders KM, Zusman RM, Healy AR, Cheema F, Lasko NB, et al. Pilot study of secondary

prevention of posttraumatic stress disorder with propranolol. Biol Psychiatry. 2002; 51(2):189–192.

26 Stein M, Kerridge C, Dimsdale J, Hoy D. Pharmacotherapy to prevent PTSD: results from a randomized controlled proof-of-concept trial in physically injured patients. J Trauma Stress. 2007; 20(6):923–932.

27 Froehlich J, Hausauer B, Rasmussen D. Combining naltrexone and prazosin in a single oral medication decreases alcohol drinking more effectively than does either drug alone. Alcohol Clin Expl Res. 2013; 37(10):1763–1770.

28 Iribarren J, Prolo P, Neagos N, Chiappelli F. Post-traumatic stress disorder: evidence-based research for the third millennium. Evid Based Complement Alternat Med. 2005; 2(4):503–512.

29 Rose S, Bisson J, Churchill R, Wessely S. Psychological debriefing for preventing posttraumatic stress disorder (PTSD). Cochrane Database Syst Rev. 2002; (2):CD000560.

30 Novakovic V, Sher L, Lapidus K, Mindes J, A Golier J, Yehuda R. Brain stimulation in posttraumatic stress disorder. Eur J Psychotraumatol. 2011; 2.

31 Warner CH, Warner CM, Appenzeller GN, Hoge CW. Identifying and managing posttraumatic stress disorder. Am Fam Physician. 2013; 88(12): 827–834.

32 Kennedy SH, Lam RW, Parikh SV, Patten SB, Ravindran AV. Canadian Network for Mood and Anxiety Treatments (CANMAT) clinical guidelines for the management of major depressive disorder in adults. J Affect Disord. 2009; 117 Suppl 1:S1–S2.

Adjustment Disorder

Introduction

Adjustment disorder is covered in the "Trauma- and Stressor-Related Disorders" chapter in the DSM-5 as it is a stress-response after exposure to a distressing event, or a psychological disorder that results from an inability to cope with a major stressor such as a life change or a feeling of loss of control. It can be perceived as a benign condition that will resolve naturally. However, if the stressor and its consequences are not addressed and resolved, it can lead to secondary depression or other chronic conditions. Adjustment disorder can be very disabling and costly, not to mention a frustrating venture for both patients and professionals. For primary care providers, a common presentation of adjustment disorder is a patient who has come in for workplace absence due to conflict in the workplace. Initially, the patient's state may not have crossed the threshold of significant distress to interference with functioning; however, if the conflict is not addressed, for example through an informal or more formal conflict-resolution process (e.g., meetings of parties involved or a more complex alternative dispute resolution process [ADR] with or without the help of a third party), the conflict can result in an adjustment disorder and is a common cause for long-term disability. Patients will have difficulty reintegrating into the workplace, and physicians will be asked to provide recommendations in relation to the individual's ability to work. Specialists opine that the individual is completely disabled unless the trigger or stressor is removed or addressed. The longer the conflict is left to fester, the less likely there will be a favorable outcome.

Health care professionals can have a positive impact on the course and chronicity of the illness by providing recommendations at early stages of the conflict for the parties involved to attempt to resolve the issues.

Symptoms are real and consequences can be extremely important (e.g., suicidal potential, hospitalization).[1,2,3] To learn about adjustment disorder, you can follow the diagnosis, treatment, and management of our patient, Mr. CF. You can progress through the practice case study from start to finish, or you can select your own learning path in the Practice Case Study Index, p. xxv. The choice is yours.

Clinical Presentation

A person develops adjustment disorder when they are experiencing an inability to cope with a particular event or situation (stressor). It consists of the following:[4]

- Emotional or behavioral symptoms that develop within 3 months of the onset of stressors and end within 6 months of the end of the stressors.
- The patient's distress exceeds what would normally be caused by the stressor.
- The symptoms are not caused by bereavement.
- Social and occupational or other important areas of functioning are significantly impaired.
- The criteria do not indicate another disorder such as MDD or bereavement.

Typically, the person experiences[5] the following:

- Worry
- Anxiety
- Insomnia
- Poor concentration
- Loss of self-esteem, hopelessness, feeling trapped, feeling isolated

Specifiers are as follows:

1. Subtypes:
   - With depressed mood (the most common subtype)
   - With anxious mood
   - With mixed anxiety and depressed mood
   - With disturbance of conduct
   - With mixed disturbance of emotions and conduct
   - Unspecified
2. Acute (less than 6 months) versus chronic (longer than 6 months)

Adjustment disorder can include, for example, the following:

- Conflict in the workplace
- An unwanted move
- Financial difficulties
- Marital discord
- A disappointment or failure
- A serious medical illness (e.g., cancer)

Differentiating from Other Disorders

Because adjustment disorder (AD) involves a stressor as a trigger, it can be confused with PTSD, depression, and normal stress reaction. The stressor may not always be obvious, and a frequent presentation in primary care is somatization, or depressed mood, which in the latter, can be misdiagnosed as major depressive disorder.[6] To differentiate AD from PTSD, depressed mood and normal stress reaction, refer to Table 10.1.

The diagnostic criteria for AD can be found in Appendix XXXII, p. 227.

Prevalence

Due to scarce prevalence studies, the reported prevalence of AD varies from 12–23%.[7, 8]

TABLE 10.1 DIFFERENTIATING ADJUSTMENT DISORDER (AD) FROM OTHER CONDITIONS

ADJUSTMENT DISORDER VS. COMMON DISORDERS	
AD vs. PTSD	Stressor involves major life events but not to the point that meets the criteria for PTSD (e.g., threatened death or serious injury, witnessing a death).
	AD begins within 3 months of onset of stressor and terminates within 6 months of end of stressor.
AD vs. Depressed mood	In AD, there is inadequate DSM-5 criteria for major depression.
AD vs. Normal stress reaction	In AD, there is distress in excess of what would be expected from exposure to a stressor.
	Significant impairment in social, occupational, educational, and home functioning.

Adjustment disorder is highly comorbid. Common comorbidity includes:

- Major depressive disorder (MDD)
- Substance use disorder

- Other anxiety disorders
- Personality disorder

Reports of the prevalence ratio between women and men are conflicting; more studies are required to provide accurate data.[9, 10, 11, 12]

Adjustment Disorder Case Study: Meet Mr. CF

Mr. CF is 43 years old, married with 2 adult children, and works as a carpenter. He is sitting on the examining table looking at the floor. He's been in to see you twice in the past month. Over the last 6 months, he has been having trouble at work to the point that his boss spoke to him because he was making mistakes that were costly to the company. This caused tension between him and his boss. He began missing a few days here and there at work, which prompted his boss to schedule a performance appraisal meeting. Tensions kept building to the point that he tells you, "Doctor, I don't think I can work there. My boss treats me unfairly." In addition, he presents with the following complaints:

- He is unhappy in his marriage.
- He has trouble sleeping.
- He is experiencing fatigue.
- He generally does not enjoy life because he is unable to relax.
- Thinking about all the things that bother him makes him quite angry and agitated.

Mr. CF's family is well known to you, as you treated his older brother for 2 years and his mother for major depressive disorder 3 years ago. He is visibly agitated and speaks angrily with a stern look on his face. His body is tense.

> » What should or can you do?
> » What are your options?

ASSESSMENT: SCREENING AND PROVISIONAL DIAGNOSIS

If you are pressed for time and there is no safety risk or clinical judgment of urgency, you can tell him you understand his suffering and will help. Ask him to schedule an appointment when you have time to assess him properly and to return should his condition get worse in the meantime. This is a very important step, particularly if time is an issue. This takes 1–2 minutes and reassures him that even if you don't have time to spend with him this visit, you are concerned about him and want to take the time to address his complaints properly. He feels heard and relieved that someone will help. This lessens his distress while gaining his trust.

Note: You can arrange for an investigative workup to rule out underlying non-psychiatric medical conditions as appropriate and schedule a follow-up appointment. Some medical conditions and/or factors can present with anxiety symptoms, but rarely to the point of a complete disorder. Refer to Chapter 2, p. 16, for further information on factors to consider when assessing anxiety symptoms, or go directly to Factors to Consider When Assessing Anxiety Symptoms (Appendix I, p. 155).

Mr. CF's Assessment

Mr. CF rarely comes to see you; therefore, you suspect his complaints may be emotionally based. However, you cover all your bases by conducting a full exam and sending him for a routine investigative workup.

QUESTION	OPTIONS	FEEDBACK
What further history should you obtain?	Other symptoms	He sleeps 10 hours a night and naps from 5–7 p.m.
		He is not suicidal. He's begun having panic attacks.
		He brightens up when people are around.
		He has been feeling low on energy lately.
		He experiences bouts of weeping or tearfulness.
	Past history	He has no prior history of depression.
	Family history	His mother and brother had depression 3 years ago, which you treated. His mother's sister has bipolar disorder.
	Medical history	He has osteoarthritis of the lumbar spine, hyperlipidemia, and HBP. He takes atorvastatin 40 mg OD, and perindopril 8 mg OD.
	Caffeine intake	He drinks 2 cups of coffee first thing in the morning and 1 more in the late afternoon.
What additional tests would you request?	TSH	TSH is within normal limits.
	Liver function test	A liver function test alone is unlikely to help.
	Investigative workup as appropriate	Further investigation reveals no abnormalities.
What are the most likely differential diagnoses?	Alcohol use disorder	He reports minimal use of alcohol with his friends on the weekends, maybe 3–4 beers per week at most and has no history to suggest abuse.
	MDD	He only has 4 of the 9 criteria for depressive symptoms: a) pleasure loss, b) insomnia, d) agitation, e) loss of energy.
	Bipolar disorder	Information does not support bipolar disorder.
	Panic disorder	His panic attacks began during the stressful event and are likely a consequence of it. However, you are well aware that this is an important specifier as a prognostic factor and document this as a reminder to yourself to treat more aggressively should he not respond to initial treatment.
	Dysthymic disorder	He presents with mood reactivity, insomnia, anger, and irritability, which started after tensions began at work. He had no symptoms prior to that, so his condition is not consistent with dysthymia.

Screening for Anxiety and Related Disorders

You are considering an anxiety or related disorder, keeping in mind that depressive disorders are comorbid 60% of the time.

> » How do you screen for common anxiety and related disorders?
> » How do you screen for common comorbid mental disorders?
> » What is the provisional diagnosis?

TOOLS FOR ASSESSMENT

Refer to the "Provisional Diagnosis" section of Chapter 2, p. 17, for information on screening for anxiety and related disorders and comorbid conditions, or go directly to the Patient Self-Report Screening Tool for Mental Illnesses (Appendix VI, p. 161). Physicians can subsequently review responses with patients to verify accuracy.

You can also review the "Anxiety and Related Disorders: Types and Subtypes" section of Chapter 2, p. 17, which includes a useful tool to help differentiate anxiety disorders, or go directly to Differentiating Anxiety Disorders, Obsessive-Compulsive, and Trauma- and Stressor-Related Disorders (Appendix II, p. 156).

Provisional Diagnosis

Mr. CF provides the following answers to the questions in section 9 of the Patient Self-Report Screening Tool for Mental Illnesses (Appendix VI, p. 161), which supports your suspicion that Mr. CF may be suffering from an adjustment disorder:

Have you experienced a stressful event recently?	"Oh, yes, definitely. Troubles started at home and then also not long after at work. Come to think of it, I think my troubles with my wife were as a result of my work displeasure. I was taking it out on her."
Are you having trouble coping with the stressful situation?	"Yes. I can't relax, I cry, and I feel tense and worried."
Did the distress symptoms begin within 3 months of the stressful event?	"Yes, I know what I am feeling is due to the tension between me and my boss."
Have you been affected or unable to do the things you normally do in your professional, home, or social life due to your current emotional state?	"I suppose so. I am so worried this is controlling me and I don't know how to stop. I am also angry at my boss. I have always done a great job. This is the first time I am making mistakes. My boss should give me a break. I can't work, and I can't get along with my wife. I would say yes."

Based on his responses, you make a preliminary diagnosis of adjustment disorder:
- Emotional symptoms started within 3 months of the onset of the stressor, and he appears to be overwhelmed by symptoms that affect his functioning.
- Although Mr. CF has a depressed mood, he does not meet criteria for MDD.
- Panic attacks began during the stressful event and so are part of the adjustment disorder (specifier).
- There is no sign of alcohol abuse.

In this case, adjustment disorder is indicated.

CONFIRMING THE DIAGNOSIS

The next step is to confirm MR. CF's diagnosis.

The diagnosis of adjustment disorder can be confirmed by using the DSM-5 criteria for adjustment disorder[13] (see Appendix XXXII, p. 227).

> » What factors must you consider to confirm Mr. CF has adjustment disorder?
> » What instruments can be used to confirm the diagnosis?

Adjustment disorder self-report tools reflecting the new DSM-5 criteria require further studies on reliability and on other aspects of validity. The Diagnostic Interview Adjustment Disorder (DIAD) currently under development and validation to diagnose AD shows promise.[14] Until validated diagnostic tools are developed, AD diagnosis relies on medical skills, careful history taking, and clinical judgment. The Patient Self-Report Screening Tool for Mental Illnesses (Appendix VI, p. 161), although not validated, serves as a memory aid to recall diagnostic features and can be a useful screener to be reviewed against the DSM-5 criteria.

In Mr. CF's case, the DSM-5 supports your diagnosis of AD with mixed anxiety and depressed mood.

BASELINE ASSESSMENT

The next step is to conduct a baseline assessment. This will provide you and your patient with important information to tailor a treatment plan specific to your patient.

> » What should be included in a baseline assessment?
> » What tools are useful at baseline and follow-up visits?

Patient self-report tools are used in primary care for many medical conditions. These practical, time-efficient tools can be used in mental health assessments as well; however, responses should be interpreted by clinicians together with DSM-5 criteria and clinical judgment. A careful assessment and rating of each of the following parameters will also establish a baseline from which to measure treatment response:

- Safety (suicide) assessment
- Symptom or illness severity
- Comorbid conditions
- Somatic complaints; Symptom Assessment Checklist (Appendix VIII, p. 167)
- Functional impairment; Functional Impairment Assessment Scale (Appendix IX, p. 168)

Validated self-report assessment and monitoring tools specific to AD need more robust research supporting their use. However, studies are underway, and these tools will become available. For this reason, severity assessment in our patient case study will be based on clinical symptoms and functional capacity. As new information becomes available, this will be incorporated into future editions.

If your patient presents with a subtype (depressed mood, anxiety), administering an assessment scale specific to the subtype can help assess the severity and monitor clinical change over the course of treatment. Self-report scales such as the PHQ-9 (depressed mood, see Appendix VII, p. 165) and GAD-7 (anxiety, see Appendix V, p. 160) can be useful, time-efficient scales for this purpose.

You can also refer to the "Baseline Assessment" section of Chapter 2, p. 18.

Mr. CF's Baseline Assessment

Mr. CF completes the baseline assessment scales. The results are that he denies having suicidal thoughts. In this case, you choose to administer the GAD-7 as a severity assessment measure as the anxiety symptoms predominate the depressed mood. He scores 10 (mild) on the GAD-7. Although Mr. CF has a depressed mood, he does not meet the criteria for MDD. He has panic attacks, though they began during the stressful event and are therefore cued by the adjustment disorder.

In addition, on the Symptom Assessment Checklist, he rates the following: decreased interest in sex (2), insomnia (2), fatigue (2), and tenseness (3).

Functional capacity is also a good option for measuring illness severity. Despite presenting symptoms, Mr. CF's functioning is mildly affected; he rates functioning at work at 80% and home life at 70%. He tells you that his home life is not terribly affected other than he is unhappy in his marriage, which he feels is normal. "I think I am just in a rut," he tells you. He is not interested in sexual activities but is still able to perform.

With a diagnosis of adjustment disorder, anxiety, and depressed mood subtype, you tell Mr. CF, "This is a common problem when there is a conflict in the workplace and will often affect the relationship with the person's partner. We will work together to help you cope with the situation."

MANAGEMENT GUIDELINES

Now that you have confirmed the diagnosis of adjustment disorder and have a general idea of illness severity and how this affects Mr. CF, you begin to develop a care plan. Information collected to date will guide your management plan; however, the choice of treatment will depend on several factors, for example:[15, 16]

- Patient's opinions about treatment
- Receptivity to counseling
- Receptivity to medication
- Severity of symptoms
- Comorbidity
- Previous response (or lack of response) to treatment
- Availability of resources in the community

You can also refer to Chapter 3: Management, p. 25.

Studies are emerging on the optimal treatment for AD; however, recommendations are varied, and there is no consensus on how to best manage this disorder. Ideally, addressing the stressor early is key (e.g., marital counseling for marital difficulties, informal or formal conflict resolution for workplace conflict). However, this is not always possible or easy. In this case, non-pharmacological treatment is the primary intervention, in particular brief psychotherapy, unless the stressor is prolonged. Medications may not be appropriate unless AD is complicated by another disorder such as MDD. More studies are required to provide evidence surrounding the efficacy of medications in AD.

Self-Management Strategies

If available, patients can access community programs that offer self-management strategies, as well as online resources or self-help books to learn emotion- and problem-focused coping skills.[17] Emotion-focused coping strategies are useful when a person *does not have control* over the stressor. The goal is to maximize emotional self-regulation and avoid maladaptive coping measures.

Management strategies focus on the arousal caused by stress and try to reduce the negative emotional responses associated with it. Emotion-focused coping strategies may include the following:

- Keeping busy to take one's mind off the issue
- Venting
- Reaching for spiritual guidance and strength
- Distracting oneself (eating, watching TV)

Substance misuse—alcohol or drugs—is also an emotion-focused coping strategy, though a negative one.

Problem-focused coping strategies are useful when a person *has control* over the stressor. They target the root of the problem or the cause of stress. Individuals learn to tackle the stressful situation directly with the goal of reducing or eliminating it. Problem-focused coping strategies include

- Taking control—changing the relationship between the source of stress and the person by clarifying the meaning of the stressor for the patient (i.e., asking, "What does that mean for me? Is it really important to me?")
- Reframing the meaning of the stressor
- Understanding the stress—trying to understand the situation and making a conscious effort to prevent the situation from reoccurring or reducing the stressful situation
- Evaluating the pros and cons—weighing different options for dealing with a stressor and deciding if it can be eliminated or minimized (problem solving).

These strategies are more effective in the long run because the individual deals with the stressor head-on, working towards reducing or removing it.

Psychotherapy

Among non-pharmacological treatments, CBT is the first line of therapy—working with a psychotherapist to help reduce the significance of the stressor and learn coping strategies (emotion- and problem-focused strategies). Patients regain perspective on the stressor, establish support systems, and learn to manage the stressful situation better. The following approaches can also be helpful:

- Crisis intervention
- Family and group therapies

- Support groups specific to the stressor
- Interpersonal psychotherapy

Pharmacotherapy

More studies are required to evaluate the effectiveness of agents and additional novel treatments in treating adjustment disorder. If another comorbid psychiatric disorder is present, treat the disorder that predominates.

VISIT-BY-VISIT GUIDE: MILD ADJUSTMENT DISORDER

Having confirmed AD, with mixed anxiety and depressed mood, you address Mr. CF's sleep difficulties. You elect to avoid hypnotics for now, but maintain it as an option. You alert him to sleep hygiene techniques.

Your recommendation is to initiate a CBT self-management strategies program. Mr. CF tells you he is not interested in a self-management program. You also ask if there is some informal or formal resolution process at his workplace, and with his permission, send this recommendation to his supervisor. Because the AD may also be affecting his marriage, you advise him to seek marital counseling. However, he is not receptive to this option either at this time. Fortunately, Mr. CF is eager to manage the stressful situation better and strengthen his coping skills to feel better at his job, so he accepts the referral to a psychotherapist and is willing to participate in a conflict-resolution process.

> What treatment should you consider out of the choices provided below?
> » Self-management strategies program
> » CBT alone
> » Pharmacotherapy alone
> » CBT plus pharmacotherapy

You schedule an appointment in 2 weeks and ask him to complete the GAD-7 (Appendix V, p. 160), the Functional Impairment Assessment Scale (Appendix IX, p. 168), and the Symptom Assessment Checklist (Appendix VIII, p. 167) the night before the appointment.

After 2 weekly CBT sessions, Mr. CF improves slightly. The GAD-7 score remains unchanged at 10 (mild). You learn of an informal conflict-resolution meeting scheduled in 2 weeks with his supervisor, which he feels quite happy about. He is feeling less alone and is making an effort to rebuild his relationship with his wife. He is also sleeping a bit better. Finally, after 18 sessions of psychotherapy to build coping skills and family support, plus having worked out the issues between him and his boss, his symptoms subside altogether. You see him monthly at first, and then according to his needs.

VISIT-BY-VISIT GUIDE: MODERATE ADJUSTMENT DISORDER

First Visit Five months later, Mr. CF returns, having relapsed. He explains that tensions are mounting again at work. He admits to calling in sick intermittently. He asked for time off over the summer, but his boss refused, stating that there would be too many people off on vacation. This triggered an outburst in which Mr. CF told off his boss and walked out. He immediately comes to see you and says that his boss is hard on him; he feels targeted and is asked to perform many tasks above and beyond his mandate and what is asked of his colleagues. He left work angry and not sure if he is able to return at this point. He gets angry each time he thinks about going to work; he tells you that he feels the heat rising in his face and becomes very stressed out. "I am overwhelmed. I can't sleep at night. I think of facing my boss, and I get agitated and irritable."

You reassess comorbidity using the Patient Self-Report Screening Tool for Mental Illnesses (Appendix VI, p. 161) and administer the Functional Impairment Assessment Scale (Appendix IX, p. 168) and the Symptom Assessment Checklist (Appendix VIII, p. 167). Again, the screen is positive for AD and has now reached the threshold for comorbid clinical depression. Mr. CF is experiencing tenseness and panic attacks but does not meet the criteria for panic disorder. He denies having suicidal thoughts. He appears quite agitated in your office and becomes very emotional as he is describing the turn of events. Illness severity is assessed with the PHQ-9 (Appendix VII, p. 165) and the GAD-7 (Appendix V, p. 160), which yield scores of 7 and 15 respectively (mild depression, moderate anxiety severity).

Somatic complaints include reduced interest in sex (3), hypersomnia (2), fatigue (3), and tenseness (3). He rates his functional capacity at 50% in the social and family categories and has missed 10 intermittent days of work (about 50% of the time).

You consider the possible pharmacological therapies as the depressed mood has crossed the threshold to MDD and start sertraline 50 mg daily. You also strongly encourage him to attend booster sessions for CBT and, with his permission, provide a recommendation to his workplace to initiate a formal alternative dispute resolution (ADR) process for the escalating conflict between him and his supervisor. You also advise Mr. CF that the goal is to return to the workplace as soon as possible. "Is there an option to work temporarily under another supervisor in a different environment?" you ask. He replies that he is not sure, and once again with his permission, you provide this recommendation to his workplace.

Second Visit After 2 weeks of CBT and sertraline 50 mg daily, Mr. CF returns showing a partial response. He is feeling alone and starting to blame himself for his troubles. His sleep is now affected, and he wakes up in the middle of the night worried about all aspects of his life. The thought of returning to work is overwhelming.

Mr. CF's score on the GAD-7 is 14 (moderate), and his PHQ-9 score remains unchanged; he answers "sometimes" when asked if he thinks he'd be better off dead. However, he says he's convinced suicide is not an option. He's exhausted from thinking things through but can't seem to follow the sleep hygiene directions. He denies having other stressors. Working closely with his psychotherapist, you learn that he

- criticizes himself

- tries to keep his feelings inside

- doesn't stand his ground with his wife

- talked to someone about his situation (you)

- made a plan to enhance his problem-solving coping skills and follows it.

The psychotherapist is helping him focus on how he could change his communication and assertiveness with his boss. Total absence from the workplace raises concerns, however Human Resources (HR) is exploring the possibility of having him report to a different supervisor. You raise the sertraline dose to 100 mg daily and prescribe zopiclone 7.5 mg to help him sleep, hoping that helping Mr. CF sleep better will improve his problem-solving ability. He makes a plan to talk to his boss and to report back any examples of lack of assertiveness at the next visit.

Third Visit	The hypnotic was a "big help." Mr. CF plucked up the courage to talk to his boss, who was truly sorry for being a "big grump" and confided to him that he went through quite an adjustment period at work and personally since managing the unit. Mr. CF feels "a lot stronger" and feels he is "being a good husband and father" again. His GAD-7 score is down to 9, and he no longer feels that life is not worth living. He tells you, however, that he has no interest in sex and wishes to stop the sertraline. You show him the baseline data, telling him this symptom was present and rated as problematic before he started the drug. You both look at the Symptom Assessment Checklist (Appendix VIII, p. 167) he rated at baseline, where he rated 3 in the symptom box "Decreased interest in sex." He is surprised, but realizes suddenly that this is true, so he agrees to continue sertraline.
	The psychotherapist reports that he has been working on Mr. CF's lack of assertiveness with role-playing alternatives. Mr. CF agrees to continue the work at home, as well as keeping communication open with his wife. You offer to see his wife also, with him or without. You ask him to return in 2 weeks and refill the hypnotic for another 2 weeks, but tell him he can stop it sooner if he wishes.
	He is able to return to work, gradually increasing his tasks and number of hours to full capacity.
Fourth Visit	Mr. CF's wife, Joanne, comes in for a visit. You put her at ease by saying it must be difficult when Mr. CF returns from these long visits. She accepts your cue and talks about how angry it makes her feel when she returns from work "and it seems that he and Bill, their son, haven't even spoken all day." She acknowledges that he takes things out on her, knowing that she is sensitive to criticism.
	Mr. CF has shown his wife the work he and the psychotherapist have done together, and she has identified for herself that she is self-critical and does not talk about her feelings. "If we can sort this out, Doctor," she says, "it will help us." She and Mr. CF are now receptive to marital counseling, which you arrange. She denies having any other concerns.
Fifth Visit	Mr. CF comes in with Joanne. They're pleased with their progress and feel they can manage alone from here. Mr. CF's GAD-7, PHQ-9, and Functional Impairment Assessment Scale scores are consistent with remission. He stopped the hypnotic and is sleeping fine. You ask him to return in 2 weeks for a last visit and congratulate them on their problem solving.
Sixth Visit	Mr. CF returns. He continues to "do better than he ever did before." You review with him the usual assessment scales he has completed in the waiting room. You note that he continues to practice the effective coping techniques. You caution him to continue practicing the good sleep hygiene techniques to promote good mental health. The goal is to withdraw the sertraline after 6 months of full remission of illness.
Maintenance Visits	Mr. CF is advised that the next visit will be scheduled in 6 months to withdraw the sertraline.

VISIT-BY-VISIT GUIDE: SEVERE ADJUSTMENT DISORDER

First Visit	Unfortunately, Mr. CF's positive dynamics with his boss were short-lived. Five months after remission, Mr. CF has a setback. In addition to all his previous symptoms, he now • avoids people at work altogether • completely withdraws from his friends • cannot have professional interaction with his boss • lashes out in anger at his wife and co-workers. His GAD-7 score has risen to 20 (severe), and the PHQ-9 confirms a comorbid MDD (score 25; severe). On the Functional Impairment Assessment Scale, he has not been at work for the past 3 days, which you support with a medical leave from work until the situation is sorted out. You consider adding mirtazapine starting at 15 mg daily to be increased to 30 mg daily in 1 week. You feel that Mr. CF is getting quite discouraged, and your gut feeling is that that you need to maintain his gains at all cost. You felt that mirtazapine was a good option as he did report problematic low interest in intercourse, and studies show that mirtazapine has a lower incidence of sexual dysfunction side effects. You expect that, given his irritability, Mr. CF would benefit from booster sessions of psychotherapeutic intervention. You schedule an appointment for 2 weeks later and ask him to complete the GAD-7 as your chosen severity assessment tool (anxiety symptoms predominate), the Functional Impairment Assessment Scale (Appendix IX, p. 168), and the Symptom Assessment Checklist (Appendix VIII, p. 167) the night before the appointment.
Subsequent Visits	When he returns, his side effects are minimal, and he has responded partially. An alternative dispute resolution process had already been initiated by Human Resources at work. He reports that he now sees things differently and has realized that he contributed to the stress and problems in the workplace as well. He is working very hard to change this. On the Functional Impairment Assessment Scale, you notice he is back at work and his relationship with his wife has improved; his functionality score is 80% (moderate). Given the severity of his symptoms, you plan to monitor Mr. CF more closely. Fortunately, he responds after 10 weeks.
Maintenance Visits	Given the extreme severity of anxiety from the adjustment disorder, resulting in secondary MDD, you decide to continue pharmacotherapy for 1 year, reassessing him at least every 2 months and subsequently once a year. You also encourage him to practice the coping strategies he learned, while scheduling booster sessions as needed.

Note: In this case, AD did result in secondary comorbid depression, for which Mr. CF was treated. The situation or its consequences, if addressed early in the course of treatment, have higher odds of resolution, and if so, the symptoms would not persist for more than an additional 6 months once the stressor or its consequences have terminated (DSM-5 criteria).

SUMMARY
You have completed a case study illustrating the screening, diagnosis, treatment, and management of AD. This case study is only a guide. Decision making should be individualized and based on clinical judgment.

There are no accepted standards for treatment guidelines. The guidelines here should be used in conjunction with your own clinical judgment.

AD KEY POINTS

- AD is under-researched but frequently seen in family practice.
- The patient's distress exceeds what the stressor should cause and includes problems in functioning in important areas of the individual's life (work, education, home, socially).
- If secondary or comorbid MDD develops (i.e., DSM-5 criteria are met), treat for MDD, whether or not stressors are present; the same applies for secondary (or comorbid) anxiety disorder.
- Psychotherapy can help prevent further progression of symptoms and dysfunction.
- Conflict in the workplace is a common presentation in primary care; collaborate with the workplace (HR and other) to explore informal or formal conflict resolution processes.

NOTES

1 Schnyder U, Valach L. Suicide attempters in a psychiatric emergency room population. Gen Hosp Psychiatry. 1997; 19(2):119–129.

2 Fernández A, Mendive J, Salvador-Carulla L, Rubio-Valera M, Luciano J, Pinto-Meza A, et al. Adjustment disorders in primary care: prevalence, recognition and use of services. Br J Psychiatry. 2012; 201:137–142.

3 Armed Forces Health Surveillance Center (AFHSC). Summary of mental disorders hospitalizations, active and reserve components, U.S. Armed Forces, 2000–2012. MSMR. 2013 Jul; 20(7):4–11.

4 American Psychiatric Association. Diagnostic and statistical manual of mental disorders (DSM-5). 5th ed. Arlington, VA: American Psychiatric Association; 2013.

5 Casey P, Bailey S. Adjustment disorders: the state of the art. World Psychiatry. 2001; 10(1):11–18.

6 Grassi L, Mangelli L, Fava GA, Grandi S, Ottolini F, Porcelli P, et al. Psychosomatic characterization of adjustment disorders in the medical setting: some suggestions for DSM-V. J Affect Disord. 2007; 101(1):251–254.

7 Carta M, Balestrieri M, Murru A, Hardoy M. Adjustment disorder: epidemiology, diagnosis and treatment. Clin Prac Epidemiol Ment Health. 2009 Jun 26; 5:15.

8 Fernández A, Mendive J, Salvador-Carulla L, Rubio-Valera M, Luciano J, Pinto-Meza A, et al. Adjustment disorders in primary care: prevalence, recognition and use of services. Br J Psychiatry. 2012; 201:137–142.

9 American Psychiatric Association. Diagnostic and statistical manual of mental disorders (DSM-5). 5th ed. Arlington, VA: American Psychiatric Association; 2013.

10 Casey P. Adjustment disorder: epidemiology, diagnosis and treatment. CNS Drugs 2009; 23(11):927–938.

11 Carta M, Balestrieri M, Murru A, Hardoy M. Adjustment disorder: epidemiology, diagnosis and treatment. Clin Prac Epidemiol Ment Health. 2009 Jun 26; 5:15.

12 Fernández A, Mendive J, Salvador-Carulla L, Rubio-Valera M, Luciano J, Pinto-Meza A, et al. Adjustment disorders in primary care: prevalence, recognition and use of services. Br J Psychiatry. 2012; 201:137–142.

13 American Psychiatric Association. Diagnostic and statistical manual of mental disorders (DSM-5). 5th ed. Arlington, VA: American Psychiatric Association; 2013.

14 Cornelius L, Brouwer S, Boer M, Groothoff J, Klink J. Development and validation of the Diagnostic Interview Adjustment Disorder (DIAD). Int J Methods Psychiatr Res. 2014; 23(2):192–207.

15 Evans M, Bradwejn J, Dunn L, editors. Ontario guidelines for the management of anxiety disorders in primary care. 1st ed. Toronto: Queen's Printer of Ontario; 2000.

16 Kennedy SH, Lam RW, Parikh SV, Patten SB, Ravindran AV. Canadian Network for Mood and Anxiety Treatments (CANMAT) clinical guidelines for the management of major depressive disorder in adults. J Affect Disord. 2009; 117 Suppl 1:S1–S2.

17 TruReach Health [Internet]. [Place unknown]: TruReach Health; 2015 [cited 2015 October 30]. Available from: http://www.trureachhealth.com/

Appendices

Appendix I

Factors to Consider When Assessing Anxiety Symptoms

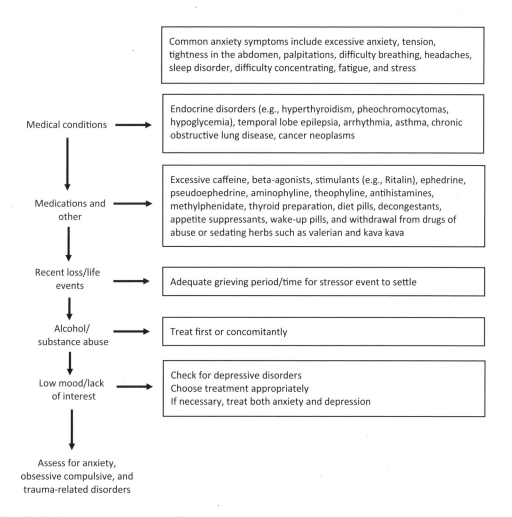

Note: This list is indicative, but not exhaustive.

Appendix II

Differentiating Anxiety, Obsessive-Compulsive, and Trauma- and Stressor-Related Disorders

Note to providers: *A print-ready version of this tool is available on the CD included with this book and downloadable from www.brusheducation.ca/toolkit.*

Note: *Panic attacks that are cued by any anxiety or related disorder would be a specifier of the disorder (as opposed to a hallmark feature in panic disorder).*

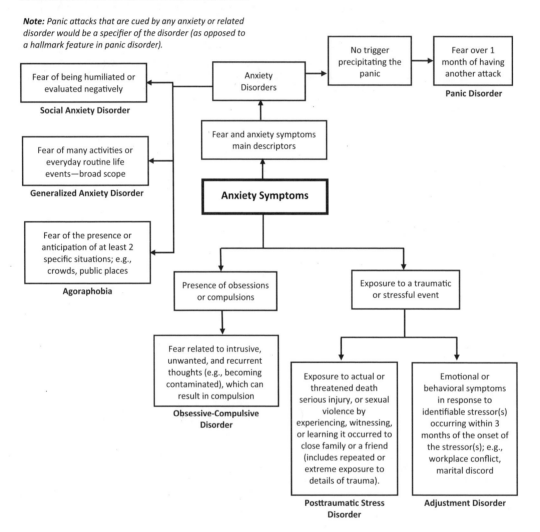

Note: *Only the disorders included in this manual are listed. Each DSM-5 chapter includes additional conditions. For a complete list, refer to the DSM-5. American Psychiatric Association. Diagnostic and Statistical Manual of Mental Disorders (DSM-5). 5th ed. Arlington, VA: American Psychiatric Association; 2013.*

Appendix III

Suicide Assessment Questionnaire

Note to providers: *A print-ready version of this tool is available on the CD included with this book and downloadable from www.brusheducation.ca/toolkit.*

In the past month did you . . .			Points
Think that you would be better off dead or wish you were dead?	No	Yes	1
Want to harm yourself?	No	Yes	2
Think about suicide?	No	Yes	6
Have a suicide plan?	No	Yes	10
Attempt suicide?	No	Yes	10
In your lifetime did you . . .			
Ever make a suicide attempt?	No	Yes	4
		Total:	

Total the points for all Yes answers.

- Low suicide risk = 5 points or less
- Moderate suicide risk = 6–9 points
- High suicide risk = 10 points or more

There are no validated suicide risk assessment tools to date. The risk scores, including low risk, are to be interpreted in conjunction with clinical judgment. If the answer to the question "Are you thinking about killing yourself" is yes, and the person has a plan, take the person seriously and ensure their safety immediately.

Appendix IV

Suicide Risk Factors Summary

Note to providers: *A print-ready version of this tool is available on the CD included with this book and downloadable from www.brusheducation.ca/toolkit.*

PERSONAL FACTORS	SYMPTOMS	CLINICAL PRESENTATION
Male gender	Depression	Recent use of substances
Past suicide attempt	Feelings of hopelessness	Suicidal ideation
Youth (age 15–35) and the elderly (age >65)	Feelings of worthlessness	Suicidal intent
Family history of suicide	Anhedonia (inability to experience pleasure)	Suicidal plan
		Access to a lethal means
Psychiatric illness	Severe anxiety/panic attacks	Past suicidal behavior
Chronic medical illness	Agitation, anger, impulsivity	
Substance use disorder	Psychosis (particularly dangerous command hallucinations)	Current situation, circumstance, or problem seems unsolvable
Poor social supports, isolation, problematic environment		Severe socio-cultural-familial stress, perceived or threatened interpersonal loss or humiliation
Abuse: psychological, sexual, physical, emotional		

Note to providers: *Indicate risk factors followed by patient's description of risk factors.*

	YES	NO
Male gender		
Past suicide attempt		
Youth (age 15–35) and elderly (age >65)		
Family history of suicide		
Psychiatric illness		
Chronic medical illness		
Substance use disorder		
Poor social supports, isolation, problematic environment		
Abuse: psychological, sexual, physical, emotional		
Depression		
Feelings of hopelessness		
Feelings of worthlessness		

	YES	NO
Severe anxiety, panic attacks		
Agitation, anger, impulsivity		
Anhedonia (inability to experience pleasure)		
Psychosis (particularly dangerous command hallucinations)		
Recent use of substances		
Suicidal ideation		
Suicidal intent		
Suicidal plan		
Access to a lethal means		
Past suicidal behavior		
Current situation, circumstance, or problem seems unsolvable		
Severe socio-cultural-familial stress, perceived or threatened interpersonal loss or humiliation		

Notes:

_____

_____

_____

_____

_____

_____

_____

_____

_____

_____

_____

_____

_____

_____

_____

_____

_____

_____

_____

_____

_____

_____

Appendix V

GAD-7*

Note to providers: *The print-ready version of this tool on the CD included with this book and downloadable from www.brusheducation.ca/toolkit includes scoring instructions and assessment scales on separate pages. You can quickly refer to the scoring legend while minimizing patient response biases induced by seeing the scoring information.*

GAD-7				
OVER THE LAST 2 WEEKS, HOW OFTEN HAVE YOU BEEN BOTHERED BY THE FOLLOWING PROBLEMS? *(USE A "✔" TO INDICATE YOUR ANSWER)*	NOT AT ALL	SEVERAL DAYS	MORE THAN HALF THE DAYS	NEARLY EVERY DAY
1. Feeling nervous, anxious, or on edge	0	1	2	3
2. Not being able to stop or control worrying	0	1	2	3
3. Worrying too much about different things	0	1	2	3
4. Trouble relaxing	0	1	2	3
5. Being so restless that it is hard to sit still	0	1	2	3
6. Becoming easily annoyed or irritable	0	1	2	3
7. Feeling afraid as if something awful might happen	0	1	2	3
Add the score for each column	0	+	+	+

Total Score

If you checked off any problems, how difficult have these made it for you to do your work, take care of things at home, or get along with other people?

Not difficult at all _____

Somewhat difficult _____

Very difficult _____

Extremely difficult _____

Scoring

0–4 no anxiety/remission

5–9 mild anxiety

10–14 moderate anxiety

>15 severe anxiety

*Developed by Drs. Robert L. Spitzer, Janet B.W. Williams, Kurt Kroenke and colleagues, with an educational grant from Pfizer Inc.[1]

Appendix VI

Patient Self-Report Screening Tool for Mental Illnesses

Note to providers: *A print-ready version of this tool is available on the CD included with this book and downloadable from www.brusheducation.ca/toolkit.*

Patient's Name: _____ Birthdate: _____

Questionnaire Date: _____

The following questions are meant as screening questions only. A positive answer does not confirm a diagnosis. Your physician will be conducting a more in-depth assessment; this screening tool is solely meant to help your physician focus on the most distressing symptoms.

DISORDER	QUESTION	YES	NO
1. Depression	Have you felt "down," most of the day, nearly every day, for the past 2 weeks?		
	In the past 2 weeks, have you been less interested in most things or less able to enjoy the things you used to enjoy most of the time?		
	Do you have low self-esteem or feelings of guilt?		
	In the past month, did you think that you would be better off dead or wished you were dead?		
2. Generalized Anxiety Disorder	Have you worried excessively, or been anxious, about several things with regard to day-to-day life while at work, at home, or in your close circle, which is out of proportion considering your life circumstances for at least the last 6 months?		
	(If you answered "Yes," tell your health care provider what you worry about.)		
	Are you by nature a worrier or is this new for you?		
	Do you think you worry more than most other people?		
	Have you been unable to stop or control your worrying, or to let go of your worries, holding them inside?		
	In the last 6 months, have you been feeling physically unwell because of your worrying (feeling exhausted, having problems sleeping, getting headaches, having trouble focusing, having sore muscles)?		
	Do your worries get in the way of your day-to-day life at home, work, or when you are with friends?		
	On a scale of 0 to 10, how problematic is this for you?		

DISORDER	QUESTION	YES	NO
3. Panic Attacks	Have you had an unprovoked ("out of the blue") attack or spell during which you suddenly felt anxious, frightened, uncomfortable, or uneasy, even in situations in which most people would not feel this way?		
	Are the attacks of fear or panic so intense you had to do something to stop them or were so physically distressing you thought you might collapse or die?		
	Do these attacks peak quickly within minutes?		
	If you answered "Yes," describe to your health care provider what happens when you get these attacks.		
	Do you experience at least 4 of the following: palpitations, chest pains, chills, sweating, dizziness, hot flashes, or difficulty breathing during these spells?		
	How often do you get these attacks?		
4. Panic Disorder	After an attack, do you worry for at least 1 month about having another attack?		
	Are the attacks brought on by any triggers; for example, social situations?		
	Does this fear of having attacks prevent you from doing certain things or interfere with your life; for example, do you avoid the "panic" triggers (going to the mall or crowded places)?		
5. Agoraphobia	Do you feel anxious or particularly uneasy in places or situations from which you might find it difficult to leave or escape and where help might not be available (e.g., in a crowd, standing in line, when you are alone away from home or alone at home, or when crossing a bridge in a bus, train, or car)?		
	Do you fear these situations so much that you avoid them, suffer through them, or need a companion to face them?		
	Has this lasted more than 6 months for most days?		
	Is the anxiety out of proportion to the actual danger or threat in the situation?		
6. Social Anxiety Disorder	Do unfamiliar social situations cause you to feel anxious, distressed, or panicky?		
	Are you fearful of being humiliated or embarrassed in social situations or when you are "performing," such as speaking in public, being watched, or eating?		
	Are you uncomfortable or embarrassed at being the center of attention?		
	Do you blush, sweat, and/or tremble when speaking in public or in social situations such as eating or writing?		

DISORDER	QUESTION	YES	NO
	What types of social situations make you feel anxious or panicky (e.g., giving a speech, introducing yourself, talking in a group, eating in public, walking into a gathering of unfamiliar people, someone watching you do things such as writing)?		
	Are there things you avoid or activities that you cannot or will not do because of your worries or your fears?		
7. Obsessive-Compulsive Disorder	Are you experiencing intrusive or repetitive thoughts, images, or urges that you cannot stop; for example, thoughts of dirt, germs, or violent or disturbing sexual thoughts?		
	Do these thoughts cause you to do things repeatedly or compulsively, such as excessive washing or checking something until it feels right?		
	Do you believe that this will actually happen (e.g., if you do not keep washing your hands repeatedly, you will be full of germs, or your hands will not be clean)?		
	Do these thoughts interfere with your normal routine at home, work, school, or socially?		
8. Posttraumatic Stress Disorder	Have you experienced, witnessed, or had to deal with an extremely traumatic event that included actual or threatened death or serious injury to you or someone else?		
	Are you having anxiety symptoms related to a past traumatic event?		
	Are you having recurrent recollections of the events; for example, memories, flashbacks, or dreams?		
	Are you re-experiencing the event in a distressing way (such as nightmares, intense recollections, or physical reactions and reminders of trauma)?		
	Do you avoid stimuli associated with the trauma (e.g., memories, places)?		
	Do you feel emotionally numb, feel emotionally detached from your loved ones, or have you lost interest in activities you used to enjoy?		
	Have you been jumpy or agitated?		
	Does this interfere with your life?		
9. Adjustment Disorder	Have you experienced a stressful event recently?		
	Are you having trouble coping with the stressful situation?		
	Did the distress symptoms begin within 3 months of the stressful event?		
	Have you been affected or unable to do the things you normally do in your professional, home, or social life due to your current emotional state?		

DISORDER	QUESTION	YES	NO
10. Substance Use Disorder	In the past 12 months, have you had 3 or more alcoholic drinks within a 3-hour period on 3 or more occasions?		
	In the past 12 months, have you taken non-prescribed medication or street drugs?		
11. Bipolar Disorder	In the past month, have you		
	– felt high or had a "big" mood or irritability?		
	– been more confident?		
	– had more energy or sex drive?		
	– needed less sleep?		
12. Psychosis	Have you ever heard voices that no one else can hear?		
	Have you ever seen things or people that no one else can see, or they say that nothing is there?		
	Do you feel that people are watching or trying to harm you?		

For each section in which you answered "Yes" to any of the questions, indicate for how many years you have been bothered by these symptoms in the table that follows.

SECTION	NUMBER OF YEARS	APPROXIMATE YEAR SYMPTOMS STARTED	HOW PROBLEMATIC IS THIS FOR YOU? INSERT ✔ IF SYMPTOMS INTERFERE WITH YOUR DAY-TO-DAY FUNCTIONS AT		
			HOME	WORK	SOCIAL LIFE
1.					
2.					
3.					
4.					
5.					
6.					
7.					
8.					
9.					
10.					
11.					
12.					

Appendix VII

*Patient Health Questionnaire-9 (PHQ-9)**

Note to providers: *The print-ready version of this tool on the CD included with this book and downloadable from www.brusheducation.ca/toolkit includes scoring instructions and assessment scales on separate pages. You can quickly refer to the scoring legend while minimizing patient response biases induced by seeing the scoring information.*

Over the **last 2 weeks**, how often have you been bothered by any of the following problems? Use ✔ to indicate your answers.

	NOT AT ALL	SEVERAL DAYS	MORE THAN HALF THE DAYS	NEARLY EVERY DAY
1. Little interest or pleasure in doing things	0	1	2	3
2. Feeling down, depressed, or hopeless	0	1	2	3
3. Trouble falling or staying asleep, or sleeping too much	0	1	2	3
4. Feeling tired or having little energy	0	1	2	3
5. Poor appetite or overeating	0	1	2	3
6. Feeling bad about yourself or that you are a failure or have let yourself or your family down	0	1	2	3
7. Trouble concentrating on things, such as reading the newspaper or watching television	0	1	2	3
8. Moving or speaking so slowly that other people could have noticed. Or the opposite— being so fidgety or restless that you have been moving around a lot more than usual	0	1	2	3
9. Thoughts that you would be better off dead or of hurting yourself in some way	0	1	2	3

FOR OFFICE CODING   0   + _____   + _____   + _____

= Total Score: _____

10. If you checked off **any** problems, how **difficult** have these problems made it for you to do your work, take care of things at home, or get along with other people?

Not difficult at all	Somewhat difficult	Very difficult	Extremely difficult
☐	☐	☐	☐

*Developed by Drs. Robert L. Spitzer, Janet B.W. Williams, Kurt Kroenke, and colleagues, with an educational grant from Pfizer Inc.[1]

SCORING LEGEND

Major depressive disorder is suggested if:

1. Question 1 or 2: Need 1 or both of the first 2 questions endorsed as 2 = "More than half the days" or 3 = "Nearly every day"
2. Need a total of 5 or more of the 9 items endorsed within the shaded area of the form (questions 1–8 must be endorsed as a 2 or a 3; question 9 must be endorsed as a 1, a 2, or a 3)
3. Question 10 must be endorsed as "Somewhat difficult," "Very difficult," or "Extremely difficult"

USE OF THE PHQ-9 TO ASSESS SEVERITY AND MONITOR TREATMENT:

Add the total score. The scoring interpretation is as follows:

0–4 = not depressed

5–9 = mild depression

10–14 = moderate depression

15–19 = moderate-severe depression

20–27 = severe depression

Appendix VIII

Symptom Assessment Checklist

Note to providers: *A print-ready version of this tool is available on the CD included with this book and downloadable from www.brusheducation.ca/toolkit.*

SYMPTOM ASSESSMENT FOR PATIENTS—RATE SYMPTOM(S)* OVER THE PAST WEEK:

* Symptom Rating:

0 = Absent

1 = Present/not problematic

2 = Problematic/no impairment

3 = Problematic/with impairment

SYMPTOM	0	1	2	3	SYMPTOM	0	1	2	3	SYMPTOM	0	1	2	3
Headache					Confusion/ reduced or lack of concentration					Constipation				
Drowsiness					Blurred vision					Urination problems				
Weak/tired					Dry mouth					Sleep problems				
Sweating					Nervous/tense					Dizziness				
Nausea					Skin rash					Decreased interest in sex				
Weight gain					Diarrhea					Erectile problems				
Acne					Stomach pain					Absent or delayed orgasm/ejaculation				
Unsteadiness					Other:									

NOTES:

Appendix IX

Functional Impairment Assessment Scale

Note to providers: *A print-ready version of this tool is available on the CD included with this book and downloadable from www.brusheducation.ca/toolkit.*

Patient Name: _____

What best describes your situation now?
Your anxiety symptoms need to be the factor interfering with your daily functioning. Do not score high simply because you have not been in the situation. Try to imagine yourself in the situation and see if the anxiety would interfere with work, social life, and so on.

Work

During the past week, how many days of work have you lost due to your mood problem? _____

During the past week, how would you rate your ability, on a scale of 0–100, to work to your potential?

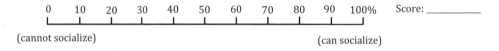

(cannot work)   (can work to full potential)

Social Life/Leisure Activities
During the past week, how would you rate your ability, on a scale of 0–100, to socialize with other people at parties, socializing, visiting, dating, outings, clubs, entertaining?

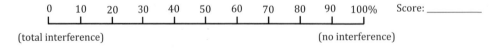

(cannot socialize)   (can socialize)

Family Life/Home Responsibilities
During the past week, how would you rate your ability, on a scale of 0–100, to relate to your home responsibilities (family members, paying bills, managing home, shopping, and cleaning)?

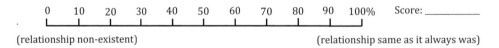

(total interference)   (no interference)

Relationship with Spouse/Partner
During the past week, how would you rate your relationship, on a scale of 0–100, with your partner/spouse?

(relationship non-existent)   (relationship same as it always was)

Assessment Scoring

Providers can use this tool to monitor specific areas of daily functioning affected by the disorders. Providers can also monitor overall functioning. To obtain an overall functioning score, total the scores in all four domains. Improvements in dysfunction caused by disorders will be reflected by increasing total scores. There are no cut-off scores.

Appendix X

Pharmacological Therapies
Disclaimer: This information is believed to be reliable and generally in accord with the accepted standards at the time of its publication. Due to the possibility of human error and changes in medical sciences, use this information as a guide in conjunction with product monographs to be updated continuously as new information becomes available.

ANTIDEPRESSANT GENERIC OPTION	TYPICAL EFFECTIVE DOSE (MG/D)*	MAXIMUM DOSE (MG/D)*	INITIAL SUGGESTED DOSE**	TITRATION SCHEDULE*	ADVANTAGES	DISADVANTAGES
Selective Serotonin Reuptake Inhibitors (SSRIs)						
Citalopram	20–40	40 (20 in patients >60 years old)	20 mg in a.m. w/food (10 mg in elderly, those w/sensitivity to drug or those w/panic disorder)	Maintain initial dose as per treatment guide before dose increase. If no response, increase in 10 mg increments q 7 days as tolerated.		
Escitalopram	10–20	20	10 mg	Maintain initial dose as per treatment guide before dose increase. If no response, increase in 5–10 mg increments q 7 days as tolerated.	More potent s-enantiomer of citalopram, 10 mg dose effective for most. FDA approved for GAD.	More expensive than citalopram.
Fluoxetine	20–60	80	20 mg in the a.m. w/food (10 mg in elderly, those w/sensitivity to drug, or those w/comorbid panic disorder)	Maintain initial dose as per treatment guide. Increase in 10 mg increments at 7-day intervals. If significant side effects occur w/in 7 days, lower dose or change med.	Effective in most anxiety and related disorders. Long half-life good for poor adherence, missed doses; less frequent discontinuation syndrome. Reduces all 3 symptom groups of PTSD (studies done as per DSM-IV criteria; dissociative reactions and avoidance were combined in DSM-IV).	Slower to reach steady state and eliminate when discontinued. Sometimes too stimulating. Active metabolite half-life ~10 days, renal elimination. Inhibits cytochrome P450 2D6 and 3A4. Use cautiously in elderly and patients on multiple meds.

ANTIDEPRESSANT GENERIC OPTION	TYPICAL EFFECTIVE DOSE (MG/D)*	MAXIMUM DOSE (MG/D)*	INITIAL SUGGESTED DOSE**	TITRATION SCHEDULE*	ADVANTAGES	DISADVANTAGES
Paroxetine	20–50 (20–40 in elderly)	60	20 mg once daily, usually in the a.m. w/food (10 mg in elderly, those w/ sensitivity to drug, or those w/comorbid panic disorder)	Maintain initial dose as per treatment guide before dose increase. Increase in 10 mg increments at intervals of ~7 days up to maximum dose of 60 mg/day (40 mg in elderly).	FDA labeling for most anxiety and related disorders. Reduces all 3 symptom groups of PTSD (studies done as per DSM-IV criteria; dissociative reactions and avoidance were combined in DSM-IV).	Sometimes sedating. Anticholinergic effects can be troublesome. Inhibitor of CYP2D6.
Paroxetine CR	25–62.5 (25–50 in elderly)	75	25 mg daily (12.5 mg in elderly, those w/sensitivity to drug, or those w/panic disorder)	Maintain at initial dose for suggested number of weeks as per treatment guide before dose increase. Increase by 12.5 mg at weekly intervals.	May cause less nausea and GI distress.	More expensive than paroxetine.
Sertraline	50–200	200	50 mg once daily, usually in the a.m. w/food (25 mg for elderly or those w/sensitivity to drug)	Maintain initial dose as per treatment guide before dose increase. Increase in 25–50 mg increments at 7-day intervals as tolerated.	FDA labeling for anxiety and related disorders including PTSD. Safety shown post-MI.	Weak inhibitor of CYP2D6. Drug interactions less likely.
Fluvoxamine	100–300	300	50 mg/day (25 mg/day for elderly or those w/sensitivity to drug)	Maintain initial dose as per treatment guide before dose increase. Increase every 5–7 days by 50 mg/day as tolerated.		Side effects may hinder rapid dose escalation.

Drug	Dose range	Max dose	Initial dose	Titration		
Fluvoxamine CR	100–300	300	100 mg at bedtime	Maintain initial dose as per treatment guide before dose increase. Increase every 7 days by 50 mg/day as tolerated.	Studies show consistently earlier onset of action than other SSRIs. Allows more aggressive dose titration.	
Noradrenergic and Specific Serotonergic Antidepressants (NaSSAs)						
Mirtazapine	15–45	45	15 mg at bedtime	Maintain initial dose as per treatment guide before dose increase. Increase in 15 mg increments (7.5 mg in elderly) as tolerated.	Few drug interactions. Less sedation as dose increases. May stimulate appetite.	Sedation at low doses only (<15 mg). Weight gain due to appetite stimulation.
Norepinephrine and Dopamine Reuptake Inhibitors						
Bupropion	200–300	450	100 mg twice a day (100 mg once a day in elderly)	Maintain initial dose as per treatment guide before dose increase. Increase to 100 mg TID as tolerated. Increase to maximum 150 mg TID.	Can be stimulating. Less or no sexual dysfunction. Does not appear to cause weight gain.	Contraindicated in patients w/seizures, CNS lesions, recent head trauma, or eating disorder. Stimulating effect can increase anxiety/insomnia.

ANTIDEPRESSANT GENERIC OPTION	TYPICAL EFFECTIVE DOSE (MG/D)*	MAXIMUM DOSE (MG/D)*	INITIAL SUGGESTED DOSE**	TITRATION SCHEDULE*	ADVANTAGES	DISADVANTAGES
Bupropion SR	200–400	400	150 mg once a day (100 mg in elderly)	Maintain initial dose as per treatment guide before dose increase. Increase to 150 mg BID (100 BID in elderly). Increase to a maximum of 200 mg BID (150 BID in elderly).	Dose slowly released in 12 hours. Also indicated for smoking cessation (Zyban). Does not appear to cause weight gain.	Interval of at least 8 hours between successive doses. Do not split or crush SR products.
Bupropion XL	300–450	450	150 mg once daily (in the morning)	Maintain initial dose as per treatment guide before dose increase. Increase to 300 mg daily. Increase to maximum 450 mg once daily.	Dose released for period of 24 hours. Less or no sexual dysfunction. Does not appear to cause weight gain.	Contraindicated in patients w/seizures, CNS lesions, recent head trauma, or eating disorder. Can cause insomnia. Do not split or crush XL products.
Serotonin and Norepinephrine Reuptake Inhibitors						
Venlafaxine Venlafaxine XR	75–225	225	75 mg w/food; 37.5 mg if anxious, elderly, panic disorder.	IR: divide dose BID or TID. XR: once daily.	Helpful also for neuropathic pain and vasomotor symptoms.	May increase BP at higher doses. Greater cardiotoxicity. Risk for drug interactions similar to fluoxetine.

				If initial dose is 37.5 mg, consider increase to 75 mg in 4–7 days as tolerated. Maintain dose as per treatment guide before dose increase. Increase no sooner than q 4 days by 75 mg to maximum dose of 225 mg.	
Desvenlafaxine	50	50	50 mg once daily	No evidence that higher doses are associated w/greater effect. Some experts suggest that should it be considered necessary, an escalation to 100 mg/day can be tried.[2]	Active metabolite of venlafaxine.
Duloxetine	30–120	120	60 mg as a single or divided doses (30–60 mg in elderly)	Dose can be increased after 1 week. Maximum dose 120 mg/day, although doses >60 mg/day not more effective in studies.	Also approved for pain from diabetic neuropathy and fibromyalgia. May increase BP at higher doses. Greater cardiotoxicity.

ANTIDEPRESSANT GENERIC OPTION	TYPICAL EFFECTIVE DOSE (MG/D)*	MAXIMUM DOSE (MG/D)*	INITIAL SUGGESTED DOSE**	TITRATION SCHEDULE*	ADVANTAGES	DISADVANTAGES
Milnacipran	12.5–100	200	12.5 mg	Increase to 12.5 mg twice daily in 2–3 days, then to 50 mg twice daily q 7 days as tolerated. Maintain dose as per treatment guide before dose increase. Increase to maximum 200 mg in divided doses (BID).	Also effective in fibromyalgia.	May increase BP at higher doses. Greater cardiotoxicity.
Serotonin Antagonist and Reuptake Inhibitors						
Trazadone	50–150	400	25–50 mg HS	Increase initial dose to 150 mg/d as tolerated in divided doses (TID). Maintain 150 mg as per treatment guide before dose increase. Increase in 50 mg increments at 4–7-day intervals as tolerated to maximum dose.	Can be helpful for insomnia.	
Norepinephrine Reuptake Inhibitors						
Atomoxetine	40–100	100	40 (can be OD or divided dose (BID)	Initial dose can be increased after ≥3 days to 80 mg PO OD or in divided doses BID.	Effective for comorbid ADHD.	May only be effective in social anxiety disorder.

May be increased to 100 mg if optimal response is not achieved.

Tricyclic Antidepressants: Secondary Amines					
Desipramine	100–200 (25–100 in elderly)	300	25–50 mg in a.m. (10 or 25 mg in elderly)	Increase in 25 to 50 mg increments q 3–7 days to initial target dose of 150 mg (75 or 100 mg in elderly). Target serum concentration: 115–300 ng/mL. Maintain 150 mg as per treatment guide before dose increase. Increase in 25–50 mg increments at 4–7-day intervals as tolerated to maximum dose.	More effect on norepinephrine than serotonin. Effective for diabetic neuropathy and neuropathic pain. Compliance and effective dose can be verified by serum concentration.	May not be helpful for anticipatory anxiety. Can be stimulating, but sedating in some patients. Anticholinergic, cardiac, hypotensive; caution in patients w/BPH, cardiac conduction disorder, or CHF.
Nortriptyline	50–150	150	25 mg in p.m. (10 mg in elderly)	Increase initial dose in 10–25 mg increments every 5–7 days as tolerated to initial target dose of 75 mg/day. Obtain serum concentration after 4 wks; target range: 50–150 ng/mL.	Less jitteriness than imipramine. Less orthostatic hypotension than other tricyclics. Compliance and effective dose can be verified by serum concentration.	May not be helpful for anticipatory anxiety. Anticholinergic, cardiac, and hypotensive; caution in patients w/BPH, cardiac conduction disorder, or CHF.

ANTIDEPRESSANT GENERIC OPTION	TYPICAL EFFECTIVE DOSE (MG/D)*	MAXIMUM DOSE (MG/D)*	INITIAL SUGGESTED DOSE**	TITRATION SCHEDULE*	ADVANTAGES	DISADVANTAGES
Imipramine	150–250	300	10–25 mg at bedtime	Increase dose 10 mg every day until dose of 50 mg/day reached. Increase 25 mg every third day up to 100 mg. After 1 week, dose can be increased by 25–50 mg as tolerated every third day to maximum dose of 300 mg/day (increments of 10 mg may be required.)	Slowly metabolized; can be taken once daily, usually at bedtime.	May experience more general anxiety the first few days up to 3 weeks.
Clomipramine	150–300	300	25 mg in p.m. (10 mg in elderly)	Increase initial dose by 25 mg increments q 3–4 days to 100 mg/day. Maintain 100 mg as per treatment guide before dose increase. Increase in 25 mg increments at 4–7-day intervals as tolerated to maximum dose.	Helps control OCD. Usually taken in 1 dose.	May experience more general anxiety the first few days up to 3 weeks. Can take 4–6 weeks to work.

Mood Stabilizers/Anticonvulsants						
Pregabalin	150–600	600	150 mg in divided doses (BID)	Initial dose may be increased in 75–150 mg increments as tolerated to maximum dose.	No clinically significant laboratory, electrocardiogram, or other treatment-related safety findings.	Weight gain (19–24.4%).[3] Dizziness (12.5%), somnolence, headache, insomnia, balance disorder, tremor, confusional state, coordination abnormal (use with caution in the elderly population). Increased seizure frequency may occur in patients with seizure disorders if rapidly discontinued.
Gabapentin	900–1800 in divided doses (TID)	3600	300 mg in divided doses (TID)	Initial dose can be increased to 300 mg BID, then TID within 3–7 days. Further increase as tolerated to maximum dose (in divided doses — TID).	Can be effective in concurrent epilepsy, postherpetic neuraldia, and restless leg syndrome.	TID schedule; maximum time between doses should not exceed 12 hours.

ANTIDEPRESSANT GENERIC OPTION	TYPICAL EFFECTIVE DOSE (MG/D)*	MAXIMUM DOSE (MG/D)*	INITIAL SUGGESTED DOSE**	TITRATION SCHEDULE*	ADVANTAGES	DISADVANTAGES
Reversible inhibitor of monoamine oxidase						
Moclobemide	300–600 in divided doses (BID or TID)	600	150 mg after meals	Increase initial dose by increments of 150 mg q 1–2 weeks.	Better tolerated than MAOI; less concern with diet.	Multiple dosing schedule.
Monoamine Oxidase Inhibitors						
Phenelzine	45–90	90 in divided doses (BID to TID)	15 mg TID; lower initial dose may be required in some patients; e.g., elderly (15 mg OD)	If needed, initial dose can be increased to at least 60 mg/day fairly quickly as tolerated.		Hypertensive crises w/ingestion of foods with a high concentration of tyramine or dopamine.
Tranylcypromine	30–40 in divided doses (BID)	60	10 mg BID; lower initial dose may be required in some patients; e.g., elderly (10 mg OD)	If no response after 2–3 weeks, increase initial dose by increments of 10 mg/day q 1–3 weeks (may need to increase by 5 mg/day in elderly).		Hypertensive crises w/ingestion of foods with high concentration of tyramine or dopamine.
Anxiolytics						
Hydroxyzine (antihistamine)	50–100 in divided doses (QID)	100	50 mg in divided doses (may need to start at lower dose of 25 mg in elderly)		Also used in allergic reactions or urticaria.	Higher rates of sleepiness/ drowsiness than benzodiazepines and buspirone. Contraindicated in pregnancy.
Other						
Agomelatine (melatonin agonist)	25–50 taken at bedtime	50	25 mg HS	After 2 weeks at initial dose, dose may be increased to 50 mg once daily at bedtime.	Usually no adjustment in recommended dose for elderly solely based on age.	Contraindicated in hepatic disease.

Reboxetine (selective noradrenergic reuptake inhibitor)	6–8	Usually 8 mg in divided doses (BID) May increase to 10 mg as necessary Elderly 2 mg BID	2 mg	Initial dosage can be increased by 2 mg/day weekly to a maximum dosage of 8 mg/day. Can be increased more rapidly if tolerated as soon as 5 days. Elderly may increase to 6 mg/day in divided doses (BID) after 3 weeks.	Limited clinical data on patients >75 years of age; not recommended in this group. May not be as effective as paroxetine in addressing panic attacks.
Buspirone	20–30	30	7.5 mg BID	Increased every 2–3 days in increments of 2.5 mg twice daily to a maximum of 30 mg twice daily. Divided doses BID and TID can be used.	Approved as second-line monotherapy for GAD. Significant delay in the onset of clinical activity, which can vary from 2 weeks to much longer.

IR: Immediate release

XL: Extended release (release of dose for extended period in a day)

SR: Sustained release (slowly released in body throughout the day, maintaining constant drug concentration)

*Consult drug monograph if renal, hepatic impairment, or medically ill patient, pregnancy, breastfeeding, and elderly; dose adjustment may be warranted or drug could be contraindicated.

**If initial dose is lower than minimum effective dose (e.g., in elderly), increase to minimum effective dose as tolerated and maintain as per treatment guide. In some disorders (e.g., OCD, PTSD), consider increasing to target dose and then maintain as per treatment guide.

Note: Black box warning for all antidepressant medications: Increased risks of suicidal thinking and behavior in young adults 18–24 years old during the first 1–2 months of treatment. Scientific data does not show increased risk in adults >24 years of age; adults >65 years of age show decreased risk.

Appendix XI

DSM-5 Diagnostic Criteria for Generalized Anxiety Disorder 300.02 (F41.1)*

A. Excessive anxiety and worry (apprehensive expectation), occurring more days than not for at least 6 months, about a number of events or activities (such as work or school performance).

B. The individual finds it difficult to control the worry.

C. The anxiety and worry are associated with three (or more) of the following six symptoms (with at least some symptoms having been present for more days than not for the past 6 months):

   Note: Only one item is required in children.

   1. Restlessness or feeling keyed up or on edge.
   2. Being easily fatigued.
   3. Difficulty concentrating or mind going blank.
   4. Irritability.
   5. Muscle tension.
   6. Sleep disturbance (difficulty falling or staying asleep, or restless, unsatisfying sleep).

D. The anxiety, worry, or physical symptoms cause clinically significant distress or impairment in social, occupational, or other important areas of functioning.

E. The disturbance is not attributable to the physiological effects of a substance (e.g., a drug of abuse, a medication) or another medical condition (e.g., hyperthyroidism).

F. The disturbance is not better explained by another mental disorder (e.g., anxiety or worry about having panic attacks in panic disorder, negative evaluation in social anxiety disorder (social phobia), contamination or other obsessions in obsessive-compulsive disorder, separation from attachment figures in separation anxiety disorder, reminders of traumatic events in posttraumatic stress disorder, gaining weight in anorexia nervosa, physical complaints in somatic symptom disorder, perceived appearance flaws in body dysmorphic disorder, having a serious illness in illness anxiety disorder, or the content of delusional beliefs in schizophrenia or delusional disorder).

Appendix XII

Generalized Anxiety Disorder Treatment Guide Summary

CONDITION	OPTIONS
If GAD mild to moderate and no comorbid condition	Start with psychotherapy intervention alone
If GAD severe or comorbid condition	Start with psychotherapy intervention + first-line medication* (see Table 4.1 on p. 51)
	Start with first-line medication alone
Wait 6–8 weeks to assess response, assessing every 2 weeks. If no response or partial response and using first-line medication, titrate every 2 weeks until maximum dose is reached.	
If no response or partial response to psychotherapy intervention alone	Add a first-line medication
If no response or partial response to first-line medication	Add psychotherapy intervention; allow 8–12 weeks for response
If no response or partial response to first-line medication, with or without psychotherapy intervention	Switch to another first-line medication
	Consider add-on medication (see Table 4.1 on p. 51)
If no response to second first-line medication	Consider add-on medication
If no response to second first-line medication plus add-on medication, with or without psychotherapy intervention	Switch to second-line medication (see Table 4.1 on p. 51)
If no response to 3 medication trials (first-line medications or add-on), with or without psychotherapy intervention	Consider referral
If response	Continue treatment for a minimum of 1 year

*Allow 6–8 week trial at minimum dose, then titrate every 2 weeks until maximum dose.

Appendix XIII

Criteria for Panic Attack

A panic attack is an abrupt surge of intense fear or intense discomfort that reaches a peak within minutes, in which 4 (or more) of the following symptoms develop abruptly. The abrupt surge can occur from either a calm or an anxious state:

- Palpitations, pounding heart, or accelerated heart rate
- Sweating
- Trembling or shaking
- Sensation of shortness of breath or smothering
- Feeling of choking
- Chest pain or discomfort
- Nausea or abdominal distress
- Feeling dizzy, unsteady, lightheaded, or faint
- Chills or heat sensation
- Paresthesia (numbness or tingling sensation)
- Derealization (feelings of unreality) or depersonalization (being detached from oneself)
- Fear of losing control or going crazy
- Fear of dying

Appendix XIV

DSM-5 Diagnostic Criteria for Panic Disorder 300.01 (F41.0)*

A. Recurrent unexpected panic attacks. A panic attack is an abrupt surge of intense fear or intense discomfort that reaches a peak within minutes, and during which time four (or more) of the following symptoms occur:

Note: The abrupt surge can occur from a calm state or an anxious state.

1. Palpitations, pounding heart, or accelerated heart rate.
2. Sweating.
3. Trembling or shaking.
4. Sensations of shortness of breath or smothering.
5. Feelings of choking.
6. Chest pain or discomfort.
7. Nausea or abdominal distress.
8. Feeling dizzy, unsteady, light-headed, or faint.
9. Chills or heat sensations.
10. Paresthesias (numbness or tingling sensations).
11. Derealization (feelings of unreality) or depersonalization (being detached from oneself).
12. Fear of losing control or "going crazy."
13. Fear of dying.

Note: Culture-specific symptoms (e.g., tinnitus, neck soreness, headache, uncontrollable screaming, or crying) may be seen. Such symptoms should not count as one of the four required symptoms.

B. At least one of the attacks has been followed by 1 month (or more) of one or both of the following:

1. Persistent concern or worry about additional panic attacks or their consequences (e.g., losing control, having a heart attack, "going crazy").

2. A significant maladaptive change in behavior related to the attacks (e.g., behaviors designed to avoid having panic attacks, such as avoidance of exercise or unfamiliar situations).

C. The disturbance is not attributable to the physiological effects of a substance (e.g., a drug of abuse, a medication) or another medical condition (e.g., hyperthyroidism, cardiopulmonary disorders).

D. The disturbance is not better explained by another mental disorder (e.g., the panic attacks do not occur only in response to feared social situations, as in social anxiety disorder; in response to circumscribed phobic objects or situations, as in specific phobia; in response to obsessions, as in obsessive-compulsive disorder; in response to reminders of traumatic events, as in post-traumatic stress disorder; or in response to separation from attachment figures, as in separation anxiety disorder).

Appendix XV

*Panic Disorder Self-Report Scale**

Note to providers: The print-ready version of this tool on the CD included with this book and downloadable from www.brusheducation.ca/toolkit includes scoring instructions and assessment scales on separate pages. You can quickly refer to the scoring legend while minimizing patient response biases induced by seeing the scoring information.

> Panic attacks are discrete episodes of intense fear, apprehension, or terror that are accompanied by several physical symptoms. Panic attacks can either occur for no apparent reason (spontaneously) or upon entering into or being in situations which have become associated with them (e.g., long lines, closed spaces, driving over bridges). Do not consider fear to be a panic attack if it lasts several hours or most of the day.

---

1. During the last 6 months, have you had a panic attack or a sudden rush of intense fear or anxiety? (Circle your answer)   No   Yes
   When was the most recent time this occurred?   Date: _____

If NO (you have not experienced a panic attack), please leave the remainder of this form blank. If YES, please continue.

2. Was at least 1 panic attack unexpected, as if it came out of the blue?   No   Yes
3. Did it happen more than once?   No   Yes
4. If YES to 3, approximately how many panic attacks have you had in your lifetime? _____

If NO to 1, 2, and 3, please leave the remainder of this form blank, otherwise continue.

5. Have you ever worried a lot (for at least 1 month) about having another panic attack?   No   Yes
6. Have you ever worried a lot (at least 1 month) that having the attacks meant you were losing control, going crazy, having a heart attack, seriously ill, etcetera?   No   Yes
7. Did you ever change your behavior or do something different (for at least 1 month) because of the attacks?   No   Yes

If YES to 5, 6 OR 7 please answer the following questions:

Think back to your most severe panic attack. Did you experience any of the following symptoms?

8. Shortness of breath or smothering sensations?   No   Yes
9. Feeling dizzy, unsteady, lightheaded, or faint?   No   Yes
10. Palpitations, pounding heart, or rapid heart rate?   No   Yes
11. Trembling or shaking?   No   Yes

12. Sweating?   No   Yes

13. Feelings of choking?   No   Yes

14. Nausea or abdominal distress?   No   Yes

15. Numbness or tingling sensations?   No   Yes

16. Flushes (hot flashes) or chills?   No   Yes

17. Chest pain or discomfort?   No   Yes

18. Fear of dying?   No   Yes

19. Fear of going crazy or doing something uncontrolled?   No   Yes

20. How much do these symptoms interfere with your daily functioning? (Circle one)

0	1	2	3	4
|	|	|	|	|
Not at all	Mildly	Moderately	Severely	Very severely/ disabling

21. How distressing do you find these symptoms? (Circle one)

0	1	2	3	4
|	|	|	|	|
No distress	Mild distress	Moderate distress	Severe distress	Very severe distress

22. When you have bad panic attacks, does it often take **minutes** from the point at which the attack begins to the point at which it reaches a peak or becomes most intense?   No   Yes

23. Just before you began having panic attacks, were you taking any drugs or excessive amounts (more than 4 cups daily) of stimulants (e.g., coffee, tea, or cola with caffeine)?   No   Yes

    a. If YES, what were you were taking? _____

    b. How much of it were you taking (in cups, cans, etc.)? _____

24. Have you ever been diagnosed with a medical problem (hyperthyroidism, a seizure or cardiac condition, etc.) that could have caused your panic symptoms?   No   Yes

Note: Self-report tools should be reviewed by clinicians and interpreted against DSM-5 criteria in conjunction with clinical judgment.

Note: Question 22 has been modified to reflect DSM-5 criteria; that is, in the DSM-5, wording "reaches a peak in **less than 10 minutes**" has been changed to "**peaks within minutes**."

*Reproduced with permission from Dr. Michelle Newman. Newman MG, Holmes M, Zuellig AR, Kachin KE, Behar E. The Reliability and Validity of the Panic Disorder Self-Report: A New Diagnostic Screening Measure of Panic Disorder. Psychol Assess. 2006; 18 (1), 49–61.

Summary of Scoring Legend (detailed scoring legend appears below)

If Yes to 1, 2, 3, **and** 22

AND

If Yes to 5, 6, **or** 7

AND

If Yes to >4 symptoms from questions 8–19

AND

If 20 **or** 21 is scored a minimum of 2

AND

If No to 23 **or** 24

THEN

Results are consistent with a diagnosis of panic disorder.

Detailed Rational for Scoring Legend

The scoring system for the PDSR was devised to create a score that would best enable detection of the presence of panic disorder. For items 1, 2, 3, 5–19, and 22, "Yes" answers were coded as 1 and "No" answers as 0. If items 1–3 were not all answered "Yes," participants were instructed not to complete the remainder of the questionnaire, as the initial 3 criteria are essential to the diagnosis of panic disorder. Items 20 and 21 were each divided by 2. Any unanswered questions were coded as 0.

Items 4, 23, and 24 were not included in the scoring system. The rationale for this scoring system was to allot 1 point to any item required for the diagnosis of panic disorder (i.e., items 1, 2, 3, and 22), as well as to items relevant to meeting diagnostic criteria (i.e., items 5–19), even if endorsing all of the items in a particular section was not required for diagnosis (i.e., for diagnosis, only 1 of items 5–7 is required and only 4 of items 8–19 are required). The latter decision was reached because we suspected that participants who endorsed a greater number of items 5–19 were more likely to meet criteria for the disorder.

The values for items 20–21 (which measure distress and interference) were divided in half because these are the only items for which the face value reaches a maximum of 4. This ensured that these items would not outweigh 1-point items too heavily. Thus, for items 20–21, participants received 1 point for moderate distress/interference (minimum required for diagnosis) and 2 points for very severe distress or interference. Similar to the reasoning above, this decision was based on the suspicion that endorsing greater severity and interference would suggest a greater likelihood that a participant would meet diagnostic criteria for panic disorder.

Item 4 was not included in the scoring system because the total number of panic attacks experienced is not crucial to meeting diagnostic criteria as long as an individual has experienced more than 1 panic attack, and this criterion is already covered by item 3. Items 23 and 24 were not included in scoring because the determination as to whether a medical condition caused panic disorder or whether intoxication or withdrawal from substances is the current cause of panic attacks requires detailed questioning. Also, the exclusion of these items from the overall score of the measure did not decrease the overall sensitivity and specificity of the measure when the structured interview was used as the standard for comparison. Nonetheless, these items were retained in the questionnaire as items that could be explored with additional interviewing.

Appendix XVI

Panic Disorder Severity Scale Self-Report Form*

Note to providers: *The print-ready version of this tool on the CD included with this book and downloadable from www.brusheducation.ca/toolkit includes scoring instructions and assessment scales on separate pages. You can quickly refer to the scoring legend while minimizing patient response biases induced by seeing the scoring information.*

Name: _____ Date: _____

Several of the following questions refer to panic attacks and limited symptom attacks. For this questionnaire, we define a panic attack as a sudden *rush of fear* or discomfort accompanied *by at least 4 of the symptoms listed below*. To qualify as a sudden rush, the symptoms must peak within minutes. Episodes like panic attacks but having fewer than 4 of the listed symptoms are called limited symptom attacks. Here are the symptoms to count:

- Rapid or pounding heartbeat
- Sweating
- Trembling or shaking
- Breathlessness
- Feeling of choking

- Chest pain or discomfort
- Nausea
- Dizziness or faintness
- Feelings of unreality
- Numbness or tingling

- Chills or hot flushes
- Fear of losing control or going crazy
- Fear of dying

1. How many panic and limited symptom attacks did you have during the week?

    0   No panic or limited symptom episodes
    1   Mild: no full panic attacks and no more than 1 limited symptom attack/day
    2   Moderate: 1 or 2 full panic attacks and/or multiple limited symptom attacks/day
    3   Severe: more than 2 full attacks but not more than 1/day on average
    4   Extreme: full panic attacks occurred more than once a day, more days than not

2. If you had any panic attacks during the past week, how distressing (uncomfortable, frightening) were they **while they were happening**? (If you had more than one, give an average rating. If you didn't have any panic attacks but did have limited symptom attacks, answer for the limited symptom attacks.)

    0   Not at all distressing, or no panic or limited symptom attacks during the past week
    1   Mildly distressing (not too intense)
    2   Moderately distressing (intense but still manageable)
    3   Severely distressing (very intense)
    4   Extremely distressing (extreme distress during all attacks)

Shear M, Brown T, Barlow D, Money R, Sholomskas D, Woods S, et al. Multicenter collaborative panic disorder severity scale. Am J Psychiatry. 1997; 154(11):1571–1575.

3. During the past week, how much have you worried or felt anxious **about when your next panic attack would occur or about fears related to the attacks** (e.g., that they could mean you have physical or mental health problems or could cause you social embarrassment)?

   0   Not at all
   1   Occasionally or only mildly
   2   Frequently or moderately
   3   Very often or to a very disturbing degree
   4   Nearly constantly and to a disabling extent

4. During the past week, were there any **places or situations** (e.g., public transportation, movie theaters, crowds, bridges, tunnels, shopping malls, being alone) you avoided or felt afraid of (uncomfortable in, wanted to avoid or leave) **because of fear of having a panic attack?** Are there any other situations that you would have avoided or been afraid of if they had come up during the week, for the same reason? If yes to either question, please rate your level of fear and avoidance this past week.

   0   None: no fear or avoidance.
   1   Mild: occasional fear and/or avoidance, but I could usually confront or endure the situation. There was little or no modification of my lifestyle due to this.
   2   Moderate: noticeable fear and/or avoidance but still manageable. I avoided some situations, but I could confront them with a companion. There was some modification of my lifestyle because of this, but my overall functioning was not impaired.
   3   Severe: extensive avoidance. Substantial modification of my lifestyle was required to accommodate the avoidance, making it difficult to manage usual activities.
   4   Extreme: pervasive, disabling fear and/or avoidance. Extensive modification of my lifestyle was required such that important tasks were not performed.

5. During the past week, were there any **activities** (e.g., physical exertion, sexual relations, taking a hot shower or bath, drinking coffee, watching an exciting or scary movie) that you avoided, or felt afraid of (uncomfortable doing, wanted to avoid or stop) **because they caused physical sensations like those you feel during panic attacks or that you were afraid might trigger a panic attack?** Are there any other activities that you would have avoided or been afraid of if they had come up during the week for that reason? If yes to either question, please rate your level of fear and avoidance of those activities this past week.

   0   No fear or avoidance of situations or activities because of distressing physical sensations.
   1   Mild: occasional fear and/or avoidance, but usually I could confront or endure with little distress activities that cause physical sensations. There was little modification of my lifestyle due to this.
   2   Moderate: noticeable avoidance but still manageable. There was definite, but limited, modification of my lifestyle such that my overall functioning was not impaired.
   3   Severe: extensive avoidance. There was substantial modification of my lifestyle or interference in my functioning.
   4   Extreme: pervasive and disabling avoidance. There was extensive modification in my lifestyle due to this such that important tasks or activities were not performed.

6. During the past week, how much did the above symptoms altogether (panic and limited symptom attacks, worry about attacks, and fear of situations and activities because of attacks) interfere with your **ability to work or carry out your responsibilities at home?** (If your work or home responsibilities were less than usual this past week, answer how you think you would have done if the responsibilities had been usual.)

0   No interference with work or home responsibilities.
1   Slight interference with work or home responsibilities, but I could do nearly everything I could if I didn't have these problems.
2   Significant interference with work or home responsibilities, but I still could manage to do the things I needed to do.
3   Substantial impairment in work or home responsibilities; there were many important things I couldn't do because of these problems.
4   Extreme, incapacitating impairment such that I was essentially unable to manage any work or home responsibilities.

7. During the past week, how much did panic and limited symptom attacks, worry about attacks, and fear of situations and activities because of attacks interfere with your **social life?** (If you didn't have many opportunities to socialize this past week, answer how you think you would have done if you did have opportunities.)

0   No interference.
1   Slight interference with social activities, but I could do nearly everything I could if I didn't have these problems.
2   Significant interference with social activities, but I could manage to do most things if I made the effort.
3   Substantial impairment in social activities; there are many social things I couldn't do because of these problems.
4   Extreme, incapacitating impairment such that there was hardly anything social I could do.

Scoring the Panic Disorder Severity Scale Self-Report Form

In scoring the Panic Disorder Severity Scale, items are rated on a scale of 0 to 4. A composite score is established by averaging the scores of the 7 items. The table below can be used to convert raw scores (the sum of individual item scores) into composite scores.

RAW SCORE	COMPOSITE SCORE	RAW SCORE	COMPOSITE SCORE	RAW SCORE	COMPOSITE SCORE	RAW SCORE	COMPOSITE SCORE
0	0	7	1.00	14	2.00	21	3.00
1	.14	8	1.14	15	2.14	22	3.14
2	.28	9	1.28	16	2.28	23	3.28
3	.42	10	1.42	17	2.42	24	3.42
4	.57	11	1.57	18	2.57	25	3.57
5	.71	12	1.71	19	2.71	26	3.71
6	.85	13	1.85	20	2.85	27	3.85
						28	4.00

Appendix XVII

Panic Disorder Treatment Guide Summary[5,6]

CONDITION	OPTIONS
Panic disorder	Start with psychotherapy + first-line antidepressant +/− benzodiazepine (see Table 5.3, p. 64)
	Start with first-line medication +/− benzodiazepine if patient unable or unreceptive to psychotherapy; encourage psychotherapy
	Start with psychotherapy alone if mild
Wait 8 weeks to assess response. With drug therapy, if evidence of response, titrate every 2 weeks until optimum response or maximum dose is reached. For any options above, allow 12 weeks as improvement may not plateau until 12 weeks of treatment.	
If no response or partial response to psychotherapy alone	Add first-line medication +/− benzodiazepine
If partial response to first-line medication alone	Add adjunctive medication
	Switch to another first-line antidepressant (see Table 5.3, p. 64)
	Add psychotherapy
If no response to first-line medication alone	Switch to another first-line antidepressant
	Consider adding psychotherapy
If partial response to second first-line medication, with or without psychotherapy	Add adjunctive medication
	Add psychotherapy if not started
If no response to second first-line medication, with or without psychotherapy	Switch to second-line +/− adjunctive therapy
	Add psychotherapy if not started
	Refer
If response	Continue treatment for a minimum of 6 months after remission and longer if long-standing condition, treatment resistant disorder, or prior relapse to treatment discontinuation.

Medication Guidelines

If using benzodiazepines, give TID rather than PRN and withdraw gradually when anticipatory and panic attacks resolve. Give antidepressant an 8-week trial at minimum dose, then titrate every 2 weeks until maximum dose is reached.

First-line psychotherapy consists of CBT, delivered in any format: individual, group, Internet, telephone coaching, or self-help books.

Other Considerations

Psychotherapy intervention should be encouraged at any point in treatment if the patient is receptive.

Appendix XVIII

DSM-5 Diagnostic Criteria for Agoraphobia 300.22 (F40.00)*

A. Marked fear or anxiety about two (or more) of the following five situations:

   1. Using public transportation (e.g., automobiles, buses, trains, ships, planes).
   2. Being in open spaces (e.g., parking lots, marketplaces, bridges).
   3. Being in enclosed places (e.g., shops, theaters, cinemas).
   4. Standing in line or being in a crowd.
   5. Being outside of the home alone.

B. The individual fears or avoids these situations because of thoughts that escape might be difficult or help might not be available in the event of developing panic-like symptoms or other incapacitating or embarrassing symptoms (e.g., fear of falling in the elderly; fear of incontinence).

C. The agoraphobic situations almost always provoke fear or anxiety.

D. The agoraphobic situations are actively avoided, require the presence of a companion, or are endured with intense fear or anxiety.

E. The fear or anxiety is out of proportion to the actual danger posed by the agoraphobic situations and to the sociocultural context.

F. The fear, anxiety, or avoidance is persistent, typically lasting for 6 months or more.

G. The fear, anxiety, or avoidance causes clinically significant distress or impairment in social, occupational, or other important areas of functioning.

H. If another medical condition (e.g., inflammatory bowel disease, Parkinson's disease) is present, the fear, anxiety, or avoidance is clearly excessive.

I. The fear, anxiety, or avoidance is not better explained by the symptoms of another mental disorder—for example, the symptoms are not confined to specific phobia, situational type; do not involve only social situations (as in social anxiety disorder); and are not related exclusively to obsessions (as in obsessive-compulsive disorder), perceived defects or flaws in physical appearance (as in body dysmorphic disorder), reminders of traumatic events (as in posttraumatic stress disorder), or fear of separation (as in separation anxiety disorder).

Note: Agoraphobia is diagnosed irrespective of the presence of panic disorder. If an individual's presentation meets criteria for panic disorder and agoraphobia, both diagnoses should be assigned.

*Reprinted with permission from the American Psychiatric Association. Diagnostic and Statistical Manual of Mental Disorders, 5th ed. Copyright © 2013 American Psychiatric Association. All Rights Reserved.[4]

Appendix XIX

Patient-Directed Agoraphobia Self-Report Tool

Note to providers: *A print-ready version of this tool is available on the CD included with this book and downloadable from www.brusheducation.ca/toolkit.*

	YES	NO
1. Were there places where you felt afraid or that you avoided because you thought it could be difficult to get help or to easily leave?		
2. Did you have intense fear or anxiety about at least 2 of the following 5 groups of situations?		
(1) Public transportation (e.g., traveling in automobiles, buses, trains, ships, or planes)		
(2) Open spaces (e.g., parking lots, marketplaces, or bridges)		
(3) Being in shops, theaters, or cinemas		
(4) Standing in line or being in a crowd		
(5) Being outside the home alone in other situations		
3. Did you fear or avoid these situations due to thoughts that escape might be difficult or help might not be available in the event of panic-like symptoms or other incapacitating or embarrassing symptoms (e.g., fear of falling in the elderly; fear of incontinence)?		
4. Did you require the presence of a companion or endure the situation with marked fear or anxiety?		
5. Was the fear or anxiety out of proportion to the actual danger posed by the agoraphobic situation?		
6. Did the fear, anxiety, or avoidance persist, typically lasting longer than 6 months?		

If 1–6 are coded Yes, the results are consistent with a diagnosis of agoraphobia, with further assessment required.

Appendix XX

Severity Measure for Agoraphobia—Adult

Note to providers: *The print-ready version of this tool on the CD included with this book and downloadable from www.brusheducation.ca/toolkit includes scoring instructions and assessment scales on separate pages. You can quickly refer to the scoring legend while minimizing patient response biases induced by seeing the scoring information.*

Name: _____ Age: _____

Male _____ Female _____ Date: _____

Instructions: The following questions ask about thoughts, feelings, and behaviors you may have had in the following situations: crowds, public places, using transportation (e.g., buses, planes, trains), traveling alone, or away from home. **Please respond to each item by marking (√ or x) one box per row.**

	DURING THE PAST 7 DAYS, I HAVE . . .	NEVER	OCCASIONALLY	HALF OF THE TIME	MOST OF THE TIME	ALL OF THE TIME	CLINICIAN USE — ITEM SCORE
1.	felt moments of sudden terror, fear, or fright in these situations	☐ 0	☐ 1	☐ 2	☐ 3	☐ 4	
2.	felt anxious, worried, or nervous about these situations	☐ 0	☐ 1	☐ 2	☐ 3	☐ 4	
3.	had thoughts about panic attacks, uncomfortable physical sensations, getting lost, or being overcome with fear in these situations	☐ 0	☐ 1	☐ 2	☐ 3	☐ 4	
4.	felt a racing heart, sweaty, trouble breathing, faint, or shaky in these situations	☐ 0	☐ 1	☐ 2	☐ 3	☐ 4	
5.	felt tense muscles, felt on edge or restless, or had trouble relaxing in these situations	☐ 0	☐ 1	☐ 2	☐ 3	☐ 4	
6.	avoided, or did not approach or enter, these situations	☐ 0	☐ 1	☐ 2	☐ 3	☐ 4	
7.	moved away from these situations, left them early, or remained close to the exits	☐ 0	☐ 1	☐ 2	☐ 3	☐ 4	

	DURING THE PAST 7 DAYS, I HAVE . . .	NEVER	OCCASIONALLY	HALF OF THE TIME	MOST OF THE TIME	ALL OF THE TIME	CLINICIAN USE
							ITEM SCORE
8.	spent a lot of time preparing for, or procrastinating about (putting off), these situations	☐ 0	☐ 1	☐ 2	☐ 3	☐ 4	
9.	distracted myself to avoid thinking about these situations	☐ 0	☐ 1	☐ 2	☐ 3	☐ 4	
10.	needed help to cope with these situations (e.g., alcohol or medication, superstitious objects, other people)	☐ 0	☐ 1	☐ 2	☐ 3	☐ 4	
	Total/Partial Raw Score:						
	Prorated Total Raw Score (if 1–2 items left unanswered):						
	Average Total Score:						

Scoring and Interpretation

To use when a diagnosis of agoraphobia has been made for an individual aged 18 or over. Total score can range from 0–40; higher scores indicate higher severity.

Clinician indicates the raw score for each item in the "Clinician Use" section.

Calculate the Average Total Score, reducing the overall score to a 5-point scale; this allows the clinician to think of the severity of the individual's agoraphobia in terms of none (0), mild (1), moderate (2), severe (3), or extreme (4).

The Average Total Score is calculated by dividing the Total Raw Score by the number of items in the measure (i.e., 10).

Note: If 3 or more items are left unanswered, the total score on the measure should not be calculated. If 1–2 items are left unanswered, you are asked to calculate and use a Prorated Total Raw Score as the Total Raw Score.

The Prorated Total Raw Score is calculated by summing the scores of items that were answered to get a Partial Raw Score. The formula for prorating the Partial Raw Score to the Total Raw Score is:

$$\frac{(\text{Partial raw score} \times 10)}{\text{Number of items that were actually answered (8–9)}}$$

If the result is a fraction, round to the nearest whole number. Use this prorated score as the Total Raw Score and calculate the average score as instructed above.

Appendix XXI

DSM-5 Diagnostic Criteria for Social Anxiety Disorder (Social Phobia) 300.23 (F40.10)*

A. Marked fear or anxiety about one or more social situations in which the individual is exposed to possible scrutiny by others. Examples include social interactions (e.g., having a conversation, meeting unfamiliar people), being observed (e.g., eating or drinking), and performing in front of others (e.g., giving a speech).

    Note: In children, the anxiety must occur in peer settings and not just during interactions with adults.

B. The individual fears that he or she will act in a way or show anxiety symptoms that will be negatively evaluated (i.e., will be humiliating or embarrassing; will lead to rejection or offend others).

C. The social situations almost always provoke fear or anxiety.

    Note: In children, the fear or anxiety may be expressed by crying, tantrums, freezing, clinging, shrinking, or failing to speak in social situations.

D. The social situations are avoided or endured with intense fear or anxiety.

E. The fear or anxiety is out of proportion to the actual threat posed by the social situation and to the sociocultural context.

F. The fear, anxiety, or avoidance is persistent, typically lasting for 6 months or more.

G. The fear, anxiety, or avoidance causes clinically significant distress or impairment in social, occupational, or other important areas of functioning.

H. The fear, anxiety, or avoidance is not attributable to the physiological effects of a substance (e.g., a drug of abuse, a medication) or another medical condition.

I. The fear, anxiety, or avoidance is not better explained by the symptoms of another mental disorder, such as panic disorder, body dysmorphic disorder, or autism spectrum disorder.

J. If another medical condition (e.g., Parkinson's disease, obesity, disfigurement from burns or injury) is present, the fear, anxiety, or avoidance is clearly unrelated or is excessive.

    Specify if: Performance only: If the fear is restricted to speaking or performing in public.

Appendix XXII

Social Phobia Diagnostic Questionnaire (SPDQ)*

Note to providers: *The print-ready version of this tool on the CD included with this book and downloadable from www.brusheducation.ca/toolkit includes scoring instructions and assessment scales on separate pages. You can quickly refer to the scoring legend while minimizing patient response biases induced by seeing the scoring information.*

1. In social situations where it is possible that you will be noticed or evaluated by other people, do you feel excessively nervous, fearful, or uncomfortable?	No	Yes
2. Do you tend to be overly worried that you may act in a way that might embarrass or humiliate yourself in front of other people, or that others may not think well of you?	No	Yes
3. Do you try to avoid social situations?	No	Yes

Below is a list of some situations that are fear provoking for some people. Rate the severity of your anxiety and avoidance on the following scales:

0 = No fear	0 = Never avoid
1 = Mild fear	1 = Rarely avoid
2 = Moderate fear	2 = Sometimes avoid
3 = Severe fear	3 = Often avoid
4 = Very severe fear	4 = Always avoid

	a) Fear	b) Avoidance
4. Parties	0 1 2 3 4	0 1 2 3 4
5. Meetings	0 1 2 3 4	0 1 2 3 4
6. Eating in a public location	0 1 2 3 4	0 1 2 3 4
7. Using public bathrooms when others are present	0 1 2 3 4	0 1 2 3 4
8. Becoming the focus of attention	0 1 2 3 4	0 1 2 3 4
9. Writing in front of other people (signing checks, filling out forms)	0 1 2 3 4	0 1 2 3 4
10. Dating circumstances	0 1 2 3 4	0 1 2 3 4
11. A first date	0 1 2 3 4	0 1 2 3 4
12. Meeting people in authority	0 1 2 3 4	0 1 2 3 4
13. Speaking with people in authority	0 1 2 3 4	0 1 2 3 4

*Adapted with permission to reflect changes in the DSM-5. Newman MG, Kachin KE, Zuellig AR, Constantino MJ, Cashman L. The social phobia diagnostic questionnaire: preliminary validation of a new self-report diagnostic measure of social phobia. Psychol Med. 2003; 33(4):623–635.

	0 = No fear	0 = Never avoid
	1 = Mild fear	1 = Rarely avoid
	2 = Moderate fear	2 = Sometimes avoid
	3 = Severe fear	3 = Often avoid
	4 = Very severe fear	4 = Always avoid
	a) Fear	b) Avoidance
14. Saying "no" to an unreasonable request	0 1 2 3 4	0 1 2 3 4
15. Asking others to do something differently	0 1 2 3 4	0 1 2 3 4
16. Being introduced	0 1 2 3 4	0 1 2 3 4
17. Initiating a conversation	0 1 2 3 4	0 1 2 3 4
18. Keeping a conversation going	0 1 2 3 4	0 1 2 3 4
19. Giving a speech	0 1 2 3 4	0 1 2 3 4
20. Using the telephone	0 1 2 3 4	0 1 2 3 4
21. Others judging you	0 1 2 3 4	0 1 2 3 4
22. Being under observation by others	0 1 2 3 4	0 1 2 3 4
23. Being teased	0 1 2 3 4	0 1 2 3 4

24. Do you tend to experience fear each time you are in feared social situations?   No   Yes

25. Does the fear come on as soon as you encounter feared social situations?   No   Yes

26. Would you say your social fear is excessive or unreasonable?   No   Yes

27. Circle the degree to which your social fear interferes with your life, work, social activities, family, etc. (Circle one)

0	1	2	3	4	5	6	7	8
|	|	|	|	|	|	|	|	|
Not at all		Mildly		Moderately		Severely		Very severely/ Disabling

28. How distressing do you find your social fear? (Circle one)

0	1	2	3	4	5	6	7	8
|	|	|	|	|	|	|	|	|
No distress		Mild distress		Moderate distress		Severe distress		Very severe distress

29. Has what you have been able to achieve in your job or in school been negatively affected by your social fear?   No   Yes

Note: Questions 4–23 provide clinicians with additional information on specific feared situations.

Note: In the DSM-5, it is no longer required that the individual recognize that their anxiety is excessive or unreasonable. It is now the clinician's judgment. (Individuals with these disorders often overestimate the danger in "phobic" situations, and older individuals often misattribute "phobic" fears to aging.) The following follow-up questions (30–32)—not part of the original scale—have been added by the author to reflect criteria in the DSM-5.

Clinician assessment follow-up questions (Yes/No):

30.	Is social fear out of proportion to the actual threat posed by the social situation and to the sociocultural context? (DSM-5 deletion of requirement that person feels the fear is excessive or unreasonable—clinician evaluation of question 26 of the scale.)	No	Yes
31.	Have these symptoms been present for 6 months or more?	No	Yes
32.	Can the fear be better explained by another psychiatric or medical condition or substance (e.g., drug, substance use disorder)?	No	Yes

Provisional Diagnosis Legend (can be used to recall DSM-5 criteria, requires validation through research)

If Yes to 1, 2, 24 or 25, 30, **and** 31

AND

If Yes to 3 **or** 28 ≥4

AND

27 ≥4

AND

If No to 32

THEN

Results are consistent with social anxiety disorder. Consider further evaluation and review with DSM-5 criteria.

Total Score Legend (validated as follows)

Screening for social anxiety disorder: **Total Score >7.38** (85% specificity, sensitivity 82%)
Detecting social anxiety disorder: **Total Score >12.13** (94% specificity, sensitivity 47%)
To create a total score:

1. All Yes answers are coded 1, "No" answers 0.
2. Only items in the "a" column from 4–23 are summed and divided by 4.
3. Items 27 and 28 are summed and divided by 2.

Note: Avoidance scores (b column, 4–23) and item 29 are not factored in the total score; avoidance scores were not found to add anything to the scoring.

Appendix XXIII

Social Phobia Inventory (SPIN)*

Note to providers: *The print-ready version of this tool is available on the CD included with this book and downloadable from www.brusheducation.ca/toolkit.*

Please indicate how much the following problems have bothered you **during the past week**. Mark only one box for each problem, and be sure to answer all items.

	NOT AT ALL	A LITTLE BIT	SOME-WHAT	VERY MUCH	EXTREMELY
1. I am afraid of people in authority.	☐	☐	☐	☐	☐
2. I am bothered by blushing in front of people.	☐	☐	☐	☐	☐
3. Parties and social events scare me.	☐	☐	☐	☐	☐
4. I avoid talking to people I don't know.	☐	☐	☐	☐	☐
5. Being criticized scares me a lot.	☐	☐	☐	☐	☐
6. Fear of embarrassment causes me to avoid doing things or speaking to people.	☐	☐	☐	☐	☐
7. Sweating in front of people causes me distress.	☐	☐	☐	☐	☐
8. I avoid going to parties.	☐	☐	☐	☐	☐
9. I avoid activities in which I am the center of attention.	☐	☐	☐	☐	☐
10. Talking to strangers scares me.	☐	☐	☐	☐	☐
11. I avoid having to give speeches.	☐	☐	☐	☐	☐
12. I would do anything to avoid being criticized.	☐	☐	☐	☐	☐
13. Heart palpitations bother me when I am around people.	☐	☐	☐	☐	☐
14. I am afraid of doing things when people might be watching.	☐	☐	☐	☐	☐
15. Being embarrassed or looking stupid is among my worst fears.	☐	☐	☐	☐	☐
16. I avoid speaking to anyone in authority.	☐	☐	☐	☐	☐
17. Trembling or shaking in front of others is distressing to me.	☐	☐	☐	☐	☐

Scoring

Severity	None/Very Mild	Mild	Moderate	Severe	Very Severe
Score	Less than 20	21–30	31–40	41–50	51 or more

A total score of ≥19 and associated dysfunction (work, home, or social) suggests a diagnosis of social anxiety disorder, to be confirmed clinically based on the DSM-5 criteria.

Appendix XXIV

Social Anxiety Disorder Treatment Guide Summary

CONDITION	OPTIONS
Social anxiety disorder	Start with first-line medication with or without psychosocial intervention
	Start with psychotherapy alone
Wait 6–8 weeks with first-line medication alone to assess response if clinically feasible.	
Wait 10–12 weeks to assess response if psychotherapy alone.	
If no response or partial response with first-line medication alone, titrate every 2 weeks until maximum dose is reached or problematic side effects occur.	
If no response or partial response to psychotherapy alone	Add a first-line medication (see Table 7.2, p. 93)
If no response or partial response to first-line medication alone	Add psychotherapy; allow 6–8 weeks for response
If no response to maximum dose of first-line medication, with psychotherapy (or without, if patient not receptive)	Switch to another first-line medication, and titrate to maximum dose or problematic side effects
	Consider mindfulness strategies
	Consider exercise regimen
If no response to optimum dose of second first-line medication, with or without psychotherapy	Switch to a second-line medication (see Table 7.2, p. 93)
If partial response to first-line or second-line medication, or unable to tolerate maximum dose, with or without psychotherapy	Consider third-line medication (see Table 7.2, p. 93)
	Add adjunctive therapy
If inadequate response to above, with or without psychotherapy	Consider referral
If response	Consider continuing treatment for a minimum of 1 year

Medication Guidelines

SSRIs are generally preferred. Consider including medication if a comorbid condition is present (e.g., OCD, or substance use disorder) or in severe or long-lasting cases. Allow a 6–8 week trial at minimum dose, then titrate every 2 weeks until maximum dose is reached.

Add-on

Add-on d-cycloserine can enhance exposure therapy for social anxiety disorder.

An add-on drug is a second-line recommendation due to the potential increase in side effects and/or drug interactions; however, an add-on has advantages in patients who took a long time to respond to keep them motivated to continue with the treatment plan, address side effects secondary to the current drug, or target residual symptoms. Physicians should weigh factors such as the patient's past history and degree of response, side effects to the initial antidepressant, and the potential side effects of the new medication.[7] Consider consulting a psychiatrist.

Other Considerations

Psychotherapy may be useful at any point in treatment. Consider individual, couples, or family treatment when indicated. Consider mindfulness strategies.

Switching: The first-line recommendation is to switch to another drug (monotherapy) over adding-on a second drug due to better tolerability and less potential for side effects. Physicians can follow the same titration schedule as for the first treatment trial; however, the dose can be increased sooner if tolerated.

Appendix XXV

DSM-5 Diagnostic Criteria for Obsessive-Compulsive Disorder 300.3 (F42)*

A. Presence of obsessions, compulsions, or both:

Obsessions are defined by (1) and (2):

1. Recurrent and persistent thoughts, urges, or images that are experienced, at some time during the disturbance, as intrusive and unwanted, and that in most individuals cause marked anxiety or distress.
2. The individual attempts to ignore or suppress such thoughts, urges, or images, or to neutralize them with some other thought or action (i.e., by performing a compulsion).

Compulsions are defined by (1) and (2):

1. Repetitive behaviors (e.g., hand washing, ordering, checking) or mental acts (e.g., praying, counting, repeating words silently) that the individual feels driven to perform in response to an obsession or according to rules that must be applied rigidly.
2. The behaviors or mental acts are aimed at preventing or reducing anxiety or distress, or preventing some dreaded event or situation; however, these behaviors or mental acts are not connected in a realistic way with what they are designed to neutralize or prevent, or are clearly excessive. Note: Young children may not be able to articulate the aims of these behaviors or mental acts.

B. The obsessions or compulsions are time-consuming (i.e., take more than 1 hour per day) or cause clinically significant distress or impairment in social, occupational, or other important areas of functioning.

C. The obsessive-compulsive symptoms are not attributable to the physiological effects of a substance (e.g., a drug of abuse, a medication) or another medical condition.

D. The disturbance is not better explained by the symptoms of another mental disorder (e.g., excessive worries, as in generalized anxiety disorder; preoccupation with appearance, as in body dysmorphic disorder; difficulty discarding or parting with possessions, as in hoarding disorder; hair pulling, as in trichotillomania [hair-pulling disorder]; skin picking, as in excoriation [skin-picking] disorder; stereotypies, as in stereotypic movement disorder; ritualized eating behavior, as in eating disorders; preoccupation with substances or gambling, as in substance-related and addictive disorders; preoccupation with having an illness, as in illness anxiety disorder; sexual urges or fantasies, as in paraphilic disorders; impulses, as in disruptive, impulse-control, and conduct disorders; guilty ruminations, as in major depressive disorder; thought insertion or delusional preoccupations, as in schizophrenia spectrum and other psychotic disorders; or repetitive patterns of behavior, as in autism spectrum disorder).

SPECIFY IF:
With good or fair insight: The individual recognizes that obsessive-compulsive disorder beliefs are definitely or probably not true or that they may or may not be true.

With poor insight: The individual thinks obsessive-compulsive disorder beliefs are probably true.
With absent insight/delusional beliefs: The individual is completely convinced that obsessive-compulsive disorder beliefs are true.

SPECIFY IF:
Tic-related: The individual has a current or past history of a tic disorder.

Appendix XXVI

Brief Obsessive-Compulsive Scale (BOCS)*

Note to providers: *A print-ready version of this tool is available on the CD included with this book and downloadable from www.brusheducation.ca/toolkit.*

The BOCS has been validated for the DSM-IV criteria only. For example, in item 14, dealing with somatic obsessions, preoccupation with appearance is more in keeping with body dysmorphic disorder; therefore, a positive response requires further assessment. Nonetheless, the tool can be of value to clinicians as a guide until such time as a validated tool in keeping with DSM-5 criteria is available, as most criteria remain unchanged. If this tool is used, clinicians should note that in the DSM-5, the word "impulse" (which appears in this original scale) has been replaced with the word "urge" to describe obsessions more accurately, and the word "inappropriate" when referring to obsessions, has been replaced with the word "unwanted" (the meaning of "inappropriate" can vary with culture, gender, age, and other factors).

See page 108 for important information about the use of the BOCS scale for use in provisional diagnosis.

Scoring Legend and Interpretation

Endorsement of 2 or more items in the checklist or a mean score of 1.5 or above on the severity scale suggests OCD.

Higher mean scores on the severity scale (questions 1–6) starting on page 4 indicate higher severity.

Brief Obsessive-Compulsive Scale (BOCS)

By S. Bejerot. Based on Wayne Goodman's Yale-Brown Obsessive-Compulsive Scale and Children's Yale-Brown Obsessive-Compulsive Scale

Name: _____   Patient ID: _____

Date: _____

Clinician: _____

The patient (>15 years of age) can complete the checklist as a self-rating procedure, while the information from younger children should be obtained by interview. The questions on page 4 are to be completed by the clinician in an interview setting.

The terms *obsessions* and *compulsions* may be described in the following way:

> *Obsessions* are distressing thoughts, ideas, feelings, fantasies, images (pictures), or impulses that keep coming into your mind even though you do not want them to. Since obsessions cause distress, compulsions are sometimes carried out to reduce the distress.

> *Compulsions* are habits, rituals, or behaviors you feel you have to do, although you may know that they do not make sense or are excessive. At times you may try to stop from doing them, but this might not be possible. While most compulsions are observable behaviors, some compulsions may be hidden mental acts, such as silent checking or repeating certain words to yourself each time you have disturbing thoughts.

Check the obsessions and compulsions that trouble you **right now** (during the past week) in the "Current" box. If they have occurred previously but not any longer, check the box marked "Past." There are examples of each symptom to help you decide if you have an obsessive-compulsive symptom. If you never have had the obsession or compulsion, check the box marked "Never."

	Current	**Past**	**Never**
Contamination/Cleanness			
1. I am worried about dirt, germs, and viruses.	☐	☐	☐
Ex. Fear of getting germs from touching door handles or shaking hands or sitting in certain chairs or seats or fear of getting AIDS.			
2. I wash my hands very often or in a special way to be sure I am not dirty or contaminated.	☐	☐	☐
Ex. Washing one's hands many times a day or for long periods after touching, or thinking one has touched, a contaminated object.			
Harming obsessions			
3. I fear that my actions might harm others.	☐	☐	☐
Ex. Fear of poisoning others' food, fear of hurting babies, fear of pushing someone in front of a train, fear of causing harm by giving bad advice.			
4. I fear I will lose control and do something I don't want to do.	☐	☐	☐
Ex. Fear of driving into a tree, fear of running over someone, fear of stabbing someone.			

	Current	Past	Never

Sexual obsessions

5. I have unpleasant, forbidden, or perverse sexual thoughts, images, or impulses that frighten me.   ☐   ☐   ☐

Ex. Unwanted bad sexual thoughts about strangers, family members, children, or friends.

Checking

6. I must check the stove or other electrical appliances, that I have locked the door, or to make sure things have not disappeared.   ☐   ☐   ☐

Ex. Repeated checking of door locks, the stove, the iron, or electrical outlets before leaving home; repeated checking that one's cupboard at school is locked, or if one is properly dressed.

Religion/Magical thoughts/Superstition

7. My dirty words, thoughts, and curses directed towards God bother me; I have a fear of offending God.   ☐   ☐   ☐

Ex. Worries about being punished for such sins and thoughts now, later in life, or after death.

8. To prevent something terrible from happening, I must have special thoughts or acts done in a special way.   ☐   ☐   ☐

Ex. Touching an object like a telephone ensures that someone in the family will not get sick.

Morality and Justice

9. I am occupied with morality issues, justice, or what is right or wrong.   ☐   ☐   ☐

Ex. Worries about always doing "the right thing," having told a lie, or having cheated someone.

Symmetry/Exactness/Ordering

10. How things are placed or how they are positioned is important to me. It needs to feel "just right" (but isn't associated with magical thinking).   ☐   ☐   ☐

Ex. Worries about papers and books being neatly placed; worries about calculations or handwriting being perfect or not evening up.

11. I get a compelling urge to put my things in a special order.   ☐   ☐   ☐

Ex. Straightening paper and pens on a desktop or books in a bookcase; wasting hours arranging or lining up things in the house in "order" and then becoming very upset if this order is disturbed.

Just right/Repeating rituals/Counting

12. I have a compelling urge to repeat certain actions until it feels "just right."   ☐   ☐   ☐

Ex. Repeating activities like turning the tap or appliances on and off, combing one's hair, going in and out of a doorway.

	Current	Past	Never

Hoarding and saving

13. I must follow strong impulses to collect and hoard things.   ☐   ☐   ☐

   Ex. Saving old newspapers, notes, cans, paper towels, and wrappers for fear that if one throws them away, one may some day need them; picking up useless objects from the street.

Somatic obsessions

14. I have worries that I look peculiar; I am concerned that something is wrong with my looks.   ☐   ☐   ☐

   Ex. Worries that one's face, ears, nose, eyes, or another part of the body is hideously ugly, despite reassurance to the contrary.

Self-damaging behaviors

15. I do things that injure my body.   ☐   ☐   ☐

   Ex. Scratching and tearing the skin, cutting oneself or banging one's head.

If you have other obsessive-compulsive problems (obsessions/thoughts, compulsions/habits) that are not included in the checklist, enter them here:

1. _____

2. _____

3. _____

Mark the *most troublesome* obsessive-compulsive problems and enter them here:

1. _____

2. _____

3. _____

What is worse, your obsessions or your compulsions?

*Please respond to **either** question A or B.*

A. If you separate your obsessions and your compulsions, what percent are the former and what the latter?

   Obsessions: _____%

   Compulsions: _____%

B. Obsessions and compulsions should together fill the circle.

Please fill in the sections that correspond to your compulsions/habits.

The empty sections correspond to your obsessions/thoughts.

☐ = Obsessions/thoughts

▨ = Compulsions/habits

For Clinician Use

Review the current **obsessive-compulsive problems** (obsessions/thoughts and compulsions/ habits). Ask the patient to respond according to the situation during the last 7 days (including today).

1. Approximately how much of your time is occupied by obsessive-compulsive problems?
   0 = None
   1 = Occasional symptoms or less than 1 hour per day
   2 = Frequent obsessive-compulsive symptoms or 1–3 hours per day
   3 = Very frequent symptoms or more than 3 and up to 8 hours a day
   4 = Almost constantly or more than 8 hours a day

2. On average, what is the longest amount of consecutive waking hours per day that you are completely free of obsessive-compulsive problems?
   0 = No symptoms
   1 = Long symptom-free interval; more than 8 consecutive hours/day symptom-free
   2 = Moderately long symptom-free interval; more than 3 and up to 8 consecutive hours/day symptom-free
   3 = Short symptom-free interval; from 1 to 3 consecutive hours/day symptom-free
   4 = Extremely short symptom-free interval; less than 1 consecutive hour/day symptom-free

3. How much do your obsessive-compulsive problems interfere with your everyday life, work or school, or social functioning?
   0 = No interference
   1 = Mild; slight interference with social or occupational/school activities, but overall performance not impaired
   2 = Moderate; definite interference with social or occupational/school performance, but still manageable
   3 = Severe interference; causes substantial impairment in social or occupational/school performance
   4 = Extreme; incapacitating interference

4. How much distress do your obsessive-compulsive problems cause you?
   0 = None
   1 = Mild; not too disturbing
   2 = Moderate; disturbing, but still manageable
   3 = Severe; very disturbing distress
   4 = Extreme; near constant and disabling distress

5. How much control do you have over your obsessive-compulsive problems? How successful are you in stopping or diverting them? If you rarely try to resist, please think about those rare occasions in which you did try. *(Note: Do not include here obsessions stopped by doing compulsions.)*
   0 = Complete control
   1 = Much control; usually able to stop or divert obsessive-compulsive problems with some effort/concentration
   2 = Moderate control; sometimes able to stop or divert obsessive-compulsive problems only with difficulty

3 = Little control; rarely successful in stopping or dismissing obsessive-compulsive problems, but they can be delayed for the moment

4 = No control; are rarely able, even momentarily, to ignore obsessions or refrain from performing compulsions; they cannot even be delayed for the moment

6. Have you been avoiding doing anything, going anyplace, or being with anyone to avoid your obsessive-compulsive problems?

0 = No deliberate avoidance

1 = Mild; minimal avoidance

2 = Moderate; some avoidance; clearly present

3 = Severe; much avoidance; avoidance prominent

4 = Extreme; very extensive avoidance; patient does almost everything he/she can to avoid triggering symptoms

Obsessions: _____ %   **BOCS TOTAL (add items 1–6):** _____
Compulsions: _____%

(refer to the question on page 3 of the patient questionnaire)

Appendix XXVII

Level 2—Repetitive Thoughts and Behaviors—Adult*

Note to providers: *The print-ready version of this tool on the CD included with this book and downloadable from www.brusheducation.ca/toolkit includes scoring instructions and assessment scales on separate pages. You can quickly refer to the scoring legend while minimizing patient response biases induced by seeing the scoring information.*

In "Instructions" on the patient questionnaire that begins on page 216, you will find a reference to the Level 1 Cross-Cutting Questionnaire, which can be downloaded directly from http://www.psychiatry.org/psychiatrists/practice/dsm/dsm-5/online-assessment-measures: Level 1 Cross-Cutting Symptom Measures–Adult. **If your patient has not completed the Level 1 Cross-Cutting Questionnaire**, ask your patient the following:

During the past 2 weeks, have you been bothered by "unwanted repeated thoughts, images, or urges" and/or "being driven to perform certain behaviors or mental acts over and over" at a mild or greater level of severity?

Scoring and Interpretation

To use when a diagnosis of obsessive-compulsive behaviour is made for an individual aged 18 and older. The total score can range from 0–20, with higher scores indicating higher severity.

The clinician reviews the score of each item and indicates the raw score for each item in the "Clinician Use" section, and summed up to obtain a total raw score. If the individual has a raw score of 8 or higher, you may want to consider a more detailed assessment for an obsessive compulsive disorder.

Calculate the Average Total Score, reducing the overall score to a 5-point scale, which allows the clinician to think of the severity of the individual's repetitive thoughts and behavior in terms of none (0), mild (1), moderate (2), severe (3), or extreme (4).

The Average Total Score is calculated by dividing the Total Raw Score by the number of items in the measure (i.e., 5).

Note: If 2 or more items are left unanswered, the total score on the measure should not be calculated. If 1 item is left unanswered, you are asked to calculate and use a Prorated Total Raw Score as the Total Raw Score.

The prorated score is calculated by summing the scores of the items that were answered to get a partial raw score. The formula to prorate the partial raw score to the Total Raw Score is:

$$\frac{(\text{Partial raw score} \times 5)}{\text{Number of items that were actually answered (4)}}$$

If the result is a fraction, round to the nearest whole number. Use this prorated score as the Total Raw Score, and calculate the average score as instructed above.

*Adapted from the Florida Obsessive-Compulsive Inventory (FOCI) Severity Scale (Part B) © 1994. Wayne K. Goodman, MD, and Eric Storch, PhD. This material can be reproduced without permission by clinicians for use with their own patients. Any other use, including electronic use, requires written permission from Dr. Goodman (wkgood@gmail.com).

Level 2—Repetitive Thoughts and Behaviors—Adult*

Name: _____   Age: ___   Sex: ❑ Male ❑ Female   Date: _____

If the measure is being completed by an informant, what is your relationship with the individual receiving care? _____

In a typical week, approximately how much time do you spend with the individual receiving care? _____ (hours/week)

Instructions: When you spoke with your doctor, or on the DSM-5 Level 1 cross-cutting questionnaire (or other) that you just completed, you indicated that **during the past 2 weeks** you have been bothered by "unwanted repeated thoughts, images, or urges" and/or "being driven to perform certain behaviors or mental acts over and over" at a mild or greater level of severity. The questions below ask about these feelings in more detail and especially how often you have been bothered by a list of symptoms **during the past 7 days**. Please respond to each item by marking (✓ or x) in one box per row.

					CLINICIAN USE
DURING THE PAST SEVEN (7) DAYS . . .					**ITEM SCORE**
1. On average, how much time is occupied by these thoughts or behaviors each day?					
❑	❑	❑	❑	❑	
0—None	1—Mild (Less than 1 hour a day)	2—Moderate (1–3 hours a day)	3—Severe (3–8 hours a day)	4—Extreme (more than 8 hours a day)	
2. How much distress do these thoughts or behaviors cause you?					
❑	❑	❑	❑	❑	
0—None	1—Mild (slightly disturbing)	2—Moderate (disturbing but still manageable)	3—Severe (very disturbing)	4—Extreme (overwhelming distress)	
3. How hard is it for you to control these thoughts or behaviors?					
❑	❑	❑	❑	❑	
0—Complete control	1—Much control (usually able to control thoughts or behaviors)	2—Moderate control (sometimes able to control thoughts or behaviors)	3—Little control (infrequently able to control thoughts or behaviors)	4—No control (unable to control thoughts or behaviors)	
4. How much do these thoughts or behaviors cause you to avoid doing anything, going anyplace, or being with anyone?					
❑	❑	❑	❑	❑	
0—No avoidance	1—Mild (occasional avoidance)	2—Moderate (regularly avoid doing these things)	3—Severe (frequent and extensive avoidance)	4—Extreme (nearly complete avoidance; house-bound)	

	CLINICIAN USE
DURING THE PAST SEVEN (7) DAYS . . .	**ITEM SCORE**

5. How much do these thoughts or behaviors interfere with school, work, or your social or family life?

❑	❑	❑	❑	❑	
0—None	1—Mild (slight interference)	2—Moderate (definite interference with functioning, but still manageable)	3—Severe (substantial interference)	4—Extreme (near-total interference; incapacitated)	

Total/Partial Raw Score:	
Prorated Total Raw Score (if 1 item is left unanswered):	
Average Total Score:	

*Adapted from the Florida Obsessive-Compulsive Inventory (FOCI) Severity Scale (Part B) © 1994. Wayne K. Goodman, MD, and Eric Storch, PhD. This material can be reproduced without permission by clinicians for use with their own patients. Any other use, including electronic use, requires written permission from Dr. Goodman (wkgood@gmail.com).

Appendix XXVIII

Obsessive-Compulsive Disorder Treatment Guide Summary

CONDITION	OPTIONS
If OCD mild or pregnant patient	Start with CBT alone
If OCD more severe in adolescent or adult	Start with first-line medication alone (see Table 8.2 on p. 112)
	Start with CBT + first-line medication
If CBT alone, allow 12–15 weeks to assess response.	
If using medication, titrate to typical average effective dose (target dose) or lowest effective dose. Onset of clinical response is commonly delayed up to 8 weeks. Wait this time, assessing every 2 weeks. If no response or partial response, titrate every 1–2 weeks until maximum dose is reached.	
Note: An adequate medication trial for OCD is 10–12 weeks or longer depending on individual circumstances (with minimum 4 weeks on maximum tolerated dose).	
If no response or partial response to CBT alone	Add a first-line medication
If no response or partial response to first-line medication alone	Add CBT
If no response or partial response to combined CBT and first-line medication	Switch to another first-line medication
	Augment with another medication
If no response to first-line medication plus add-on, or to second first-line medication, with or without psychotherapy	Consider referral
	Switch to a second-line medication (see Table 8.2 on p. 218)
If no response or partial response to 3 therapies total, with or without CBT	Referral
If response	Continue treatment for 1–3 years, depending on severity

Medication Guidelines

Fluvoxamine is widely considered the treatment of choice. Give first-line medication a 6–10 week trial at the average target or lowest effective dose to assess response, and usually a 12–15-week trial (total). OCD requires higher mean doses than other anxiety disorders.

Clomipramine is as effective but is considered second-line due to tolerability and safety issues.

Referral Guidelines

Consider referral if you feel uncomfortable with any part of this suggested management (e.g., substance use disorder comorbidity, augmentation).

Appendix XXIX

DSM-5 Diagnostic Criteria for Posttraumatic Stress Disorder 309.81 (F43.10)*

Note: The following criteria apply to adults, adolescents, and children older than 6 years.

A. Exposure to actual or threatened death, serious injury, or sexual violence in one (or more) of the following ways:

1. Directly experiencing the traumatic event(s).
2. Witnessing, in person, the event(s) as it occurred to others.
3. Learning that the traumatic event(s) occurred to a close family member or close friend. In cases of actual or threatened death of a family member or friend, the event(s) must have been violent or accidental.
4. Experiencing repeated or extreme exposure to aversive details of the traumatic event(s) (e.g., first responders collecting human remains; police officers repeatedly exposed to details of child abuse).

   Note: Criterion A4 does not apply to exposure through electronic media, television, movies, or pictures, unless this exposure is work related.

B. Presence of one (or more) of the following intrusion symptoms associated with the traumatic event(s), beginning after the traumatic event(s) occurred:

1. Recurrent, involuntary, and intrusive distressing memories of the traumatic event(s).

   Note: In children older than 6 years, repetitive play may occur in which themes or aspects of the traumatic event(s) are expressed.

2. Recurrent distressing dreams in which the content and/or affect of the dream are related to the traumatic event(s).

   Note: In children, there may be frightening dreams without recognizable content.

3. Dissociative reactions (e.g., flashbacks) in which the individual feels or acts as if the traumatic event(s) were recurring. (Such reactions may occur on a continuum, with the most extreme expression being a complete loss of awareness of present surroundings.)

   Note: In children, trauma-specific reenactment may occur in play.

4. Intense or prolonged psychological distress at exposure to internal or external cues that symbolize or resemble an aspect of the traumatic event(s).
5. Marked physiological reactions to internal or external cues that symbolize or resemble an aspect of the traumatic event(s).

C. Persistent avoidance of stimuli associated with the traumatic event(s), beginning after the traumatic event(s) occurred, as evidenced by one or both of the following:

1. Avoidance of or efforts to avoid distressing memories, thoughts, or feelings about or closely associated with the traumatic event(s).
2. Avoidance of or efforts to avoid external reminders (people, places, conversations, activities, objects, situations) that arouse distressing memories, thoughts, or feelings about or closely associated with the traumatic event(s).

D. Negative alterations in cognitions and mood associated with the traumatic event(s), beginning or worsening after the traumatic event(s) occurred, as evidenced by two (or more) of the following:

1. Inability to remember an important aspect of the traumatic event(s) (typically due to dissociative amnesia and not to other factors such as head injury, alcohol, or drugs).
2. Persistent and exaggerated negative beliefs or expectations about oneself, others, or the world (e.g., "I am bad," "No one can be trusted," "The world is completely dangerous," "My whole nervous system is permanently ruined").
3. Persistent, distorted cognitions about the cause or consequences of the traumatic event(s) that lead the individual to blame himself/herself or others.
4. Persistent negative emotional state (e.g., fear, horror, anger, guilt, or shame).
5. Markedly diminished interest or participation in significant activities.
6. Feelings of detachment or estrangement from others.
7. Persistent inability to experience positive emotions (e.g., inability to experience happiness, satisfaction, or loving feelings).

E. Marked alterations in arousal and reactivity associated with the traumatic event(s), beginning or worsening after the traumatic event(s) occurred, as evidenced by two (or more) of the following:

1. Irritable behavior and angry outbursts (with little or no provocation), typically expressed as verbal or physical aggression towards people or objects.
2. Reckless or self-destructive behavior.
3. Hypervigilance.
4. Exaggerated startle response.
5. Problems with concentration.
6. Sleep disturbance (e.g., difficulty falling or staying asleep or restless sleep).

F. Duration of the disturbance (Criteria B, C, D, and E) is more than 1 month.

G. The disturbance causes clinically significant distress or impairment in social, occupational, or other important areas of functioning.

H. The disturbance is not attributable to the physiological effects of a substance (e.g., medication, alcohol) or another medical condition.

Specify whether: With dissociative symptoms: The individual's symptoms meet the criteria for posttraumatic stress disorder, and in addition, in response to the stressor, the individual experiences persistent or recurrent symptoms of either of the following:

1. Depersonalization: Persistent or recurrent experiences of feeling detached from, and as if one were an outside observer of, one's mental processes or body (e.g., feeling as though one were in a dream; feeling a sense of unreality of self or body or of time moving slowly).
2. Derealization: Persistent or recurrent experiences of unreality of surroundings (e.g., the world around the individual is experienced as unreal, dreamlike, distant, or distorted).

Note: To use this subtype, the dissociative symptoms must not be attributable to the physiological effects of a substance (e.g., blackouts, behavior during alcohol intoxication) or another medical condition (e.g., complex partial seizures).

Specify if: With delayed expression: If the full diagnostic criteria are not met until at least 6 months after the event (although the onset and expression of some symptoms may be immediate).

Appendix XXX

Posttraumatic Stress Disorder Checklist for DSM-5 (PCL-5)*

Note to providers: *The print-ready version of this tool on the CD included with this book and downloadable from www.brusheducation.ca/toolkit includes scoring instructions and assessment scales on separate pages. You can quickly refer to the scoring legend while minimizing patient response biases induced by seeing the scoring information.*

Instructions

The table below lists problems that people sometimes have in response to extremely stressful experiences. **Keeping your worst event in mind**, please read each problem carefully and then circle one of the numbers to indicate how much you have been bothered by that problem **in the past month**.

IN THE PAST MONTH, HOW MUCH WERE YOU BOTHERED BY:	NOT AT ALL	A LITTLE BIT	MODERATELY	QUITE A BIT	EXTREMELY
1. Repeated, disturbing, and unwanted memories of the stressful experience?	0	1	2	3	4
2. Repeated, disturbing dreams of the stressful experience?	0	1	2	3	4
3. Suddenly feeling or acting as if the stressful experience were actually happening again (as if you were actually back there reliving it)?	0	1	2	3	4
4. Feeling very upset when something reminded you of the stressful experience?	0	1	2	3	4
5. Having strong physical reactions when something reminded you of the stressful experience (e.g., heart pounding, trouble breathing, sweating)?	0	1	2	3	4
6. Avoiding memories, thoughts, or feelings related to the stressful experience?	0	1	2	3	4
7. Avoiding external reminders of the stressful experience (e.g., people, places, conversations, activities, objects, or situations)?	0	1	2	3	4
8. Trouble remembering important parts of the stressful experience?	0	1	2	3	4

*PCL-5 (8/14/2013) Weathers, Litz, Keane, Palmieri, Marx, and Schnurr: National Center for PTSD[8]

IN THE PAST MONTH, HOW MUCH WERE YOU BOTHERED BY:	NOT AT ALL	A LITTLE BIT	MODERATELY	QUITE A BIT	EXTREMELY
9. Having strong negative beliefs about yourself, other people, or the world (e.g., having thoughts such as: I am bad, there is something seriously wrong with me, no one can be trusted, the world is completely dangerous)?	0	1	2	3	4
10. Blaming yourself or someone else for the stressful experience or what happened after it?	0	1	2	3	4
11. Having strong negative feelings such as fear, horror, anger, guilt, or shame?	0	1	2	3	4
12. Loss of interest in activities that you used to enjoy?	0	1	2	3	4
13. Feeling distant or cut off from other people?	0	1	2	3	4
14. Trouble experiencing positive feelings (e.g., being unable to feel happiness or have loving feelings for people close to you)?	0	1	2	3	4
15. Irritable behavior, angry outbursts, or acting aggressively?	0	1	2	3	4
16. Taking too many risks or doing things that could cause you harm?	0	1	2	3	4
17. Being "super-alert" or watchful or on guard?	0	1	2	3	4
18. Feeling jumpy or easily startled?	0	1	2	3	4
19. Having difficulty concentrating?	0	1	2	3	4
20. Trouble falling or staying asleep?	0	1	2	3	4

Scoring

SCORING SUMMARY SHEET

CRITERIA	QUESTION NUMBER							TOTALS
B	1	2	3	4	5			
C	6	7						
D	8	9	10	11	12	13	14	
E	15	16	17	18	19	20		
						Total Score		

Each item 1–20 is considered a positive symptom if rated as 2 = "Moderately" or higher.

Provisional diagnosis of PTSD

Criterion A of the DSM-5, plus
Criterion B—at least 1
Criterion C—at least 1
Criterion D—at least 2
Criterion E—at least 2

The PCL-5 can also be used to assess the severity of the illness. A total symptom severity score ranges from 0–80. A 5–10 point change represents reliable change (i.e., not due to chance), a 10–20 point change represents clinically significant change. Therefore, 5 points change is accepted as a minimum threshold for determining whether an individual has responded to treatment and 10 points as a minimum threshold for determining whether the improvement is clinically meaningful. The PCL-5 has not to date been studied in terms of severity (no, mild, moderate, severe) cut-off scores.

This assessment tool was created by government employees and is therefore not copyrighted. In accordance with the American Psychological Association's ethical guidelines, these instruments are intended for use by qualified health professionals with advanced graduate training in psychodiagnostic assessment.

Note: Self-report tools should be reviewed by clinicians to verify accuracy of response and be interpreted against DSM-5 criteria in conjunction with clinical judgment.

Appendix XXXI

Posttraumatic Stress Disorder Treatment Guide Summary

CONDITION	OPTIONS
If PTSD severe or comorbid condition	Start with trauma-focused psychotherapies + first-line medication (see Table 9.2, p. 132)
	Start with first-line medication alone
If PTSD mild to moderate and no comorbid condition	Start with TF-CBT alone
If first-line medication: The bulk of the trial should occur at the typical average effective dose (target dose). Allow a total of 4–6 weeks on average target dose to assess response, assessing every 2 weeks.	
If no response or partial response, titrate every 1–2 weeks until maximum dose is reached. Allow an additional 6–8 week trial, where appropriate, on maximum effective dose to determine effectiveness.	
If no response or partial response to TF-CBT alone	Add a first-line medication
	Add more TF-CBT with changes in approach
If no response to first-line medication, with or without TF-CBT	Switch to another first-line medication
	Add or modify TF-CBT
	Referral may be considered
If partial response to first-line medication, or unable to tolerate maximum dose, with or without TF-CBT	Consider second-line medication (see Table 9.2, p. 132)
	Add adjunctive therapy
	Add or modify TF-CBT
	Referral may be considered
If inadequate response to above	Refer*
If response	Continue treatment for a minimum of 1 year

*Consider referral if you feel uncomfortable with any part of this suggested management (e.g., substance use disorder comorbidity, augmentation).

Trauma-Focused Psychotherapies (TF-CBT)

Includes in the treatment narrative exposure, in vivo exposure (i.e., directly confronting anxiety triggers), cognitive restructuring, and relaxation techniques (may be useful at any point in treatment). Examples include prolonged exposure, cognitive processing therapy, and eye-movement desensitization and reprocessing (EMDR).

Medication Guidelines

Consider including medication if a comorbid condition is present.
Adjunctive treatment with prazosin is recommended if sleep disturbance is present.

Adjunctive treatment with benzodiazepines and atypical antipsychotics—risks may outweigh benefits; consider referral or consultation with psychiatrist.

Other Considerations

Active treatment during early stages of PTSD is important to help prevent chronic PTSD. Consider referral early to a dual diagnosis treatment program if substance use disorder is present and screen for suicidality; as many as 1 in 5 patients may attempt suicide.

Appendix XXXII

DSM-5 Diagnostic Criteria for Adjustment Disorder 309 (F43.2)*

A. The development of emotional or behavioral symptoms in response to an identifiable stressor(s) occurring within 3 months of the onset of the stressor(s).

B. These symptoms or behaviors are clinically significant, as evidenced by one or both of the following:

1. Marked distress that is out of proportion to the severity or intensity of the stressor, taking into account the external context and the cultural factors that might influence symptom severity and presentation.
2. Significant impairment in social, occupational, or other important areas of functioning.

C. The stress-related disturbance does not meet the criteria for another mental disorder and is not merely an exacerbation of a preexisting mental disorder.

D. The symptoms do not represent normal bereavement.

E. Once the stressor or its consequences have terminated, the symptoms do not persist for more than an additional 6 months.

SPECIFY WHETHER:

309.0 (F43.21) With depressed mood: Low mood, tearfulness, or feelings of hopelessness are predominant.

309.24 (F43.22) With anxiety: Nervousness, worry, jitteriness, or separation anxiety is predominant.

309.28 (F43.23) With mixed anxiety and depressed mood: A combination of depression and anxiety is predominant.

309.3 (F43.24) With disturbance of conduct: Disturbance of conduct is predominant.

309.4 (F43.25) With mixed disturbance of emotions and conduct: Both emotional symptoms (e.g., depression, anxiety) and a disturbance of conduct are predominant.

309.9 (F43.20) Unspecified: For maladaptive reactions that are not classifiable as one of the specific subtypes of adjustment disorder.

NOTES

1 Patient Health Questionnaire Screeners [Internet]. [Place unknown]: Pfizer; 2002–2016. GAD-7 Screener; n.d. [cited 2015]. Available from: http://www.phqscreeners.com

2 Warner CH, Warner CM, Appenzeller GN, Hoge CW. Identifying and managing posttraumatic stress disorder. Am Fam Physician. 2013; 88(12):827–834.

3 Montgomery S, Emir B, Haswell H, Prieto R. Long-term treatment of anxiety disorders with pregabalin: a 1 year open-label study of safety and tolerability. Curr Med Res Opin. 2013; 29(10):1223–1230.

4 American Psychiatric Association. Diagnostic and statistical manual of mental disorders (DSM-5). 5th ed. Arlington, VA: American Psychiatric Association; 2013.

5 Katzman MA, Bleau P, Blier P, Chokka P, Kjernisted K, Van Ameringen M, et al. Canadian clinical practice guidelines for the management of anxiety, posttraumatic stress and obsessive-compulsive disorders. BMC Psychiatry. 2014; 14 Suppl 1:S1.

6 Ballenger JC, Davidson JR, Lecrubier Y, Nutt DJ, Baldwin DS, et al. Consensus statement on panic disorder from the International Consensus Group on Depression and Anxiety. J Clin Psychiatry. 1998; 59 Suppl 8:47–54.

7 Kennedy SH, Lam RW, Cohen NL, Ravindran AV, et al. Clinical guidelines for the treatment of depressive disorders. IV. Medications and other biological treatments. Can J Psychiatry. 2001; 46 Suppl 1:38S–58S.

8 Weathers FW, Litz BT, Keane TM, Palmieri PA, Marx BP, Schnurr PP. The PTSD checklist for DSM-5 (PCL-5). U.S. Department of Veterans Affairs; 2013. Scale available from the National Center for PTSD at www.ptsd.va.gov

Additional Resources

Anxiety and Depression Association of America (ADAA): http://www.adaa.org/

Canadian Network for Mood and Anxiety Treatments: http://www.canmat.org/

The National Institute for Health and Care Excellence: https://www.nice.org.uk/

For patient self-management and other adult mental health tools and resources, see the General Practice Services Committee (GPSC): http://www.gpscbc.ca/what-we-do/professional-development/psp/modules/adult-mental-health

About the Author

Dr. Lauria-Horner is an associate professor at Dalhousie University, Department of Psychiatry, in Halifax, Nova Scotia, and the primary mental healthcare education leader with the department. She is extensively involved in mental health continuing medical education (CME) activities and all levels of medical training locally, nationally, and internationally.

She authored a series of school resources, *Healthy Mind Healthy Body*, with the goal to reduce stigma associated with mental health problems and mental illness and to increase mental health literacy. The series—currently used across North America—are a Nova Scotia Minister of Education–approved resource for the "Healthy Living" program. She also co-authored a national web-based training program for law enforcement first responders for dealing with and responding to Emotionally Disturbed Persons (EDPs), which received the Canadian Police Knowledge Network National Award. She has published several peer-reviewed manuscripts and abstracts, joining previous honourees of the Canadian Psychiatric Association's R.O. Jones Best Paper Awards in 2015.

Dr. Lauria-Horner has been invited to over 100 conferences and initiatives as a speaker and primary care mental health expert consultant. She is also involved in multiple research endeavours, which primarily aim to evaluate the impact of community-based mental health training programs. Concurrent to her role at Dalhousie, she worked as the officer in charge of the Atlantic Region Occupational Health and Safety Branch for the Royal Canadian Mounted Police from 2004 to 2013. She was presented with an RCMP Award of Distinction for her contribution in streamlining program processes, which improved unit efficiencies.